Visionary Leadership in Health

Visionary Leadership in Health

Delivering Superior Value

Jay Satia
Anant Kumar
and
Moi Lee Liow

$SAGE www.sagepublications.com
Los Angeles • London • New Delhi • Singapore • Washington DC

First published in 2014 by

 SAGE Publications India Pvt Ltd
B1/I-1 Mohan Cooperative Industrial Area
Mathura Road, New Delhi 110 044, India
www.sagepub.in

SAGE Publications Inc
2455 Teller Road
Thousand Oaks, California 91320, USA

SAGE Publications Ltd
1 Oliver's Yard, 55 City Road
London EC1Y 1SP, United Kingdom

SAGE Publications Asia-Pacific Pte Ltd
3 Church Street
#10-04 Samsung Hub
Singapore 049483

Published by Vivek Mehra for SAGE Publications India Pvt Ltd, typeset in 10.5/12.5 Sabon by RECTO Graphics, Delhi and printed at Saurabh Printers Pvt Ltd, New Delhi.

Library of Congress Cataloging-in-Publication Data Available

Satia, J. K. (Jayantilal K.), author.
  Visionary leadership in health : delivering superior value / Jay Satia, Anant Kumar and Moi Lee Liow.
      p. ; cm.
  Includes bibliographical references and index.
  I. Kumar, Anant, author. II. Liow, Moi-Lee, author. III. Title.
  [DNLM: 1. Delivery of Health Care. 2. Leadership. 3. Health Planning.
  4. Health Policy. 5. Public Health Administration. W 84.1]
  RA971.35   362.1068'3—dc23   2014017180

ISBN: 978-81-321-1320-1 (HB)

The **SAGE Team:** Supriya Das, Neha Sharma, Anju Saxena and Dally Verghese

All those health leaders who made a difference and improved lives.

Thank you for choosing a SAGE product! If you have any comment, observation or feedback, I would like to personally hear from you. Please write to me at contactceo@sagepub.in

—Vivek Mehra, Managing Director and CEO,
SAGE Publications India Pvt Ltd, New Delhi

Bulk Sales

SAGE India offers special discounts for purchase of books in bulk. We also make available special imprints and excerpts from our books on demand.

For orders and enquiries, write to us at

Marketing Department
SAGE Publications India Pvt Ltd
B1/I-1, Mohan Cooperative Industrial Area
Mathura Road, Post Bag 7
New Delhi 110044, India
E-mail us at marketing@sagepub.in

Get to know more about SAGE, be invited to SAGE events, get on our mailing list. Write today to marketing@sagepub.in

This book is also available as an e-book.

Contents

Part I
Leadership: Delivering Superior Results in Health

Part II
Leadership Competencies

List of Tables

List of Figures

List of Boxes

List of Abbreviations

AMRF	African Medical and Research Foundation
ART	Antiretroviral Treatment
ASPH	Association of Schools of Public Health
ASRH	Adolescent Sexual and Reproductive Health
BATNA	Best Alternative to Negotiated Agreement
BRAC	Bangladesh Rural Advancement Committee
CAFS	Centre for African Family Studies
CBCP	Cataract Blindness Control Program
CLP	Community Leadership Programme
CSDH	Commission on Social Determinants of Health
CWCS	Centre for Women and Children's Studies
DDT	Dichloro Diphenyl Trichloroethane
DFID	Department for International Development
DHS	Demographic and Health Survey
DTP	Diphtheria, Tetanus, and Pertussis
DV	Domestic Violence
FGM	Female Genital Mutilation
FRUs	First Referral Units
GAIN	Global Alliance for Improved Nutrition
GBV	Gender-Based Violence
GDP	Gross Domestic Product
HIV	Human Immunodeficiency Virus
HLEG	High Level Expert Group
ICCE	Intracapsular Cataract Extraction
ICOMP	International Council on Management of Population Programmes
ICPD	International Conference on Population and Development
ICRW	International Center for Research on Women
IEC	Information, Education, and Communication
JHU	Johns Hopkins Bloomberg School of Public Health

JSY	*Janani Suraksha Yojana*
MAP	Mobilizing for Active Participation
MDGs	Millennium Development Goals
MHRD	Ministry of Human Resources Development
MMR	Maternal Mortality Ratio
MOH	Ministry of Health
MOV	Means of Verification
MSH	Management Sciences for Health
NAFIN	Namibian Alliance for Improved Nutrition
NCDs	Noncommunicable Diseases
NGO	Nongovernmental Organization
NRHM	National Rural Health Mission
NTDs	Neural-Tube Defects
ONCCs	One Stop Crisis Centers
OR	Operational Research
ORT	Oral Rehydration Therapy
OVIs	Objectively Verifiable Indicators
PAHO	Pan American Health Organization
PDA	Population and Community Development Association
PHC	Primary Health Center
PHFI	Public Health Foundation of India
PLWHA	Person Living with HIV/AIDS
PPAT	Planned Parenthood Association of Thailand
PPD	Partners in Population and Development
RBM	Results-Based Management
RH	Reproductive Health
RTE	Right to Education
SRH	Sexual and Reproductive Health
SSA	*Sarva Shiksha Abhiyan*
STIs	Sexually Transmitted Infections
UEE	Universal Elementary Education
UHC	Universal Health Coverage
UNAIDS	Joint United Nations Programme on HIV/AIDS
UNFPA	United Nations Population Fund
UNIFEM	United Nations Development Fund for Women
VAW	Violence against Women
VCT	Voluntary Counseling and Testing Center

VECs	Village Education Committees
VLD	Visionary Leadership Development
VLP	Visionary Leadership Program
WHO	World Health Organization
WRAP	Women's Rights and Protection
XISS	Xavier Institute of Social Service
YAFS	Young Adults Fertility Survey

Foreword

The Programme of Action from the International Conference on Population and Development (ICPD), Cairo, 1994, has underscored the importance of ensuring universal access to reproductive health (RH), and three of the eight Millennium Development Goals (MDGs) are directly related to health, maternal and child mortality, and communicable diseases including malaria, tuberculosis, and HIV/AIDS. Recent evidence indicates progress toward each of the MDGs, yet the pace of progress has been slower than what is needed to achieve the targets set in the MDGs.

In this context there is also increasing recognition of the need for strengthening leadership competencies and management skills of health program managers in order for them to make significant difference in performance of the health programs. The International Council on Management of Population Programmes (ICOMP), an international non-governmental organization (NGO), dedicated to excellence in management of population programs at country, regional, and international levels, has been working with RH programs to improve their management through training, action research, and technical support. Since its establishment in 1973, it has endeavored to developing models for leadership development in population and RH and has contributed in strengthening leadership competencies and management skills of RH program managers, women leaders, youth leaders, and rural community leaders in countries of Africa and Asia.

With support from the David and Lucile Packard Foundation, ICOMP collaborated with the Partners in Population and Development (PPD) and the Centre for African Family Studies (CAFS) in creating a critical mass of 200 visionary leaders and managers in three countries in Africa (Ethiopia, Nigeria, and Sudan) and one in Asia (India) through the Visionary Leadership

Programme in Population and Development (VLP) (2001–2006). The VLP approach to leadership development was developed through a 10–12 months' advance leadership training, mentoring, and exposure program that was designed to meet the specific needs of the countries and participants. With support from United Nations Population Fund (UNFPA), ICOMP also contributed toward improving performance of RH and HIV/AIDS programs in Asia through the project on "Accelerating Improvements in Reproductive Health: Strategic Leadership Development Initiative in Asia" (2004–2007).

Furthermore, with continued support from the David and Lucile Packard Foundation, ICOMP extended its assistance in building institutional capacity in organizational excellence, developing leadership and management skills, and strengthening organizational sustainability of selected NGOs in Pakistan and the Philippines using frameworks and tools developed by ICOMP (1999–2010). ICOMP, as a lead agency, partnered with the Xavier Institute of Social Service (XISS) in implementing the "Leadership Development and Organizational Capacity Building for Reproductive Health and Family Planning in Bihar and Jharkhand, India" (LDOE) (2006–2010), aimed to create longer-term impact on the FP/RH sector through enhanced systemic impact in the two states of India by an LDOE process at three levels—NGOs, district health teams, and communities. It contributed in developing leadership competencies and management skills of district health team members from three districts in Jharkhand, and organizational effectiveness of participating NGO executives from Bihar and Jharkhand through a series of training based on LDOE modules developed by ICOMP. The Community Leadership Programme (CLP), a scaling up of the LDOE program at community level through in-country resource mobilization, was instrumental in developing leadership skills of 800 community leaders in the two states of Bihar and Jharkhand.

This book is based on training modules and materials developed under several projects on leadership development for program managers in the health sector during 2000–2010. They have their genesis in a leadership development project—the VLP implemented in four countries in Asia and Africa. Then they were adapted and improvised for use in a leadership development project for teams of program managers from six countries in Asia and the leadership development and organizational effectiveness project in India.

The ICOMP is grateful to the David and Lucile Packard Foundation and the UNFPA for providing financial support for implementation of these projects.

This book is targeted at leaders and health program managers to enable and empower them to deliver superior health results to people through enhancing their leadership competencies. The materials constitute concepts, illustrative examples, and exercises.

ICOMP wants to take this opportunity to specifically thank the team of authors—Jay Satia, Senior Advisor, Public Health Foundation of India (PHFI), and former Executive Director, ICOMP; Anant Kumar, Assistant Professor, XISS; and Moi Lee Liow, Executive Director, Asia Pacific Council on AIDS Service Organizations, Malaysia—for taking the initiative and tireless effort in putting the materials together in this book form.

It is my pleasure to introduce this book as a compilation of field-tested and ready-to-use leadership development modules. I am hopeful that the book will be useful for organizing leadership training for program managers in the health sector.

Wasim Zaman, PhD
Executive Director
ICOMP

With profound sorrow, we report that Dr Wasim Zaman passed away in an insurgent attack at Hotel Serena in Kabul, Afghanistan in March 2014.

Preface

Our Journey in Leadership Field

The International Council on Management of Population Programmes (ICOMP) had been working with RH programs to improve their management through training, action research, and technical support. However, we were dissatisfied with the results we were achieving. Something was missing. We, therefore, invited Mr Ben Lozare of the Johns Hopkins Bloomberg School of Public Health (JHU) to our international seminar of top officials of the HIV/AIDS as well as RH and population programs in 2003 held at Jinja, Uganda. Under the guidance of Dr Henry W. Mosley, they had developed a program on strategic leadership for RH. The response to his one-day seminar was overwhelming and all participants felt that they did not have this exposure to leadership, and strengthening their leadership competencies would have enhanced the performance of their programs.

This whetted our appetite for leadership field and the potential it had if we could enhance leadership competencies in the health field. Several others were also working on these lines. The Management Sciences for Health (MSH) had developed programs under the title "Managers Who Lead." They were expanding the horizons of top managers to add/refine four tasks: scan, focus, align/mobilize, and inspire complementing four management tasks: plan, organize, implement, and monitor and evaluate.

We scanned the leadership literature and successful experiences on leadership development. We learned that training alone on leadership is not enough. In addition to training, leadership development requires commitment from participants, mentoring following training, on-the-job support, and peer networking. Therefore, ICOMP along with partners—Partners in Population and Development (PPD), Dhaka, Bangladesh; Centre for African Family Studies (CAFS), Nairobi, Kenya—secured funding from the David and Lucile Packard Foundation for a visionary leadership development program (VLP) in population and development for four countries: India, Ethiopia, Nigeria, and Sudan. It incorporated the foregoing features of leadership development. More than 100 persons with potential for leadership were identified and participated in this program over a period of three years. Their journal documenting leadership journeys were both encouraging and instructive. We had a framework for visionary leadership development and had developed a way to enhance their capacities to utilize the framework for results they desired to achieve. The profiles of selected participants as well as profiles of selected leaders in population and development in Asia and Africa were documented.

However, the process of selection including an application process as well as completing a three-month self-learning phase deterred government officials to apply and almost all the participants of VLP program came from nongovernment organizations (NGOs). Building on the VLP experience and with support from the United Nations Population Fund (UNFPA), ICOMP implemented a leadership development program for teams of senior and mid-level officials on population and RH programs of 10 Asian countries. The results were mixed. Some teams were able to implement their action plans and made a difference whereas others found it difficult to bring about changes in their programs. This led us to believe that leadership development in government programs should be complemented with organizational effectiveness efforts. Indeed, several leadership development programs were structured in this fashion where the participants implemented their leadership learning over a period of time to address some specific health problems, often as a part of a donor-funded program.

Following this effort, ICOMP secured funding from the David and Lucile Packard Foundation for a Leadership Development and Organizational Effectiveness (LDOE) program to be implemented in selected districts and NGOs in Jharkhand and Bihar states of India in partnership with the Xavier Institute of Social

Service (XISS). The performance of health programs in these areas was poor and both the socioeconomic conditions as well as organizational contexts were difficult. While NGO teams had modest success in reforming their organizations, district teams had considerable difficulty in implementing their action plans and utilizing their learning. Results were quite variable.

Through these efforts over a decade, we developed and tested a visionary leadership development framework and found it useful as a vehicle to structure our leadership development efforts.

We have also learned several lessons for leadership development. Often leadership development is seen as training workshop of varying lengths offered by an outside agency. The experience shows that this is merely a beginning. The organizations need to actively participate in leadership development efforts as an integral part of their strategy to improve performance and long-term sustainability. They need to be active partners in identifying potential leaders. The leadership development efforts need to be tailored to strategic imperatives and the potential leaders need to be mentored. Leadership programs have reported greater success when some or all of these conditions were met.

Leadership development in the health field is an unfinished business. Several leadership development efforts in health have only had partial success despite leadership being considered as a critical factor for success of health programs. As they need to deliver results in a three-to-five-year time frame, donors supporting leadership development efforts soon lose interest.

We hope that our endeavor will encourage/motivate and assist public health professionals, practitioners, managers, and leaders in developing their leadership and management skills and competencies, and that they will use them to deliver superior health results—a growing expectation of people. This book can be used to organize training programs or for leadership modules of a public health educational curriculum. Therefore, it is organized around a competency framework developed by the Association of Schools of Public Health (ASPH).

Satia, Kumar, and Liow

Acknowledgments

This book is the outcome of efforts put by many individuals, organizations, institutions, and donors who share a consuming interest in leadership development as a path toward better health outcomes, especially in a developing country context.

We would like to begin by thanking fellow travelers in our journey in the leadership field. Some of them are

- PPD, Bangladesh: Dr Bruno Benavides, Dr Ishtiaq Mannan, and Dr Badrud Duza
- CAFS, Kenya: Dr Pape Syr Diagne, Florence Muindi, and Mary Majumbo
- XISS, India: Varun Kumar

We would also like to thank our donors—the David and Lucile Packard Foundation, Ford Foundation, and UNFPA—for their belief in leadership development and investing in emerging young leaders in global health as well as supporting our leadership initiatives and programs. We would specially like to thank Dr Don Lauro and Mr Lester F. Coutinho of Packard Foundation for their relentless support and guidance. Additionally, we appreciate the institutions and organizations we partnered with over the years who helped us shape and refine our thinking on leaders and leadership, and the necessary skills and competencies as are relevant to the real world of global health in developing countries.

We would like to acknowledge our colleagues at ICOMP who directly or indirectly contributed in enriching the content of this book. Our special thanks to Elmer Herradura Lighid, Neera Shrestha, and Dr Aurelio Camilo "Jun" Naraval for researching, developing, and compiling various case studies, stories, and documentation, and for their contribution in leading and managing the leadership program at ICOMP. We would also like to thank Dr Wasim Zaman, Executive Director of ICOMP, for his support and patience.

Last but not least, without whom this book would not exist, the participants of our leadership initiatives and programs in different countries—the policymakers, program managers, doctors, community leaders, health workers, and so on—deserve a special mention. Their eagerness to learn and willingness to share experiences as well as their enthusiasm to apply new leadership principles and knowledge gave us the privilege of gathering immense learning from these real-life leaders! We are humbled by so many stories of heroism, tenacity, strengths, and wisdom from these leaders, which made our efforts of writing this book so much more meaningful.

Our special thanks go to Premendra Sharma and Rekha Natrajan from SAGE Publications for their effort and support in the publication of this book.

PART I

Leadership: Delivering Superior Results in Health

One

Strengthened Leadership and Political Will for Better Health

The main reason leaders are needed is to move the organization forward, to make progress. Leadership is where tomorrow begins.
—Kouzes and Posner

Introduction

In much of the developing world, there is a wide gap between what has been achieved and what is desired in health. Technologies are available to address the various health concerns which may help in achieving the many health-related goals. However, this has not yet happened. The World Health Organization's (WHO) Framework for Action[1] underscores the importance of strengthening health systems to improve health outcomes. There is a need to emphasize the role of institution building in health systems so that access and quality of available health services can be improved.[2] However, a missing piece of this triangulation of critical factors for closing the gap and achieving desired health outcomes may as well be found in visionary leadership.

[1] WHO (2007). *Everybody's business. Strengthening health systems to improve health outcomes. WHO's framework for action.* Geneva: WHO.

[2] Satia, J. K., & Chowdhury, Tawfiq-e-Elahi (2005). *Achieving the MDGs in Asia. Policies and strategies for institutional development in population and reproductive health.* Technical Background Paper written for the Second Regional MDG Report. Bangkok and Kathmandu: UNFPA Country Technical Services Teams.

In the following section of this chapter, a case is made for strengthening leadership in health as the success in improving health has been inadequate. Progress has been slow in achieving several health-related Millennium Development Goals (MDGs) as well as in addressing communicable or noncommunicable diseases or health-sector reforms. Most reviews of progress have shown a lack of leadership and political will, and have argued for greater leadership that could lead to enhanced policy attention and resources which would result in targeted effective programs for achieving global standards such as the MDGs. The need for strengthening leadership is not new or limited to the developing countries alone. In 1994, the Milbank Memorial Fund organized a meeting on "leadership in public health."[3] In the introduction of the report, Daniel M. Fox and William L. Roper summarized the views of participants and authors as follows:

> The authors of these papers agree that problems of leadership contribute to the difficulty of making and implementing policy to improve the health of the American public. By leadership they mean the capacity of professionals to work effectively during long careers in a variety of organizations that command resources and favorable attention from elected officials and the general public. The authors, along with many of their colleagues among senior public health professionals, believe that more effective leadership would improve the translation of existing knowledge about the prevention and control of disease into policies that lead to longer and healthier lives.

Leaders can make a difference, as discussed in the third section (Leaders Can Make a Difference) of this chapter, where a case of a leader making a difference in the functioning of health center in a state in India is presented. Many such examples abound in the literature.[4] A recent example of leadership's role in Senegal's decision to offer free health care is discussed.

---

[3] Coye, M. J., Foege, W. H., & Roper, W. G. (1994). Leadership in public health. New York, USA: Milbank Memorial Fund. Available at www.milbank.org/uploads/documents/mrlead.html (accessed on January 17, 2012).
[4] For instance, International Council on Management of Population Programmes (ICOMP). (2006). Making a difference for population and

What do leaders need to do? While a lack of adequate resources is often mentioned as a key barrier to achieving better results, the examples presented in the coming section, Leaders Can Make a Difference, contradict this. We first discuss an example where a woman's life was saved despite pregnancy complications. The experience of Sri Lanka with reducing maternal mortality shows what can be achieved in resource-constrained settings. Similarly, several countries have achieved remarkable success in reversing or preventing the spread of Human Immunodeficiency Virus (HIV), including Thailand, Uganda, and Senegal. Practices which led to their success have been analyzed by Joint United Nations Programme on HIV/AIDS (UNAIDS). We map these practices through a leadership perspective leading to outcomes of shared vision, aligned values, coordinated practices/behaviors, and leveraged resources of the health system. This is the outcome leaders need to achieve.

Inadequate Progress in Improving Health: Case for Strengthened Leadership

The Millennium Development Goals

In 2000, the 189 U.N. member states met at the Millennium Summit and adopted eight goals and 18 targets to combat poverty, hunger, disease, discrimination against women, degradation of land, and illiteracy. The world development community is challenged to achieve MDGs by 2015.

The Millennium Declaration (paragraphs 11 and 12) states:[5]

> We will spare no effort to free our fellow men, women and children from the abject and dehumanising conditions of extreme poverty, to

---

development: Leaders in action. Volume 1: Profiles of emerging leaders. Volume 2: Profiles of selected visionary leaders in Asia and Africa.

[5] U.N. (2000). *Millennium Declaration*. Retrieved from www.un.org/millennium declaration/ares552e.htm.

which more than a billion of them are currently subjected. We are committed to making the right to development a reality for everyone and to freeing the entire human race from want.

We resolve therefore to create an environment—at the national and global levels—which is conducive to development and to the elimination of poverty.

Table 1.1: *The Millennium Development Goals*

No.	Goals
1	Eradicate extreme poverty and hunger
2	Achieve universal primary education
3	Promote gender equality and empower women
4	Reduce child mortality
5	Improve maternal health
6	Combat HIV/AIDS, malaria, and other diseases
7	Ensure environmental sustainability
8	Develop a global partnership for development

Source: United Nations, the Millennium Development Goals Report, 2011.

Three of the eight MDGs are health-related goals (see Table 1.1): child mortality (MDG 4), maternal health (MDG 5), and HIV/AIDS (MDG 6). In addition, gender (MDG 3) is a crosscutting issue that impacts many health issues including the three mentioned. Other MDGs such as poverty and education have a strong correlated relationship with the social determinants of health.

Inadequate Progress toward Health Millennium Development Goals

A quick review in 2004 reveals that most countries were not on track to reach health-related MDGs. According to the World Bank,[6] South Asia was off track on six goals: gender equality,

---

[6] World Bank. (2004b). *Global Monitoring Report: Policies and Actions for Achieving the Millennium Development Goals and Related Outcomes.* Washington, D.C.: World Bank.

universal primary school completion, child mortality, maternal mortality, communicable diseases, and sanitation. East Asia and the Pacific region as a whole were off track on child mortality, maternal mortality, and communicable diseases. Only about 25 percent of countries in South Asia, East Asia and the Pacific were on track to achieve under-five mortality rate. This situation is even worse for maternal mortality, where less than 15 percent of the countries were on track to reach this goal.

Although recent estimates for child mortality vary, assessments have highlighted that several countries are off track to achieve the MDG 4 which calls for a two-thirds reduction in mortality in children younger than five years between 1990 and 2015. It is estimated that worldwide mortality in children younger than five years has dropped from 11.9 million deaths in 1990 to 7.7 million deaths in 2010, a per year decline of about 2.1 percent compared to 4.4 percent per year needed to achieve MDG 4.[7] Examination of distribution of yearly rates of change in under-five mortality shows that the MDG 4 target of reduction rate of 4.4 percent per year corresponds to the performance of countries at the 67 percentile level; clearly a stretch target. This distribution of progress for child mortality also highlights that bursts of rapid decline are possible. The study by Rajratnam et al. (2010) suggests that, "For example, 66 countries have decreased child mortality by more than 30% in just 5 years during the period of this study." Such a remarkable decline provides hope that accelerated progress is possible. These robust estimates of mortality in children younger than five years show that several low-income countries have been able to achieve accelerated declines. These positive developments suggest that the progress can be accelerated in poor countries, but they may need to address leadership challenges that could lead to enhanced policy attention and resources for targeted programmes with increased effectiveness.

The MDG 5 aims to improve maternal health with a goal of reducing maternal mortality ratio (MMR), number of maternal

[7] Rajratnam, J. K. et al. (2010). Neonatal, post neonatal, childhood, and under-5 mortality for 187 countries, 1970–2010: A systematic analysis of progress towards Millennium Development Goal 4. *The Lancet, 375*(9730), 1988–2008, June 2010.

deaths per 100,000 live births, by 75 percent between 1990 and 2015. It thus seeks to achieve a 5.5 percent annual decline in MMR from 1990. The recent U.N. report[8] estimated that globally the annual percentage decline in MMR between 1990 and 2008 was only 2.3 percent, less than half of what is needed to achieve the MDG 5. An estimated 358,000 maternal deaths occurred worldwide in 2008, a 34 percent decline from the level of 1990. The U.N. report goes on to say

> The modest and encouraging progress in reducing maternal mortality is likely due to increased attention to developing and implementing policies and strategies targeting increased access to effective interventions. Such efforts need to be expanded and intensified to accelerate progress towards reducing the still very wide disparities between developing and developed countries.

We will later on discuss how Sri Lanka was able to halve their MMR in about 7 to 10 years and relate it to addressing leadership challenges. Progress at this pace in reducing MMR would have been adequate to achieve the MDG 5. This clearly shows that much needed leadership was not forthcoming.

Nowhere is the influence of leadership more visible than for HIV/AIDS programs, particularly by people living with HIV (PLHIV). The results are visible in progress toward a target of MDG 6 which aims to "combat HIV/AIDS, malaria, and other diseases." The U.N. report[9] on progress toward MDG 6 suggests that against the target—to halve infections by 2015 and begin to reverse the spread of HIV/AIDS—the spread of HIV appears to have stabilized in most regions, and more people on antiretroviral treatment (ART) have a longer survival rate. The report says, "The latest epidemiological data indicates that, globally, the spread of HIV appears to have peaked in 1996, when 3.5 million people were newly infected. By 2008, that number had dropped

[8] WHO, UNICEF, UNFPA, and the World Bank. (2011). *Trends in maternal mortality: 1990 to 2008*. Retrieved from www.who.int/pmnch, accessed in March 2014.

[9] U.N. (2010). *The millennium development goals report, United Nations*. Retrieved from www.un.org/millenniumgoals/, accessed in March 2014.

to an estimated 2.7 million." However, much more is required for rapidly reducing the new infections.

Progress is also visible towards the MDG No. 6 (a) and (c) targets—to have halted by 2015 and begun to reverse the spread of HIV/AIDS, and incidence of malaria and other major diseases—which has been largely driven by external attention and resources as evinced by the formation of the Global Fund to Fight AIDS, Tuberculosis and Malaria in 2002. The U.N. report says, "Sustained malaria control is central to achieving many of the MDGs, and available data show significant progress in scaling up prevention and treatment efforts." The report concludes, "[M]ore attention needs to be given to ensuring success in large countries that account for most malaria cases and deaths if the MDG target is to be reached." The external influence on large countries is likely to be restrained and more vigorous in-country leadership is needed to address disease burden due to malaria.

The progress on tuberculosis is inching forward as incidence rate per capita continues to decline slowly. The U.N. report concludes, "If current trends are sustained, the world as a whole will have already achieved the MDG target of halting and reversing the incidence of tuberculosis in 2004." However, because of lack of access to high-quality care, tuberculosis remains the second important cause for the number of people it kills. In 2008, 1.8 million people died from this disease.

The MDGs passed the 12-year mark in 2012 and there are three more years to go before the target year 2015. There has been progress but it has been uneven and patchy. For instance, where there have been movements toward achievements of MDG targets, there was evidence that leadership was vigorous and contributed toward the actions for desired health outcomes. So, this is the opportunity and leadership challenge for achieving MDGs by 2015.

Noncommunicable Diseases

Although no specific MDGs were set for noncommunicable diseases (NCDs), they are the cause of a majority of deaths, and the global disease burden of NCDs is increasing.

The Lancet NCD Action Group and the NCD Alliance say[10] that there is a need to create a sustained global involvement against premature deaths and preventable morbidity and disability from NCDs, mainly heart disease, stroke, cancer, diabetes, and chronic respiratory diseases. As a response, it proposes five key priority actions—leadership, prevention, treatment, international cooperation, and monitoring and accountability—in concert with five priority intervention areas. These areas are (1) tobacco control, (2) salt reduction, (3) improved diets and physical activity, (4) reduction in hazardous alcohol intake, and (5) essential drugs and technologies.

The report goes on to say,

> The first key action for success is strong and sustained political leadership at the higher national and international levels.... Individual champions and politicians will also need to take a leadership role. The health sector has a leading role in responding to NCDs but many other government sectors including finance, agriculture, foreign affairs and trade, justice, education, urban design and transport, have to be part of the whole-of-government response, along with civil society and private sector.

Clearly, the health program leadership of NCDs would have to go beyond their zone of control to influence these other sectors.

Health Sector

Health sector is facing many challenges due to medical advances as well as rapid epidemiological and economic transitions, although their nature and intensity vary from country to country. All health systems are struggling to contain costs while improving health equity.

Such a situation, in turn, poses many challenges for leaders of health sector. An independent Commission on the Education of Health Professionals for the 21st century called for a third

---

[10] Beaglehole, R. et al. (2011). Priority actions for the non-communicable disease crisis. *377*. Retrieved from www.thelancet.com.

generation of health professionals that should be system-based to improve the performance of health systems.[11]

The "education" of health professionals needs to move progressively, beginning with informative to formative and then to transformative. At the first level, informative learning involves acquiring the necessary knowledge and skills. Then, a formative learning process would socialize health professionals around a certain value system that helps define them as professionals. Finally, transformative learning involves the development of leadership attributes which is aimed at producing enlightened agents of change.

The ultimate purpose is to assure universal coverage of the high quality comprehensive services that are essential to advance opportunity for health equity within and between countries.

Health-sector reforms require not only top-level political leadership but also leadership in the health sector at various levels. This calls for leadership to make a difference in health and, thereby, accelerate progress in achieving MDGs.

Leaders Can Make a Difference

Leaders Can Do It

CASE STUDY 1: Chainpur Primary Health Center, Jharkhand, India

The Chainpur Primary Health Center (PHC) is located about 3 km from the district hospital in Palamu District of Jharkhand state in India.[12] In 2006, the PHC was in a bad shape. Grass

---

[11] Frank, J. et al. (2011). Health professionals for a new century: Transforming education to strengthen health systems in an interdependent world. *The Lancet*, 376(9756), 1923–1958.

[12] Kumar, A., & Satia, J. (2010). Rural health innovation through leadership development and organisational effectiveness. *Jharkhand Journal of Social Development*, 3(2), 1–7.

had grown in the PHC compound and the hand pump had rusted from non-use. Very few people used the PHC services. Dr A, medical officer in-charge (MOIC), and his colleague Dr G felt that not much could be done. "Who will come to Chainpur when you can go to district hospital in 20 minutes?" they said to a visiting team from an academic institute to discuss the participation of Dr A in a leadership development and organization effectiveness (LDOE) program being launched with support from a donor. Despite his reservations, Dr A agreed to participate.

Through two round tables of training and during follow-ups by LDOE team, several ideas for improvement were discussed and routinely rejected as it was felt that "not much could be done." However, Dr A and G began to feel that something should be done.

As a part of the training, Dr A participated in advanced leadership training in Malaysia and was inspired by the functioning of the Malaysian health system during a field visit. Dr A motivated his colleague Dr G that they should try to improve the PHC. As funds were available from the National Rural Health Mission (NRHM), their first attempt was to improve the then moribund delivery room.

Feedback from women was used to improve the quality of facilities and make the services user-friendly. For instance, payment of incentives for institutional delivery under a national scheme was given before the women left for homes after delivery. As district hospital was close-by, women with complications in pregnancy could be easily referred there. Consequently, the number of deliveries increased significantly.

The layout of outpatient waiting room was improved. Benches were provided and a small television and purified water dispenser were installed with community contribution. These and other measures, despite being modest in nature, led the district health officer to praise Chainpur PHC and recommend other medical officers to visit it and observe its functioning. A journalist visited Chainpur PHC and wrote about it in a newspaper. This became a model known as "Chainpur Model" in Palamu district (see Box 1.1).

Box 1.1: *Chainpur PHC*

Take Home Messages on Leadership: Chainpur PHC	
What did it take to initiate a change?	
What did it take to make a change?	
What were the costs and benefits?	

Source: Authors.

Leaders Can Get It Done

CASE STUDY 2: How Did Sierra Leone Provide Free Health Care?

On April 27, 2010, Sierra Leone started free health care for pregnant women, new mothers, and young children. John Donnelly took an in-depth look at how the war-torn nation managed it.[13]

In November 2009, Koroma, the president of Sierra Leone, announced at a donors' conference in London that he is initiating a free health-care plan on April 27, 2010, just five months away, which coincided with the 49th anniversary of the country's independence from Great Britain. Now, one year later, the results are in: the free health care plan has substantially increased services for mothers and particularly for children. The number of children treated for malaria, for instance, has roughly tripled from the previous year, a striking example of how the lack of money proved to be a barrier to care.

[13] Special Report (2011). How did Sierra Leone provide free health care? *The Lancet* 377(9775), 1393–1396. Retrieved from www.thelancet.com.

"What happened in Sierra Leone was breathtaking," said Rob Yates, a senior health economist at the UK's Department for International Development (DFID) a month after the launch. Yates has advised several governments in Africa on launching free health-care initiatives. "In five months, they were able to do a systematic reform in the Sierra Leone health system," he said. "They had leadership that galvanized the whole system. We haven't realized the full importance of what they have done. The planning was more thorough than any I have seen. Other governments can learn from Sierra Leone." In Sierra Leone, the key factor, according to those interviewed, was the president: he put the health care directive at the top of his priority list. Political will drove the process.

Although donor community was initially reluctant, they were willing to follow. There were other crucial factors. The Ministry of Health and Sanitation, which was responsible for implementation of the initiative, was fortunate to have key leaders in technical positions, such as the chief medical officer, the director of reproductive health services, and the head of human resources. They took on additional responsibilities at a time when the ministry was without a minister. This was critical to the success of the free health-care plan.

They motivated people and played the role of health diplomat. One of them, although knowing what had to be done, did not adopt a direct nature of leading. It was conciliatory, warm, and friendly. It was, "Do you think we could do this?" instead of "Why the hell has this not happened?" Another took on the role of ministry spokesperson for free health care. Just before the launch of free health care, he went on radio shows and held press conferences. Key leaders in the ministry were assigned districts and each traveled to the areas a couple of days before the launch.

The effort to bring free health care to Sierra Leone was not easy or simple, and the ministry officials readily admitted to making wrong decisions at various points. But to make the initiative a success, scores of people worked long hours for months toward a single goal that they believed in (see Box 1.2).

Box 1.2: *Sierra Leone's Free Health-Care Plan*

Take Home Messages on Leadership: Sierra Leone's Free Health-Care Plan	
What and who made the difference?	
What resources were most crucial?	
What were the costs and benefits?	

Source: Authors.

Leaders Know What Needs to Be Done

CASE STUDY 3: Woman Whose Life Was Saved: Overcoming Adversity at Maternal and Prenatal Clinic, Tarapoto Regional Health Center, San Martin[14]

Rosa Diaz Barboza is a resident of the Tabalosos District in San Martin. At 18 years of age, Rosa was a happily married woman settling down in life with her husband, life on the farm, and expecting her first child. Her remote home is located three hours from the closest health post, which is only accessible by foot and even then, when it rains, the road is sometimes completely blocked and no one is able to get in or out. However, despite all these geographical difficulties, during the first trimester of Rosa's pregnancy, outreach efforts by the regional health center were able to get to Rosa and she received prenatal education and care.

[14] Prepared by Dr Raul Estuardo Arroyo Tirado, Jr., Cahuide #143, Tarapoto, Peru. Retrieved from rarroyo@terra.com.pe. Translated by Besen Obenson, May 2002. Project funded by Pathfinders International. Case study contributed by Partners in Population and Development. With author's permission.

During a routine prenatal visit, it was discovered that Rosa's pregnancy could be a high risk one due to several factors, including anemia. Taking into consideration the potential geographical difficulties, lack of equipment, and qualified staff, Rosa was referred to the health center in San Juan de Talliquihui where she could be attended to by not only a nurse but also a qualified clinical midwife.

At the eighth month of her pregnancy, Rosa and her husband began the long journey to San Juan which involved a three-hour trek uphill to reach the closest road. In San Juan, they stayed with relatives and Rosa's husband picked up odd jobs to start saving money for the baby. At the health clinic, Rosa was examined every week and everything seemed to be progressing normally. Nevertheless, clinic staff continuously praised Rosa and her husband for planning ahead.

In the early hours of June 25, Rosa began having labor pain and the midwife was called immediately who confirmed that she was indeed in active labor. At 8:30 am, Rosa was transported to the health center where they were met by the obstetrics/gynecology nurse. By 9:30 am, Rosa was ready to give birth but unfortunately, the only comfortable bed in the center was occupied, so she was forced to give birth on a hard plank which made the labor process even more painful.

At 10:09 am, Luzmirella was born—she took her first breath and let out a loud yell. She appeared healthy and normal and Rosa seemed to be handling the situation well. Everyone was relieved and Rosa's husband quickly ran home for a pillow and blanket for his wife. Forty minutes later, the nurse observed that Rosa's placenta had still not been expelled and she was bleeding slightly. Concerned by her prior anemia diagnosis and to be on the safer side, she decided to begin the protocol to prevent shock (low-risk level) (RED ALERT—a very successful series of first aid protocols for the prevention of shock developed by the regional health center) and tried to extract the placenta manually, but she was unsuccessful.

At that point, she gathered the family members and suggested that they take Rosa to the hospital in Cuñumbuque.

This hospital, located an hour and a half away by car, has a doctor on call 24 hours a day. Initially, Rosa refused to go saying she would rather die than be moved in her current condition. After requesting privacy with his wife, Rosa's husband pleaded to her saying if not for him, she had to do it for their child. At this point, Rosa agreed to the transfer.

San Juan is a rural, remote town and, as such, community leaders have developed contingency plans for emergencies. For this situation, they decided to do two things:

1. Communicate via citizens band (CB) radios with people living along the highway to inform them about the emergency and to request a vehicle which can take a while
2. Send someone to the hospital to return with the hospital's ambulance

Due to the communities' valiant efforts, by 12:30 pm, Rosa was on her way to the hospital. At this point, she was hemorrhaging heavily and all the nurse could do was continue with the protocol, administer injections of saline solution, and massage Rosa's abdomen. Rosa was feverish and not responsive, and she slipped in and out of consciousness.

At 1:30 pm, over 3.5 hours after giving birth, they got Rosa to the hospital in Cuñumbuque. By this time, she was completely non-responsive and had lost all sensory feelings. Doctors there immediately transferred her to the operating room where they tried a manual extraction of the placenta, which at this point was halfway out. After 30 minutes, the doctor decided that Rosa needed specialized attention by a qualified surgeon with the necessary equipment.

With IVs in both arms to prevent extreme shock due the profuse blood loss, Rosa was transferred again to the Maternity and Prenatal Clinic and, it was there that at 4:00 pm, the placenta was finally extracted and Rosa was given over 4 liters of blood.

The doctor who eventually removed the placenta said that it was due to *all* the actions taken by all the parties involved that saved Rosa's life: from the health promoter who encouraged Rosa to go to the health post, to the man who practically ran all the way to the hospital to get the ambulance, and the nurse who massaged Rosa's belly for two hours. The small room where Rosa was immediately moved to was a somber gathering till she opened her eyes and asked for her baby.

Currently, Rosa and her husband are planning Luzmirella's first birthday party in June. They plan on inviting all the hospital staff who helped ensure that Luzmirella, a healthy, rambunctious 11-month old, can actually celebrate her first and hopefully many more birthdays.

Table 1.2 examines the factors related to the recovery of Rosa. Family/household, community, and government health systems not only coordinated their responses but also leveraged resources available to them. These, in turn, were guided by shared vision about life being precious and valued maternal health.

Table 1.2: *Success Factors Related to the Recovery of Rosa*

	Individual/ Household	*Community*	*Government Health System*
Vision ➤	Woman's life is precious	Save life when there are pregnancy complications	Save life
Values ➤	Proper health care can save life during pregnancy complications	Pregnancy complications need to be addressed	Continuum of care
Practices ➤	Stay near the health facility when pregnancy is due	Implement a contingency plan	Health providers, nurse, doctors all do that is needed
Resources ➤	Family contributes its resources	Community members contribute their labor	Health system uses all available resources

Source: Authors.

The above example shows that *shared vision, aligned values, coordinated practices, and leveraging resources among individuals/households, communities, and health system can* reduce maternal deaths. Achieving this is the function of leadership as discussed in the following paragraphs.

CASE STUDY 4: Reducing Maternal Mortality in Sri Lanka[15]

We know that technologies to achieve health-related goals are available, but inadequate or lack of resources is often regarded as the key barrier to better results. A World Bank study on Sri Lanka's success in reducing maternal mortality [16](Pathmanathan, et al., 2003) shows that resource constraints may not be a barrier. The Sri Lanka experience points to both the health system's development and the role of institutional development in strengthening access to and quality of available maternal health services as critical to lowering maternal mortality.

Taking the experiences of Sri Lanka and Malaysia over five decades, the World Bank study says that MDG 5 (reducing maternal mortality ratio by three-quarters between 1990 and 2015) is achievable in developing countries. However, since the 1990s, the overall progress in reducing maternal mortality globally falls short of the goal. See the second section (Inadequate Progress in Improving Health: Case for Strengthened Leadership).

What will it take to achieve MDG 5? Sri Lanka shows that reducing maternal mortality was affordable despite the country's income level and growth rate. The path it took involves these basic interventions:

1. Skilled birth attendants during childbirth

---

[15] ICOMP. (2005). *Discussion note prepared for the regional seminar on Strategic Leadership of Reproductive Health Programmes* organized by ICOMP, Kuala Lumpur, November 28–December 1, 2005.

[16] Indra, Pathmanathan et al. (2003). Investing in maternal health: learning from Malaysia and Sri Lanka. *Health, population and nutrition series*,Washington, D.C., USA: The World Bank.

2. Management of emergencies and complications from pregnancy to childbirth
3. Monitoring maternal deaths

These interventions have to be anchored by two critical developments: (1) the health system and (2) institutional changes.

1. Health system: To reduce maternal mortality, Sri Lanka adopted the following strategies for health system development:

   • Building a foundation for effective maternity care
   • Removing barriers to access
   • Improving utilization of available facilities

2. Institutional changes: To support an effective health system development, changes in certain core and complementary institutions were necessary such as:

   • Human resource development and management
   • Reaching out to the poor
   • Building a functional referral system
   • Removing barriers to access
   • Facilitating community mobilization
   • Strengthening accountability
   • Stronger organizational management including implementation of increasingly sophisticated monitoring system

Other forces were also at work. An enabling environment as a result of early gains in female education and the empowerment of women through the electoral process ensured sustained national, political, and managerial commitment to maternal health. Improvements in national transportation system also contributed to better and quicker access to health services as well as improved health-seeking behavior. Financial barriers to maternity care were removed by the government's political commitment and society's expectations of health and education services to be provided free of charge.

Oversight institutions are also known to have complemented these efforts synergistically. Civil registration of births and deaths was governed by legislation, and maternal deaths were viewed with sufficient concern to warrant special reporting by the Registrar General.

Figure 1.1 shows the conventional perspective of health system development for reducing maternal mortality. However,

Figure 1.1: *Conventional Perspective: Health System Development for Reducing Maternal Mortality*

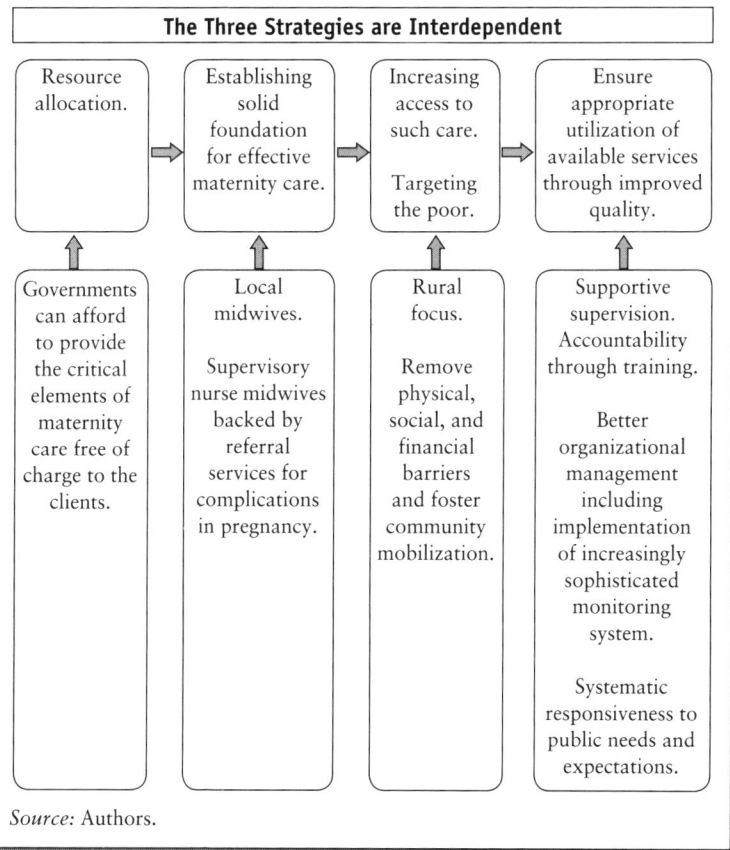

The Three Strategies are Interdependent

Resource allocation.	Establishing solid foundation for effective maternity care.	Increasing access to such care. Targeting the poor.	Ensure appropriate utilization of available services through improved quality.
Governments can afford to provide the critical elements of maternity care free of charge to the clients.	Local midwives. Supervisory nurse midwives backed by referral services for complications in pregnancy.	Rural focus. Remove physical, social, and financial barriers and foster community mobilization.	Supportive supervision. Accountability through training. Better organizational management including implementation of increasingly sophisticated monitoring system. Systematic responsiveness to public needs and expectations.

Source: Authors.

as shown in Table 1.3, these can also be seen from a leadership perspective of creating shared vision, aligning values, coordinating practices, and leveraging resources among individuals/ households and communities.

Table 1.3: *It Can Be Done: Leadership Perspective*

Tasks	Household/ Family	Community	Health System
Create shared vision	Female education		Sophisticated monitoring system and special reporting
Align values	Empower women	Political and managerial commitment	Systematic responsiveness to public needs and expectations
Coordinate practices	Remove physical, social, and financial barriers	Mobilize community	Supervisory nurse midwives backed by a referral system for complications in pregnancy
Leverage resources		Improve transport	Free of charge services

Source: Authors.

Leaders Know it Can Be Done—Leaders' Perspectives to Address HIV/AIDS

In the following paragraphs we discuss three countries[17] which had achieved notable success in combating HIV/AIDS in early stages of AIDS epidemic—Uganda, Senegal, and Thailand—which have been documented by UNAIDS as best practice case studies.

[17] ICOMP. (2005). *Discussion note prepared for the regional seminar on Strategic Leadership of Reproductive Health Programmes* organised by ICOMP, Kuala Lumpur, November 28–December 1, 2005.

Uganda

Uganda is one of the world's poorer countries and one of the most severely affected by the HIV/AIDS epidemic. In 1998, it had 21 million people, with less than 14 percent living in cities. The gross national product per capita was equivalent to about US$240. Total HIV prevalence among adults was over 8 percent.

Fortunately, Uganda is also one of the African countries where the HIV epidemic was recognized relatively early and so prevention efforts were started on a national level.[18]

- In 1986, the president publicly acknowledged the country's HIV/AIDS problem and made a commitment to mobilizing efforts against it. A national budget for the AIDS program was established early during the epidemic.
- The country adopted a multi-sectoral approach. The Uganda AIDS Commission was set up in the Office of the President and HIV/AIDS control program was established in several government ministries, including the Ministry of Health.
- Different levels of the society were involved such as political, community, and religious leaders. The Islamic Medical Association of Uganda supported community education on HIV/AIDS throughout the country, including the distribution of condoms.[19] Radio messages on HIV/AIDS were broadcast widely.
- Condom social marketing services, backed by USAID, were implemented countrywide.
- HIV voluntary counseling and testing were made available extensively and outside the formal health-care service.

---

[18] For more detailed information, see "A measure of success in Uganda: The value of monitoring both HIV prevalence and sexual behavior," Case Study UNAIDS/98.8, Geneva, May 1988.

[19] For further information, see "AIDS education through Imams: A spiritually motivated community effort in Uganda," Case Study UNAIDS/98.33, Geneva, October 1988.

Uganda's success in HIV prevention can be seen from the following:

- Percentage of adults infected declined from a peak of about 14 percent to about 6 percent in 2003.
- Steep increase in condom use: The proportion of men who said that they had ever used a condom rose from 15 percent to 55 percent. Among women, the total rose from 6 percent to 39 percent.
- Behavior change: Percentage of sexually experienced men at age 18 fell from nearly 90 percent in 1989 to 50 percent in 1995.

Senegal

Much has been written about the need to intervene early to stop the spread of HIV before it spreads to the general population. Senegal's HIV prevention program has been extensive and contains the elements of an effective program. There is good evidence that Senegal has maintained one of the lowest rates of infection in sub-Saharan Africa by changing the behavior of many of its citizens.[20]

Like Uganda, Senegal is not a rich country. In 1998, it had 9 million people, with 44 percent living in towns. Per capita income was below US$600 a year. Total HIV prevalence among adults was estimated at about 1.8 percent.

Senegal has for long emphasized prevention and primary health care. Reproductive health (RH) and child health are well-established priorities. In addition, registered sex workers are required to have regular health checkups and are treated for any curable sexually transmitted infections (STIs) that are found.

What was the response in Senegal?

- As in Uganda, politicians in Senegal were quick to move against the epidemic once the first cases appeared in the second half of the 1980s.

---

[20] For more detailed information, see "Acting early to prevent AIDS: The case of Senegal." UNAIDS Key Material, June 1999.

- Since 93 percent of Senegalese are Muslims, the government made efforts to involve religious leaders. HIV/AIDS became a regular topic in Friday sermons in mosques and senior religious figures talked about it on television and radio.
- Many other levels of Senegalese society joined in. By 1995, 200 nongovernmental organizations (NGOs) were active in the response, as were women's groups with about half a million members.
- HIV prevention was included, while sex education was introduced in schools. Parallel efforts reached out to young people who are not in school.
- HIV voluntary and confidential counseling and testing were made available.
- Programs were immediately put in place to support sex workers to persuade their clients to use condoms.
- STIs moved up on the list of health priorities. Senegal was one of the first countries in Africa to establish a national STI control program that integrated STI care into regular primary health services.

Senegal's success in HIV prevention can be seen from the following:

- HIV prevalence among pregnant women was just over 1.4 percent at the end of 1996, with no significant trend over time.
- Condom distribution rose from 500,000 pieces in 1988 to 7 million pieces in 1997.
- Median age at first sex for women in 1997 for 25–29 years age group was 17.7 years but increased to 18.7 years for 20–24 years age group.

Clearly, earlier improvements in the social structure and health services put Senegal in a good position to respond more effectively to HIV and AIDS. In addition, strong political commitment and the implementation of effective prevention activities helped keep Senegal's rates of HIV infection among the lowest in sub-Saharan Africa.

Thailand

Few countries show the link between behavior and HIV infection as clearly as Thailand.[21] Overall, behavioral changes have reduced the number of new HIV infections each year from almost 143,000 in 1991 to 29,000 in 2000. Thailand has a little over 60 million people, about 20 percent of whom live in cities. The gross national product per capita was equivalent to about US$2,700 in 1998. HIV prevalence among adults was estimated at about 1.9 percent, with higher prevalence in certain geographical areas and among certain groups. Thailand's HIV prevalence might be lower than that of Uganda's but it had a similar number of people living with HIV/AIDS.

The effective nationwide prevention program, which began in 1991, included several elements:

- The prime minister chaired the National AIDS Program.
- The Office of the Prime Minister took an active role in policy discussion, led the national public education effort using government-run mass media (that is, public, not private), and took part in monitoring.
- The Parliament established a subcommittee on AIDS.
- The National Economic and Social Development Board worked closely with the Ministry of Public Health to integrate the National AIDS Plan into the five-year National Development Plan.
- The government AIDS budget increased drastically during the following years.

[21] For more information, see "Relationships of HIV and STD declines in Thailand to behavioral change: A synthesis of existing studies," Key Material, UNAIDS/98.2, 1998. See also, "Collecting lower HIV infection rates with changes in sexual behavior in Thailand: Data collection and comparison," Case Study, UNAIDS/98. June 1998; "The success of the 100 percent Condom Promotion Programme in Thailand: Evaluation of the 100 percent Condom Promotion Programme and the validation of the decline in trends for selected STDs," Institute for Population and Social Research, Mahidol University, Thailand (funded by the Thai Ministry of Public Health and UNAIDS, February 2000).

- Each key ministry had its own AIDS plan and budget as well as a person as the AIDS focal point.
- All provincial governors led the AIDS program in their respective provinces through the provincial development planning system.
- The business community, people living with HIV/AIDS, religious leaders, and other community leaders became very involved in contributing to policy dialogue, resource mobilization, and the local implementation of activities.
- In Thailand, 1991 was the turning point for human rights protection for PLHIV. HIV was removed from the list of diseases that required notification to the health authority. The ban on entry to Thailand of people with HIV/AIDS was lifted. A set of national policy guidelines to protect the rights of PLHIV was issued.[22]

The most striking effect of the national program, famously known as 100 percent condom program, can be seen from the following:

- Total number of people living with HIV/AIDS decreased from nearly 750,000 in 1995 to 650,000 in 2000.
- Men (aged 15–49) visiting sex workers dropped from 19 percent in 1990 to 9 percent in 1993.
- Reported number of STIs in male fell from about 200,000 in 1989 to less than 20,000 in 1994.
- Consistent condom use among sex workers increased from over 50 percent in 1990 to almost 90 percent in 1996.

IT can be done: Conventional view

To demonstrate that success can be achieved even in resource-poor settings, the experiences of these three countries with differing cultures and different levels of the epidemic are discussed here. Uganda was hard hit throughout the 1980s and has had almost two million cumulative AIDS-related deaths since then.

[22] Ungphakorn, J., & Sittitrai, W. (1994). The Thai response to the HIV/AIDS epidemic. UNAIDS, 8 (Suppl.), S155–S163.

Senegal, on the other hand, had not been seriously affected by the epidemic. In Thailand, the epidemic became prominent only by the end of the 1980s, but spread rapidly once it took hold. These are three different situations, but behavioral change and some containment of the epidemic were achieved in these three developing countries even with resource constraints.

What are some essential features of effective programs which are shared by the three countries? In each one, national AIDS programs share a package of common features that UNAIDS regards as "best practice," namely:

- Strong political commitment at the highest level to deal with the epidemic (this ensures policies and funding to address the epidemic)
- Multi-sectoral approaches to prevention and care and, at the government level, involvement of multiple ministries
- Multilevel responses (at national, provincial, district, and community levels)
- Effective monitoring of the epidemic and risk behaviors, and dissemination of the findings both to improve policies and programs and to sustain awareness
- A combination of efforts aimed at the general population and focused on groups at high risk, at the same time
- Implementation on a large scale
- Integrated prevention and care

These actions proved to be effective because leadership was involved. The influence of leaders at different levels of society in each country—the president/prime minister, the ministry officials, religious and community leaders, and so on—was seen in the delivery of policy directions and program interventions according to the desired or articulated goals and objectives.

The above actions can be interpreted from the leadership perspective as shown in Figure 1.2.

Thus, the success of policies and programs is reflected through leadership actions of creating a shared vision, aligning values, coordinating practices, and leveraging resources among the individuals/households, communities, and health system, as shown in Figure 1.3.

Figure 1.2: *It Can Be Done: Leadership Perspective*

Create Shared Vision

- Uganda: Public acknowledgment, political commitment
- Senegal: Political commitment, involvement of religious groups
- Thailand: Involvement of prime minister/parliamentarians and provincial governors

Align Value:

- Uganda: Public acknowledgement, political commitment
- Senegal: Political commitment, involvement of religious and many other groups including NGOs
- Thailand: Removing stigma and discrimination

Coordinate Practices

- Uganda: Multi-sectoral approach, IEC, condom—social marketing and free distribution, voluntary counseling and testing center (VCT)
- Senegal: Schools, VCT, condom for sex workers, national STI program
- Thailand: Involvement of provincial government and businesses

Leverage Resources

- Uganda: Multi-sectoral approach, political commitment
- Senegal: National STI programs
- Thailand: National and provincial government budget, business sector

Source: Authors.

Figure 1.3: *The Leadership Perspective for Superior Results*

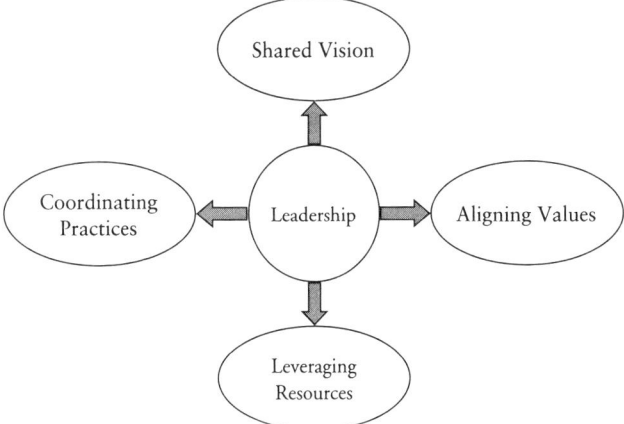

Source: Authors.

As the context changes, the leaders need to continually work on these actions to ensure sustained progress. The above mentioned early successes in HIV programs were not necessarily sustained in continuing reduction in adult prevalence of HIV infections. The HIV prevalence in Uganda has stabilized between 6.5 percent and 7 percent since 2001. The adult HIV prevalence remained low in Senegal at 2 percent or under. On the other hand in Thailand, the rate of new HIV infections decreased by more than 25 percent between 2001 and 2009. Current adult HIV prevalence is estimated to be close to 1 percent, a significant decline from a peak rate of about 2 percent in 1995.

Two

Leadership and Management: What Leaders Need to Do

There is a need for public health leadership development as an underpinning for public health effectiveness.
—Dr James Marks, Senior Vice President and
Director of the Health Group, Robert Wood Johnson Foundation

Introduction

In the previous chapter, we presented a case for leadership in health based upon inadequate performance in improving health and an analysis of some examples where leadership was effectively used. The leadership perspective that emerged says that leaders need to create shared vision among, align values of, coordinate their practices, and leverage resources of stakeholders in the health system.

The essence of effective leadership is getting others to wilfully follow you. (John Maxwell)

In this chapter, we present a visionary leadership framework on what leaders need to do to achieve the above result. There is a bewildering amount of literature on leadership. Clearly, leadership is a complex set of concepts and competencies. However, on another level, it is simple. The dictionary definition of leadership is "to go where others have not gone before" or alternatively, "to take people to a future they have not yet seen." Although this is a simple description of what leaders do, it hides many complexities and that is the source of bewildering amount of literature and advice that leadership aspirants receive. One, "to take people" means a leader is able to inspire and empower them. Two, "future" means a leader is able to visualize it and share it with people so that it becomes their vision. Three, this raises a fear of unknown and introduces uncertainty in its achievement. Therefore, a leader has to engender trust and confidence among people so that they will follow. All of this depends upon the context—how different the shared vision of future is from the present, what path will need to be taken, and how difficult will the journey be. Therefore, leadership is not only results-based but also context-dependent.

We assume that the reader is familiar with leadership literature. However, for those wishing to have a quick update, we present key strands of thoughts on leadership in Annexure 1 of this book. It is not our intent to provide a comprehensive review of the vast amount of literature on leadership.

There is considerable discussion on the literature about managers and leaders and how they differ (see the following section). However, a general consensus seems to emerge that the leadership and management are complementary. For success, both need to be exercised.

Building on the above consensus, a visionary leadership framework is presented in the third section (Framework for Visionary Leadership). This framework relates leadership and management. Leadership is seen as creating shared vision, assessing the gap between vision and reality, finding a path and strategies to bridge this gap, and inspiring and empowering stakeholders to travel on this path. The management part begins with goals and targets, planning for achieving them, organizing for implementation, and monitoring and evaluation.

The fourth section discusses how visionary leadership can deliver superior value for health. Two case studies—Global Successes in Health and African Health Leadership Initiative—illustrate how leaders deliver superior value. We conclude this chapter by highlighting the challenges of becoming a more effective visionary leader.

Leaders and Managers

Leadership requires performing leadership roles that will make a profound difference. So, circumstances and goals will dictate leadership competencies needed. This explains many different views on leadership.

How do leadership and management differ? They have distinct functions and skill sets. They are often intertwined, although they can also be mutually exclusive; that is, a leader does not need to be a manager while a manager may not be a leader.

Abraham Zaleznick, in his classical article in Harvard Business Review in 1997, argued that essential leadership elements of inspiration, vision, and human passion drive success.[1] Leaders take a personal outlook for shaping goals and change how people think about goals. Managers have an impersonal, passive outlook as they think that goals arise out of necessities. Leaders devise fresh approaches to problems which increase options but also increase risks whereas managers choose and implement the most desirable option out of a set of available options. Leaders relate to other people directly, intuitively, and empathetically, but managers use structures and processes to motivate others. Finally, leaders seek to profoundly influence or change human and economic relationships, whereas managers see themselves as a part of their organization.

At some level, whether you are a leader or a manager depends on the time you give or devote to tasks. Let's find out from a simple exercise: "What is your profile?"

Exercise What's Your profile?

Leader or manager: where would you place yourself?

On each line, put an "X" closer to the word that best describes what you do or think. The closer your X is to the word, the stronger is your behavior toward that task (see Table 2.1).

---

[1] Zaleznick, A. (2007). Managers and leaders: Are they different. *Harvard Business Review, 82*(1), 74–81.

Table 2.1: *What Is Your Profile?*

Do you...?	I am at .... (put an "X" to left or right)	Do you...?
Administer		Innovate
Maintain		Develop
Rely on control		Inspire
Focus on systems and structures		Focus on people
Have short-term view		Have long-term perspective
Ask how and when		Ask what and why
Accept status quo		Challenge the status quo
Develop detailed steps and timetables		Develop vision and strategies
Have a position provided		Take initiative to lead
Avoid risks		Take risks
Do things right		Do the right things

Source: Adapted from Bennis W. on becoming a leader.

> *Leadership complements management; it does not replace it.*
> (Kotter 1990)

Now, join up all the crosses. Where do most of your Xs fall? If you have more Xs toward the right, you have strong leadership qualities. If most of your Xs are on the left, then you are a manager by inclination. Your profile should match the tasks you need to perform. Note that task requirements vary over programs and over time, and there are always opportunities to develop leadership skills and competencies, if needed. For a new health program that requires changing people's behaviors and practices, leadership is more important, whereas for an established and well-performing program managerial tasks are critical.

Kotter argues that leadership is different from management.[2] The real challenge is to combine strong leadership and strong management and use each to balance the other. Management is

[2] Kotter, J. P. (1990). What leaders really do. *Harvard Business Review*, 1–11. Available at http://www.faithformationlearningexchange.net/uploads/5/2/4/6/5246709/what_leaders_really_do.pdf (accessed on March 10, 2014).

about coping with complexity whereas leadership is about coping with change. The former requires planning and budgeting, organizing and staffing, and controlling activities and solving problems. In comparison leadership involves setting direction, aligning people, and inspiring others.

Framework for Visionary Leadership

It is clear that leadership on its own is not enough to achieve the desired program results in the health sector. Leaders must strengthen and apply both their leadership and management skills and competencies to be both visionary and effective. The Visionary Leadership Development (VLD) framework presents a viable approach to address both sector and program challenges.

Based upon literature survey and program experiences at International Council on Management of Population Programmes (ICOMP), this VLD framework[3] for health has been developed as an analytical tool to understand both the program environment and to determine the appropriate leadership competencies necessary to address prevalent challenges. The framework consists of two circles, "leadership" on the left and "management" on the right (see Figure 2.1).

Figure 2.1: *Intersecting Circles of Leadership and Management*

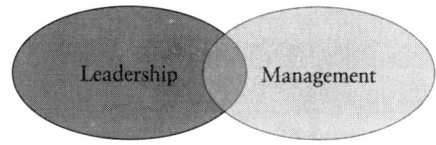

Source: Authors.

Each circle has several components, indicating an appropriate set of actions for either leadership or management. In short, the distinctions between the two can be thought of as given in Box 2.1:

---

[3] The VLD framework is developed by ICOMP and its applicability has been tested in many recent projects.

Box 2.1: *Leadership and Management Tasks*

Leadership	Doing the Right Thing >>	Having a vision, assessing the vision–reality gap, finding a path/strategy and setting goals, and inspiring and empowering to follow the path or implement the strategy.
Management	Doing Things Right >>	Setting objectives to achieve the goal, planning to achieve the objectives, implementing or organizing, and monitoring and evaluating.

Source: Authors.

Visionary leadership requires appropriate emphasis on leadership and management (Doing the Right Things Right) to achieve success.

We have learned that leadership is a very context-specific process particularly in a challenging field like health. Thus, different leadership traits and competencies are required for different situations and environments. Clearly, the challenges of realizing the desired future will differ between countries and regions.

The Components of Visionary Leadership Framework

Figure 2.2 shows the visionary leadership framework. From the experiences of applying this framework to various ICOMP projects, we have learned which leadership competencies are most relevant depends on a leader's ability to do the following:

1. Create and communicate a shared vision
2. See the big picture to analyze the vision–reality gap
3. Find the path
4. Inspire/empower stakeholders

This visionary leadership framework is developed based on our experiences of implementing two leadership projects between 2002 and 2010 and from our interactions and collaborations with other similar leadership initiatives in the field of RH, population,

Figure 2.2: *A Visionary Leadership Framework: Making a Difference in Health*

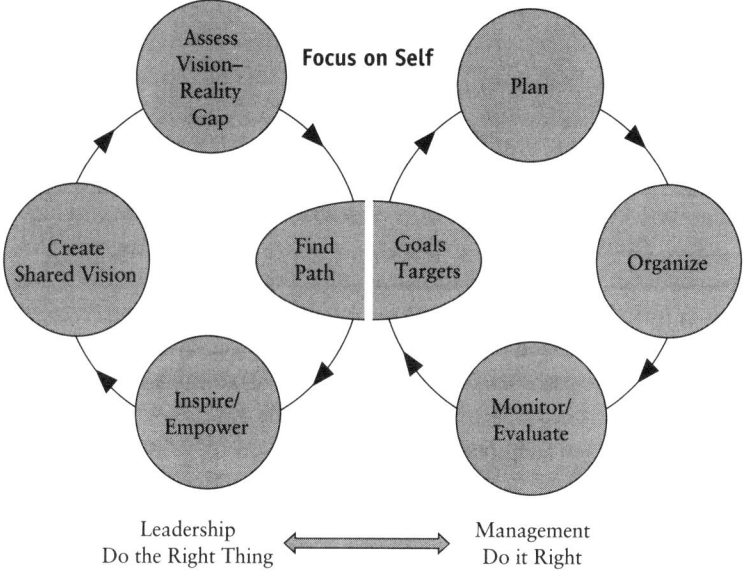

Source: Authors.

and development. The genesis of leadership in RH (left-hand side) can be found in the Visionary Leadership Program (VLP) which was implemented in Ethiopia, India, Nigeria, and Sudan by a consortium of three partners—ICOMP, Centre for African Family Studies (CAFS), Nairobi, Kenya, and Partners in Population and Development (PPD), Dhaka, Bangladesh. Lessons from the VLP support the hypothesis that management skills and organizational competencies are vital for effective leadership (right-hand side).

The framework took shape with the end of VLP in 2006.[4] It was given a chance to be operationalized through a hybrid leadership-cum-management project called LDOE which was

[4] The Association of Schools of Public Health (ASPH) describes leadership as "the ability to create and communicate a shared vision for a changing future; champion solutions to organizational and community challenges; and energize commitment to goals." Part I of this book discusses how such leadership ability can be developed. Specific leadership competencies for students in Masters in Public Health are discussed in Part II of this book.

implemented in north-eastern part of India between 2007 and 2010, in collaboration with XISS. Lessons from LDOE support two basic premises of leadership: (1) leaders are made, not born and (2) to be truly effective, leaders also need to be managers.

Creating and Communicating a Shared Vision: Most people in health interpret the need to create and communicate a shared vision to mean an "advocacy." There are several ways to create a shared vision—Information, Education, and Communication (IEC), advocacy, consultation, and cocreation. Even if one wants to advocate, it is useful to at least carry out a process of consultation. Although a shared vision has to be created, most importantly, it needs to be communicated in an effective manner as different stakeholders have their own personal/organizational vision. This is discussed in Chapter Three.

The many challenges we face in this field from weak political will, resistance from traditional cultural practices to shortage of staff make it all the more imperative that there should be a shared vision and alignment of values, support, and resources. Not only the "desired future" has to be clear but the leader has to make sure that he/she does not have to do too much "firefighting" which is a wastage of time and resource.

Assessing the Vision–Reality Gap: Often the gap between "vision" and "reality" is seen as it is here and now. However, for devising an appropriate path, visionary leaders need to see the "big picture" by considering the following:

- *Trend over time*: One needs to understand the reality and, therefore, the gap that is changing over time.
- *Differentials over geographic areas*: One needs to under-stand the reality and, therefore, the gap variation over time and space. This would show where the efforts need to be focused, as well as reasons for the variation which will help in the formulation of path/strategy.
- *See reality from different levels*: The reality maybe seen or perceived differently from village, town, district, and province levels. One needs to understand these perceptions to devise the path/strategy.
- *Relate to different levels of objectives*: Each vision, and so the reality, contributes to a higher level objective, ultimately

relating to quality of life. It helps to understand this hierarchy of objectives.

There are several advantages of seeing the "big picture." It allows us to:

1. Forecast what the gap will be if current situation continues
2. Know where our efforts should be focused if we want to create the most impact
3. Communicate the reality and the gap to different stakeholders

Assessing the vision–reality gap is discussed in Chapter Four.

Finding the Path or Strategy: Finding the right path is critical to the successful implementation and realization of a leader's vision. Assessments of the vision–reality gap will provide the appropriate and timely information to guide the leaders in their analysis of the situation and resources at their disposal to make a decision on the path to take. In Chapter Five, we present approaches to find the right "Path." A strategy is the way to progress on the chosen path.

Leaders look for ways to radically alter the status quo, for ways to create something totally new, for revolutionary new processes, for ways to beat the system. (Kouzes and Posner)

The path/strategy to bridge the vision–reality gap would not only involve creating a shared vision and aligning values, but most importantly, coordinating practices among different parts of the health system. Therefore, as a first step, visionary leaders make efforts to know about the best practices. The sources of best practices are the Internet, contacts with NGOs and peers, available reports and publications, and successes within the programs. Often leaders would identify who have been successful and why to see if these experiences can be adapted. They may also identify failures to learn what should be avoided.

Generally, the differences between the current practices and best practices (adapted, if necessary) need to be reduced to achieve the goal. This involves a careful orchestration of a change process. A change is more likely to be accepted if:

1. An urgency is felt that the current situation needs to change
2. There is consensus on direction of change
3. There is trust in the person leading the change

If the change process involves gainers and losers (which is often the case) then leaders need to develop a strategy for change. The goal needs to be set in terms of bridging the vision–reality gap. Leaders need to choose wisely, balancing the costs of under-achieving and stretching it to do the best.

Implementation of any path/strategy requires resources. First step is to see if resources are available and efficiently utilized within the current program. Then the program activities need to be reconfigured. If resources can be freed up from some other parts of the organization, they can be reallocated. Finally, additional resources may need to be mobilized.

Inspiring and Empowering: An important skill expected of an effective visionary leader is the ability to inspire and empower others. Whether it is to reduce maternal deaths, to expand RH services for young people, or address NCDs, a leader can exert influence through getting diverse stakeholders and constituencies to commit to the vision (or path), or appropriately and quickly deploying resources to match stipulated plans and activities, or sharing insights and observations with senior leaders as a way to get their support. Within the organization, the leader can empower colleagues and staff through clarity in roles and expectations, and inculcating teamwork. Some ways to inspire and empower stakeholders are discussed in Chapter Six.

Results-Based Management: While it is important to do the right thing, to achieve success, a leader should do it right through practicing results-based management which is the focus of Chapter Seven. Sometimes, the top managers may feel that the strategy is well set but results are not achieved because strategy is not executed well. If so, then the visionary leaders need to concentrate on execution. However, it is important to remember that strategies should be validated, otherwise suboptimal results will be achieved (success = doing the right things right). The execution requires three things: (1) strategies need to be converted into detailed operations, (2) people need to be motivated, and (3) an implementation plan needs to be executed.[5] Thus, the results-based management involves the following steps.

Setting Goals and Targets: Results-based management begins with the setting of clear outcome goals. The selected strategy would determine what outputs need to be targeted to realize the desired outcome goals. It is often said that output targets should be SMART (S = specific, M = measurable, A = achievable, R = relevant, and T = time-bound).

Planning: It is the process of specifying what activities need to be done to achieve the set targets, who will execute them, and what resources would be needed to carry out those activities. It is generally said that "failure to plan is to plan for failure."

Organizing and Implementing: Implementing any path or strategy involves resources. The first step is to see if current resources are efficiently utilized within the current program. Then the program activities need to be configured. Once adequate resources are ensured, the activities need to be organized and implemented according to the plan.

Monitoring and Evaluating: Whether an initiative or program is going in the right direction as planned is the goal of a monitoring and evaluation activity. Time and circumstances can bring changes, big and small, and these are often evident only from close monitoring. The leader should pay attention to monitoring throughout the course of a program or activity; if necessary with the timely information or feedback, make appropriate modifications so that the activity does not veer off the path. Thus, monitoring focuses on activities and outputs. Evaluation emphasizes whether the desired outcomes have been realized and, therefore, will give indications whether a program is well designed and implemented as per the plan in the right manner.

> Reflection: What is your "take-home" learning from this?

---

[5] Bossidy, L., Charan, R., & Burck, C. (2002). *Execution: The discipline of getting things done.* London: Random House Business Books.

Applying the Framework: Where do we start? Ideally, the process of visionary leadership begins with creating a shared vision. However, various scenarios can be present. For example, there is very weak top management or lack of political commitment for the vision. Often the response in such a situation is to resort to evidence-based advocacy with evidence derived from local, national, and international sources. However, this may take a long time.

Then one could begin with other parts of leadership circle (as above) such as inspiring/empowering stakeholders. It may be that the top manager is willing to let the staff address some operational issues which would not only inspire/empower them but also could make progress toward the "vision." In this case, teams could be formed and empowered to address related problems. Ultimately, it is important that the whole circle of leadership is completed. Therefore, it would be necessary to build on the successes of the small teams.

Sometimes top managers might feel that the strategy was good, but results were not achieved because of weak execution. In this case, a visionary leader should concentrate on execution of the strategy. It is important to remember that a strategy, however, well-designed or crafted in theory, should always be validated (success = doing the right things right).

How Does Visionary Leadership Deliver Superior Value in Health?

An effective health system, comprising the following constituents—individuals/households, communities, and public and private health service providers—makes a difference in health status of the people. The practices of these three constituents of the health system and their mutual interactions determine the effectiveness of the health system. For instance, reduction in maternal mortality requires addressing the three delays: (1) delay in individuals/households deciding to seek emergency obstetric care in case of pregnancy complication, (2) delay in reaching appropriate service facility due to lack of available transport facility in the community, and (iii) delay at the facility in providing the needed care. Minimizing all the three delays will reduce maternal mortality.

Therefore, to make a difference in health, there is a need for coordinated practices/behaviors on the part of the three constituents—individuals/households, communities, and health-care providers. Implementation of these practices or behaviors obviously needs resources. But when resources are limited, the question is how would the three constituencies leverage whatever is available for greater impact? To inspire and empower these constituencies and leveraging their resources require that they should have a shared vision for the RH issue under consideration. To sustain this vision, a foundation of aligned values is required. For instance, to reduce maternal deaths by reduction in three delays, all the three constituencies should have a shared vision on zero tolerance to maternal deaths. This shared vision must not only emanate from values of human rights but also that women's rights are human rights as well as values of gender equality and equity. Then resources available with each constituent of the health system should be leveraged.

Thus, a visionary leader, applying the visionary leadership framework, needs to perform the following roles among individuals/households, communities, and health-care providers:

1. Create a shared vision
2. Align values
3. Coordinate practices/behaviors
4. Leverage resources

While creating a shared vision is a critical part of the leadership, the path chosen should lead to coordinating practices and behaviors as well as leveraging currently or potentially available resources. While shared vision inspires, aligning values empowers stakeholders.

Figure 2.3 shows how the practices of visionary leadership will improve the health status of people.

Figure 2.3: *Visionary Leadership Making a Difference*

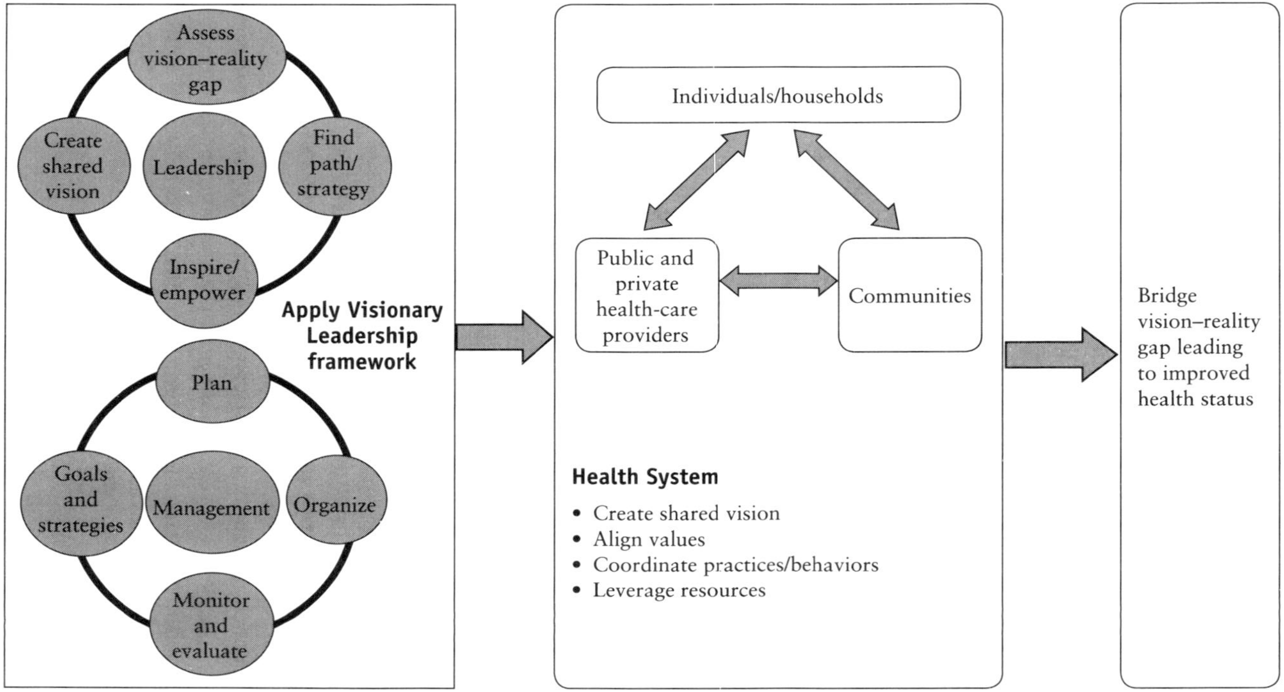

Source: Authors.

In the following paragraphs, we discuss two case studies that demonstrate the applicability of this framework.

CASE STUDY 1: **The Center for Global Development Documented 20 Evidence-Based Cases**

The Center for Global Development documented 20 evidence-based cases in "Millions Saved: Proven Successes in Global Health" in which large-scale efforts to improve health in developing countries have succeeded—saving millions of lives and preserving the livelihoods and social fabric of entire communities.[6] These include addressing communicable diseases; including small pox, HIV, tuberculosis, polio, measles, and diarrhea; preventing NCDs including tobacco use, improving health of mothers and children; and reducing morbidity due to cataracts, iodine deficiency, and neural tube defects in children.

Based upon these cases, they identified the following elements of success:

Predictable, Adequate Funding from Both International and Local Sources: Making public health programs work needs money. Steady, adequate funding is needed so that the programs can be sustained long enough to have a major impact. Almost all the successful programs managed to obtain long-term commitments of financial support (up to 20 years of funding) at levels that permitted procurement of adequate supplies and commodities and the hiring of good managers and personnel.

Political Leadership and Champions: Nearly all the cases illustrate the importance of visible high-level commitment to a cause. In few of the cases, political commitment was simply the result of a leader's particular interest in a cause. In others, political commitment came about because technical experts were able to communicate effectively that a "big win" was possible. In these instances, the ability of the technical experts to make the most of a political opening was the seed of the success.

---

[6] Center for Global Development (2004). *Millions saved: Proven successes in global health*. Case studies. Retrieved from www.cgdev.org.

Technical Innovation within an Effective Delivery System, at a Sustainable Price: Many interventions/cases used a new technology—a drug, vaccine, micronutrient supplement, or pesticide—that was appropriate to the conditions of the developing world. Typically, the new technology permitted an existing program to work more effectively and produce rapid health gains. However, development of a new health product alone is not sufficient for success. Major managerial and logistical efforts were required to ensure that the new technology reaches the target population through the existing public health system or through a dedicated distribution network.

Technical Consensus about the Appropriate Biomedical or Public Health Approach: Agreement within an expert community about the right strategy is a central factor in the appropriate design of programs. Such expert consensus occurs through regular international meetings and investment in scientific research. With such consensus, properly presented programs are seen as credible and worthy of the outlays required. "Branding" that expert consensus—as the tuberculosis community has done with directly observed therapy, short course (DOTS)—helps with advocacy for greater financial and political support.

Good Management on the Ground: Good health service delivery requires that trained and motivated workers are in place and have adequate required supplies, equipment, transportation, and supervision to do their job well. This requires both adequate funding and good management, and in some instances strong management partially compensates for budgetary restrictions.

Effective Use of Information: Information is important in four ways. First, information about the extent of a health problem raises awareness and focuses political and technical attention on finding solutions. Second, research on health behaviors and on the effectiveness of different service delivery approaches can help shape the design of a program and increase its prospects for success. Third, information motivates. In several programs, program managers were spurred to higher levels of performance through the "positive competition" that came from the knowledge that other countries or regions are making faster progress. Fourth, information facilitates mid-course corrections. Collecting information before the program begins and along the way has allowed program managers to evaluate whether the intervention is achieving its goals, and, in some cases, has signaled the need for changes in program strategy in the middle of the program.

How Do These Fit in the Visionary Leadership Framework Discussed Here?

The need for political leadership and champions is cited as one element of success. However, it is not clear what role these leaders played or if their behavior had caused something to happen. We will map these into our visionary leadership framework (see Box 2.2).

Box 2.2: *Applying Visionary Leadership Framework*

Creating shared vision	▷	There is no direct reference to creating shared vision but commitment of many funding and technical agencies and national government was obtained leading to predictable, adequate funding over more than 20 years
Assessing vision–reality gap	▷	Role of information was critical. Operations research, trials, and other country experiences were used to highlight the gap between what was possible and what the reality was.
Finding path	▷	The innovative path chosen depended not only on technical innovation within an effective delivery system at a sustainable price and technical consensus about the appropriate biomedical or public health approach, but also on forging necessary partnership among government, private sector, and communities to deliver these technical solutions.

(Box 2.2 Contd)

(Box 2.2 Contd)

Inspire/ empower	▷	Although not specifically mentioned in the elements of success, several ministries of health and other agencies were inspired by seeing other countries' experiences and role of this information was critical. The predictable and adequate funding with necessary flexibility empowered program authorities.
Results-based management	▷	Good management on the ground is cited as an element of success.

Source: Authors.

Thus, the elements of success can be mapped into visionary leadership framework. However, it is not clear whether systematic use of the framework would have added to the success. For instance, a question arises as to whether conscious efforts to create a shared vision among all stakeholders would have accelerated progress.

CASE STUDY 2: African Health Leadership Initiative[7]

A Concerted Effort across Health Systems: Even the world's most promising health technologies can hit delivery bottlenecks when they reach some developing countries. Improving health outcomes at meaningful scale requires the pairing of effective clinical interventions with efficient health systems. Without good leadership, supervision, supportive policies, sufficient infrastructure, and other factors many effective health interventions are unlikely to reach those who need them at sufficient scale or quality. Bringing effective health initiatives to fruition and scale often requires massive collaboration within government as well as coordinated efforts among government,

---

[7] Synergos. (2011). *African health leadership initiative: Strengthening health systems & leadership for improved health outcomes.* Retrieved from www.africanhealth leadership.org.

international agencies, business, civil society, and citizens. Across most of the developing world, and especially in sub-Saharan Africa, such systems are exceedingly fragile.

Leadership to Effect Meaningful Change: An essential component of strong health system is a capacity within the national health leadership to exert itself in two critical ways. First is the responsibility among leaders to articulate a compelling vision of the future, devise strategies for achieving that vision, and align and motivate people to achieve the vision. Second, leaders must ensure that actions are taken in order to realize the vision by creating appropriate plans, procedures, and programs for execution; ensuring performance and monitoring and evaluating results. The quality of leaders and leadership ultimately drives success or failure in the organizations.

The African Health Leadership Initiative: It works to bridge the implementation gap between policy formulation and front-line action. It stimulates progress on national health priorities through field-based innovation, project-based action, locally grounded scaling, and in-country leadership development. Innovation projects take an integrated approach, seeking impacts across the broader health system rather than narrow, singular interventions. It is funded by grants from the Bill & Melinda Gates Foundation and the Global Alliance for Improved Nutrition (GAIN) to the Synergos Institute. The Initiative is led by Synergos in collaboration with McKinsey & Company and the Presencing Institute.

I wish to extend our sincere gratitude for your support to the African Health Leadership Initiative. Improving the performance of our public health care system is a vital national priority and the program you are supporting could not be more timely or useful. (Right Honorable Nahas Angula, Prime Minister, Namibia)

Cultivating Leadership and Innovation Practices for Continued Success: The Initiative strengthens capacity of in-country health leaders to execute successfully national health plans and more effectively allocate and leverage human, infrastructure, and financial resources. The Initiative engages health leaders at multiple levels—from health ministry officials to frontline practitioners—as part of their regular, ongoing professional responsibilities. Through a program of action-based learning, workshops, and coaching and mentoring, the Initiative nurtures effectiveness among in-country health leaders to design and lead innovation projects, collaborate with stakeholders, scale successful projects, and ensure that efforts are integrated with national strategies and funding cycles. One example of the Initiative's work is in Namibia, which is discussed in the following section.

EXAMPLE: Namibia
Consultations with the Namibian Ministry of Health and Social Services and other in-country health leaders identified maternal health and young child nutrition as the Initiative's priority focus areas. Namibia's development and health challenges parallel those of many other African countries. The United Nations Development Programme (UNDP) ranks it at 125 out of 177 countries on its Human Development Index. Namibia has among the highest levels of income inequality in the world: over half of its population lives on less than $2 a day and health resources are often grossly unequal when viewed along socioeconomic, racial, and geographic divisions. The country's maternal mortality ratio is high at 449 per 100,000 live births and 28 percent of its children are chronically undernourished. In addition to high levels of maternal mortality and child malnutrition, Namibia has an overall HIV prevalence of 21 percent and more than two-thirds of child deaths are attributed to diarrhea, pneumonia, and malnutrition. Considering the country's relatively high health expenditures, these indicators suggest a health system whose service to health beneficiaries could improve.

The assessment found that challenges in addressing clinical causes of maternal and newborn deaths—such as eclampsia, severe infection, and pre-term birth—are compounded by health system leadership challenges such as weak alignment, unclear roles, poor communication, and lack of effective collaboration. The Initiative addresses these dual challenges through its innovation projects and its support and engagement with in-country health leaders. Health leaders design and lead innovation projects that are based on assessments, guided by national strategies, and supported by senior-level champions and officials. Innovation projects target key leverage points for improved health outcomes, while fostering more effective engagement of health leaders and demonstrating a new way of advancing toward health goals.

An Integrated Approach for Improved Outcomes: Innovation projects focus on high complexity challenges where progress depends on a combination of skills such as collaboration, political will, market understanding, and technical know-how. The Initiative's innovation projects take an integrated approach, addressing demand, access, quality, and enablers.

- Demand: Building awareness about the importance of proper maternal health and nutrition
- Access: Increasing access to maternal health and services
- Quality: Improving the quality of patient care for better health outcomes
- Enablers: Improving efficiency through ambulance service management and regular performance management

Thus, the Initiative has launched innovation projects in Namibia that address key drivers of maternal mortality and child malnutrition. Innovation projects translate national health strategy and policy intentions into context-relevant, field-based action on the ground. Designed and implemented by in-country health leaders, innovation projects respond to critical blockages and high-leverage opportunities. In addition to generating health impacts, innovation projects infuse energy into the health system and demonstrate a new way of working that is data-informed, collaborative, and action-oriented.

Central to the Initiative's maternal health activities is a core group of health leaders, who bring a diverse range of perspectives, skills, and resources. In addition, it engages an ever-evolving group that enlists specific talents as the project needs emerge. A large number of organizations are active in the Initiative's maternal and young child health activities.

As mentioned earlier, malnutrition is widespread in Namibia, with 28 percent of children under-five stunted and underweight. Chronic food insecurity, micronutrient deficiencies, recurring weather hazards—such as drought and floods—HIV/AIDS, and, more recently, rising food prices have had dire effects on people's lives and livelihoods. Immediate underlying factors of malnutrition include poor maternal nutrition and care before and during pregnancy, and non-optimal infant and young child feeding and care; for example, less than 6 percent of Namibian mothers exclusively breastfeed until six months, as recommended by WHO for infant health and nutrition.

Initiative's activities in maternal, infant, and young child nutrition are implemented by health leaders as a natural complement to its maternal health efforts. These include incorporating child nutrition as a module within educational radio programming for pregnant women, improving nurse training for Integrated Management of Acute Malnutrition, and fortifying staple foods with iron, Vitamin A, zinc, and other essential micronutrients.

Namibian Alliance for Improved Nutrition: As part of the Initiative's nutrition activities, it has created the Namibian Alliance for Improved Nutrition (NAFIN) to strategically manage and advance national nutrition activities. NAFIN is chaired by the prime minister and includes membership from key cabinet ministries, leading international agencies and corporations, and domestic organizations such as the Agronomic Board and the Millers Association. NAFIN activities focus on

- Reducing malnutrition and promoting good nutrition for all Namibians, with a focus on women and children.
- Developing capacity for service delivery across key government sectors—agriculture, health, education, gender, and child welfare—to ensure and prioritize essential

nutrition and household food security for vulnerable and disadvantaged households and communities.

- Ensuring the economic and social benefits of nutrition security are reflected in sectoral plans and policies, as well as the National Development Plans.

Strengthening Leadership and Management Skills: Through regular workshops, coaching, and mentoring, the Initiative helps the senior-most officials in the Ministry of Health and Social Services create a strong enabling environment for effective health interventions and progress on health priorities. Activities address individual health leader needs as well as the broader team or organizational culture, covering areas such as team alignment, collaboration, prioritization, and building trust and responsibility. Improved leadership and management skills are helping senior health officials and key partners to provide the ongoing leadership drive, management support, and political will required for improved health outcomes.

Challenge: Become a Better Visionary Leader

The commitment of 189 member states of the U.N. to strive toward the achievement of the MDGs by 2015 is, for all intents and purposes, commendable. But what has not been discussed was: Is there adequate leadership in health to achieve this?

The argument for visionary leadership in the health sector is an easy one to make. Leaders thrive in complex difficult environments and health is surely one of the most challenging sectors to work in.

What distinguishes leaders in health sector from those in, say, the for-profit corporate world or government sector is a combination of peculiar situational and institutional parameters. Health leaders, especially those in poor developing countries, work long hours, have limited resources, face uncertain funding flows, deal with hostile traditional groups, and face volatile policy and economic situations. In addition, there are also complex managerial demands such as inadequate organizational capacity and infrastructure, lack of trained personnel, low staff morale, to mention a few.

There is much to be done for health but we do not have enough leaders to do it. While it is easy to call for leadership (and there have been many such calls), it is not so easy to create, nurture, and sustain leaders in challenging environments such as that in health. Those currently leading programs or organizations in health simply have too much on their plate because the demands on them—time, attention, emotions, resources, results, and so on—can be overwhelming in a generally less-than-supportive context. It is a constant juggle that calls for a vast array of not only skills and competencies but emotional maturity and community sensibilities.

Perceptions on the role of leaders and about the efficacy of leadership development programs for health have also changed. Where traditionally a one-off one-time leadership training course was the norm, there is now a general consensus that this is not adequate.

Two major shifts in perceptions are evident:

1. *Developing leaders is a journey that takes time.* Therefore, an effective leadership development program has to be a training-cum-learning process constituting a mix of methodologies and implemented over a period of time.
2. *Creating and nurturing leaders require context-appropriate training and learning.* Hence, contents of leadership development curriculum need to be tailored or customized for health practitioners with concepts, frameworks, skills, and tools that are applicable to the sector and address specific needs.

Leaders in the health sector have their work cut out for them. There are enough people with the vision and passion to get things done. Often the technologies are available but that is not enough. Strengthening the health system is one critical area to focus on if the objective of improving health programs is to be achieved.

Capacity building is another area often cited for attention, and much has been done in this area though not enough. Resources are never enough but there are promising examples coming out of resource-constrained environments.

The VLD framework points to the potential of achieving health status if leadership and management elements are merged to address the many issues in health in a systematic way. The challenge in the sector is for leaders to focus on doing the right thing right and become better and more effective visionary leaders. In the chapters that follow in Part One of the book, we discuss each element of the VLD framework in detail to enable health leaders to make that journey to become more effective visionary leaders.

Three

Creating Shared Vision:
Key to Leadership

The very essence of leadership is that you have to have vision. It's got to be a vision you articulate clearly and forcefully on every occasion. You can't blow an uncertain trumpet.

—Father Theodore Hesburgh[1]

What Is Vision?

A vision is a "picture of the future that we wish to see or create." The three elements of this process are: Future, Wish to Create, and Picture. First, something in the future is unknown and, therefore, it is something that has to be imagined. So, the question is—should we accept a vision of something which is unknown because of the inherent mystery and risks? It is generally accepted, however, that the job of a vision is to articulate or propose a future that would be clearly better than our current situation. Therefore, it is a future that we want to see, create, or aspire to.

The second element is that "we wish to create" this future. This has several implications. One, the stakeholders of an organization (staff, board, shareholders, and even customers) would be willing to put in effort to support a vision in order to realize that future. Two, a vision should be "high," "lofty," or aspirational enough to inspire stakeholders to action. Three, it should engage not only the mind but the heart and spirit as well.

[1] Retrieved from www.thinkexist.com/quotes/theodore_hesburgh/, accessed on January 5, 2013.

It should provide meaning and value to the organization's work and the stakeholders' effort. They should feel that the vision is worth going for and, therefore, it should tap into their deepest personal concerns, needs, or hopes as human beings. According to Bennis and Goldsmith, a good vision is based on two deep human needs: Quality and Dedication.[2]

Thirdly, a vision is the "picture" of the future. How the leader can describe and share this "picture," that is in his/her mind as clearly and as widely as possible, is the key to developing a good vision. As the picture is related to something in the future, a vision can be grand and somewhat "cloudy" but it should be simple and memorable. The different levels of specifics (of the vision) could later be embodied in mission statements and organizational goals and objectives.

> *The future is not a result of a choice among alternative paths offered by the present, but a place that we create, first in the mind, next in will, then in action. The future is not some place where we are going, but a place we are creating. We do not discover the paths but make them, and the action of making the future changes both the maker and destination.* (Anonymous)

There are many grand and lofty forward-looking visions articulated by governments around the world, especially those in developing countries. One of the better known country-level development visions is Malaysia's "Vision 2020," a call for the country to acquire developed country status by the year 2020.[3] The articulation, sharing, and promotion of such a vision are to propel the whole country (i.e., the stakeholders) on a journey toward an aspiration (developed country status). Vision 2020 is an example of a "successful" vision as it has endured more than 20 years after its first appearance in 1991. Even with the new

---

[2] Warren, B., & Goldsmith, J. (1994). *Learning to lead: A workbook on becoming a leader.* Massachusetts,USA: Addison-Wesly, p. 126.

[3] "Vision 2020" was proposed by Mahathir Mohamad, then Prime Minister of Malaysia, when he tabled the Sixth Malaysian Plan before the Parliament in 1991. Retrieved from www.wawasan2020.com/vision/.

leadership, Malaysia today continues to use Vision 2020, modified and updated, as a national aspiration.

Traditionally, most organizations had a mission statement but now it is common that they include a vision as part of their organizational ethos. Nanus describes an organizational vision as a

> realistic, credible, attractive future of your organization…an idea so energizing that it, in effect, jump-starts the future by calling forth the skills, talents, and resources to make it happen (and) a sign-post pointing the way for all who need to understand what the organization is and where it intends to go.[4]

Finally, there are personal visions, a future that one sees for oneself. Leaders are usually individuals with strong personal visions. If they have the energy, determination, and resources to take their vision forward, they can do great things for themselves or for the organization they lead. Whichever level a vision is, what is common is the desire to realize or reach for a better and improved future, for oneself, for an organization, or for a country.

Three Levels of Vision

Ideally, vision at these three levels—personal, organizational, and societal—should be in harmony as only then can people participate whole heartedly in creating that future.

For instance, an organization working for the prevention of HIV/AIDS could, at the first level, be guided by a general societal vision of an "AIDS-free generation." Inspired by this, it could develop its own organizational vision such as "Reaching to all with HIV prevention," something that should be in harmony with all its stakeholders and, most likely, compatible with many personal visions.

---

[4] Nanus, B. (1995). *Visionary leadership: Creating a compelling sense of direction for your organization*. San Francisco, USA: Jossy Bass, p. 8.

It has always been asked: Why does vision matter? One of the best answers to that question is also very simple: "If you don't know where you're going, you might end up someplace else."[5]

Visions are powerful stuff. They can make donors part with their money "for a good cause;" investors to put their faith in "someone's dream;" or volunteers to willingly give their time because "they believe;" or employees and colleagues to work 110 percent "because we are in this together."

The Power of Vision

Leaders may come in all shapes and sizes, or they may be found in unexpected places or surfaced in times of crises and upheavals. But one thing that they all definitely have in common is—a vision. Warren Bennis, who is one of the earliest researchers to make the connection between vision and leadership, says that leaders are the most results-oriented people in the world.[6] Results attract attention and followers and believers.

According to Boyett and Boyett, the major shift in leadership thinking in recent years has been to go from the traditional strategist to the visionary.[7] Because the world has become more complex, researchers say that strategies alone are no longer enough. There is a growing consensus that hard-nosed methodical analysis of the old days cannot move people enough to commit that extra 10–20 percent to deliver superior results. It is now widely accepted that monetary or other tangible rewards can move or motivate people only to a certain extent but for commitment that is sustainable, what works is usually something intangible. Hence, "vision" has become the key to effective leadership.

---

[5] Yogi Berra Quotes. Retrieved from www.goodreads.com/authors/quotes/79014.Yogi Berra/.

[6] Bennis, W., & Nanus, B. (1985). *Leaders: The strategies for taking charge*. New York: Harper and Row, p. 28.

[7] Boyett, J., & Boyett, J. (1998). *The guru guide: The best ideas of the top management thinkers*. New York, USA: John Wiley & Sons.

Goleman[8] says it well: "Great leaders move us. They ignite our passion and inspire the best in us." What does it take to ignite that passion or give us that excitement? We believe that it is leaders who have visions. Visionary leadership has been described as a force that moves people and mobilizes resources to get things done. Vision is the glue that binds people together, that produces great teams, that acts as a catalyst to provide synergy. It is a powerful force and absolutely essential for effective leadership.

If we transpose this line of thinking to the world of health programs, we know that visionary leadership is even more vital, given the state of many such programs in developing countries, with respect to funding, resources, needs, or emerging needs, and so on. Do we have leaders with a vision? How do we know we have a vision? How do we create a shared vision and why? And what can a shared vision do for the organization we lead? These are some of the questions we address in the following sections.

An Organizational Vision

An organizational vision is guided by the purpose, goals, and rationale for which the organization exists. Most members of the organization (such as staff, board members, executives, and so on) would have a sense of a common understanding and collective responsibility for achieving its purpose and goals. However, Senge, in his well-regarded book *The Fifth Discipline*,[9] suggests that a vision is only one of four components of an organization's guiding aspiration (see Box 3.1).

We can see that while goal is specific, vision is both vague and succinct. Box 3.2 lists some examples of visions created to match specific MDGs:

---

[8] Goleman, D., Boyatzis, R., & McKee, A. (2002). *The new leaders. Transforming the art of leadership into the science of results.* London, UK: Little Brown.

[9] Senge, P. (1994). *The fifth discipline: The art and practice of a learning organization.* New York: Currency/Doubleday.

Box 3.1: *An Organization's Guiding Aspiration: Vision, Values, Purpose, and Goals*

Vision: *An image of our desired future.* It is a statement or a picture that shows where we want to go, and what we will be like when we get there. Characteristics of a good vision are

- It is appropriate for the organization and for the times.
- It sets standards of excellence and reflects high ideas.
- It clarifies purpose and directions.
- It inspires enthusiasm and encourages commitment.
- It is well-articulated and easily understood.
- It reflects the uniqueness of the organization.
- It is ambitious.

Values: Values guide us on h*ow we expect to travel to where we want to go.* Values describe how we intend to operate, on a day-by-day basis, as we pursue our vision. For instance, Gandhi said that, in all human endeavors we cannot be certain of the ends, and, therefore, we should be sure of our means.[10] Values are best expressed in terms of behavior.

Purpose or Mission: *What the organization is here to do.* It represents the fundamental reason for the organization's existence. What are we here to do together? We may never get to the ultimate purpose of our organization, but may achieve many visions along the way. There are several examples of organizational mission. A famous example is when President Kennedy gave NASA a difficult and challenging mission in 1961: "Land man on the moon within a decade."[11] This lofty and difficult mission was realized when Neil Armstrong put man's first step on the moon. A more recent example is when the Government of India launched the NRHM in 2006 to bring about architectural corrections to the government's rural health system.

Goals: *Milestones we expect to reach.* Every vision needs to be converted into specific, realizable goals. Goals represent what people commit themselves to do, often within a short period. Goals are specific outcomes we wish to achieve over a defined period of time, similar to "milestones" on a journey to a destination (vision).

Source: Senge (1994).[12]

[10] Iyer, R. (2012). Means and ends in politics. Retrieved from www.mkganchi.org/g.relevance/chap28.htm, accessed on January 25, 2012.

[11] President John F. Kennedy's speech before a joint session of Congress. The decision to go to the moon (May 25, 1961). Retrieved from http://history.nasa.gov/moondec.htm/.

[12] Senge, *The fifth discipline.*

Box 3.2: *Goals and Attributed Visions*

Millennium Development Goals	Vision (*attributed to*)
<u>MDG 1</u>: Eradicate extreme poverty and hunger <u>Target</u>: Halve the number of people living below the poverty line by 2015	"Make Poverty History" (*a slogan used by civil society organizations*)
<u>MDG 1</u>: Eradicate extreme poverty and hunger <u>Target</u>: Halve, between 1990 and 2015, the proportion of people who suffer from hunger	"No Hunger" (*President Lula of Brazil*)
<u>MDG 6</u>: Combat HIV/AIDS, malaria, and other diseases <u>Target</u>: Halt and reverse the spread of HIV/AIDS, malaria, and other major diseases by 2015	"Zero New HIV infections" (UNAIDS. World AIDS Day Report 2011)

Source: Authors.

While other theorists may differ in interpretations or definitions but generally, very similar or compatible traits have emerged to describe "vision," often as a process of thinking or a possibility or potential that exists in the future. Here are two examples (see Figure 3.1):

> *It is a terrible thing to see and have no vision.* (Helen Keller)

What do we look for in a vision? Vision should have certain characteristics before it can have the desired effect of influencing or inspiring people (see Box 3.3):

Can we "humanize" a vision and assign it specific qualities? Box 3.4 offers some suggestions:

> *The fact that we cannot achieve tomorrow what we want is the worst reason not to act today. (*Anonymous)

In haste to assign characteristics and qualities to a vision, we should recognize what a vision is or is not designed to do, see Box 3.5.

Figure 3.1: *Characteristics of a Vision*

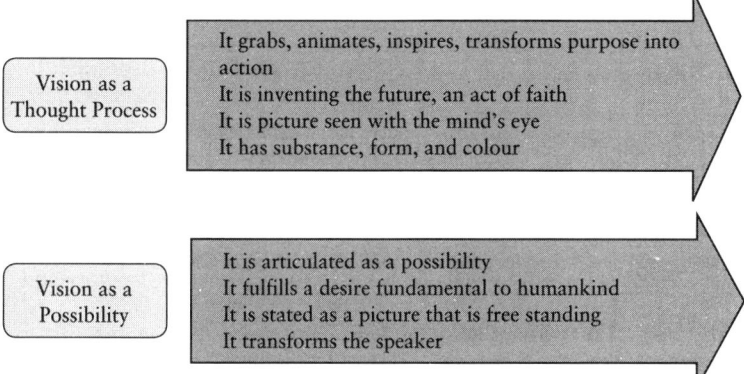

Vision as a Thought Process

It grabs, animates, inspires, transforms purpose into action
It is inventing the future, an act of faith
It is picture seen with the mind's eye
It has substance, form, and colour

Vision as a Possibility

It is articulated as a possibility
It fulfills a desire fundamental to humankind
It is stated as a picture that is free standing
It transforms the speaker

Source: Authors.

Box 3.3: *Characteristics of Good Visions*

A Good Vision

- Gives meaning to the changes expected of people
- Evokes a clear and positive mental image of a future state
- Creates pride, energy, and a sense of accomplishment
- Is ambitious, memorable, motivating, idealistic
- Offers a view of the future that is clearly and demonstrably better
- Fits the organization's history, culture, and values
- Sets standards of excellence that reflect high ideals
- Clarifies purpose and directions
- Inspires enthusiasm, encourages commitment
- Reflects the uniqueness of the organization
- Grabs attention
- Guides day-to-day activities
- Screens out the unessential
- Energizes people to transcend the bottom line
- Provides meaning and significance to daily activities
- Bridges the present and the future
- Moves people to action

Source: Boyett and Boyett (1998), p. 19.[13]

[13] Boyett and Boyett, *The guru guide.*

Box 3.4: *10 Qualities of a Vision*

1. A vision engages your heart and spirit.
2. A vision taps into embedded concerns and needs.
3. A vision asserts what you and your colleagues want to create.
4. A vision is something worth going for.
5. A vision provides meaning to the work you and your colleagues do.
6. By definition a vision is a bit cloudy and grand (if it were clear it wouldn't be a vision).
7. A vision is simple.
8. A vision is a living document that can always be expanded.
9. A vision provides a starting place from which to get to more and more levels of specificity.
10. A vision is based on two deep human needs: quality and dedication.

Source: Bennis W. and Joan Goldsmith (2010). Learning to Lead: A workbook on becoming a leader. New York, USA: Basic Books.

Box 3.5: *What a Vision Is Not?*

A Vision	
Is not a Prophecy	→ Although a vision is a mental picture of the future, it cannot predict future events.
Is not a Mission	→ A vision gives direction while a mission gives purpose.
Is not Factual	→ Because it doesn't exist in concrete terms. A vision does not deal with reality but with possible and desirable futures.
Is not a Constraint	→ On actions except for those that are not consistent with it.
Is not Static	→ Vision may change as more experience is gained or context changes significantly. As it is said that "vision is not cast in stone."
Cannot be True or False	→ As it is a picture of the future, it is neither true or false which are attributes associated with the current situation.

Source: Adapted from several sources.

It is easier to define what we do not want. Why? We have seen them. In contrast, we have not seen the future. It is harder to visualize "tomorrow" or "future." It is also more difficult to think of committing ourselves to a challenging task.

Figure 3.2: *Some Examples of Corporate Visions*

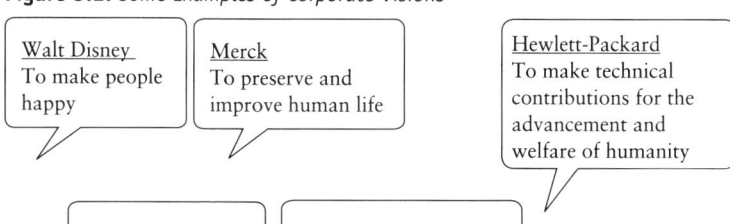

Walt Disney
To make people happy

Merck
To preserve and improve human life

Hewlett-Packard
To make technical contributions for the advancement and welfare of humanity

3M
To solve problems innovatively

Mary Kay Cosmetics
To give unlimited opportunity to women

Source: Adapted from several sources.

Some examples of visions of famous corporations are given in Figure 3.2.

Exercise Vision: Questions to Ask

When you are developing a vision for your organization, ask yourself the following questions:

- What is unique about your organization?
- What are your values and how do they shape your priorities for the future?
- What do your clients or the people you serve really need that you could provide or how do you add value to their quality of life?
- What would make people commit their mind and heart over the next three to seven years?
- What results does the organization hope to accomplish?

Exercise Developing a Vision

Write a vision of your organization, either an existing one or one you would like to see.

_____

_____

| Checklist | How Good Is Your Vision? |

How do you know if your vision is "successful" or any good? Answer the following questions with a tick (✓) in Yes or No columns in Table 3.1.

Table 3.1: *How Good Is Your Vision?*

		Yes	No
1.	Does this vision lead everyone in the organization in the best possible direction?		
2.	Will it benefit all members equally?		
3.	Will it help to sustain and protect the organization over the long term?		
4.	Can I, as a leader, articulate the mission clearly to all members of the organization?		
5.	Can the vision be expressed as a slogan?		
6.	Will the members of my group accept the vision with enthusiasm?		
7.	Am I highly enthusiastic about it myself?		
8.	Will the vision increase motivation appreciably?		
9.	Is it sufficiently visionary to work?		
10.	Is it the best vision under the circumstances?		
	Number of Yes/No		

Source: Adapted from Chapman (1989), p. 109.[14]

Scores:

- One to four Yes: Poor quality vision—try again.
- Five to seven Yes: Getting there—take another look.
- Eight or more Yes: Congratulations. You have a good and suitable vision.

[14] Chapman, E. (1989). *Leadership: What every manager needs to know.* New York: MacMillan Publishing.

Dream versus Vision

Are visions the same as dreams? Certainly, there seems to be a fine line between these two. The connection between dreams and visions is logical. But we believe there is a crucial difference. Many examples of renowned leaders' visions have elements of a dream, something grandiose, something far-reaching and fantastic that they perhaps "saw" (hence "envisioned") in their sleep. Do dreams become visions automatically? For the purpose of discussion, two examples of famous "dreams" are used: the song "Imagine" by Beatle John Lennon and "I have a dream" speech[15] by Dr Martin Luther King.

EXAMPLE 1: This is one of the most famous songs of the 20th century. Fitting for the era when it was written (the 1970s) by John Lennon, this song has been embraced by the peace movement as emblematic of its aspirations and hope.[16] It endures to this day as a messenger of peace (see Box 3.6).

EXAMPLE 2: This is one of the most famous speeches of our modern era (see Box 3.7). Even though it was specific to the conditions of race relations in the US, its message of civil rights and freedom found resonance around the world.

| Exercise | Dream versus Vision: What Is the Difference? |

Identify the difference between them. Are they the same, interchangeable or distinct and separate? What is/are the key factor(s)?

_____

_____

_____

[15] This 17-minute speech by Dr Martin Luther King, Jr, delivered on August 28, 1963 on the steps of Lincoln Memorial, calling for an end of racism in the US, was a defining moment in the American civil rights movement.

[16] Retrieved from www.metrolyrics.com/imagine-lyrics-john-lennon.html/.

Box 3.6: *The Power of a Song*

"Imagine"
Music and lyrics by John Lennon

Imagine there's no heaven
It's easy if you try, No hell below us
Above us only sky, Imagine all the
  people
Living for today...

Imagine there's no countries
It isn't hard to do. Nothing to kill or
  die for
And no religion too,
Imagine all the people, Living life in
  peace...
You may say I'm a dreamer
But I'm not the only one,
I hope someday you'll join us
And the world will be as one

Imagine no possessions
I wonder if you can
No need for greed or hunger
A brotherhood of man
Imagine all the people
Sharing all the world...

You may say I'm a dreamer
But I'm not the only one
I hope someday you'll join us
And the world will live as one

Source: www.metrolyrics.com/imagine-lyrics-john-lennon.html

Box 3.7: *Excerpt from a Speech by Dr Martin Luther King, August 1963*

"I Have a Dream"
".... I say to you today, my friends, that in spite of the difficulties and frustrations of the moment I still have a dream. It is a dream deeply rooted in the American dream.

I have a dream that one day the nation will rise up and live out the true meaning of its creed: "We hold these truths to be self-evident; that all men are created equal."

I have a dream that one day on the red hills of Georgia the sons of former slaves and the sons of former slave owners will be able to sit down together at the table of brotherhood.

I have a dream that one day even the State of Mississippi, a desert state sweltering in the heat of injustice and oppression, will be transformed into an oasis of freedom and justice.

I have a dream that my four children will one day live in a nation where they will not be judged by the color of their skin but by the content of their character.

I have a dream today...."

Source: Retrieved from www.youtube.com/.

Review	Comparing Dream and Vision

Comparison	
"Imagine"	**"I have a dream"**
It was a dream that inspired many. But John Lennon did not personally take much action for peace. Basically, the song carried the message. ↓	It was a dream that also moved millions. It turned into a critical inspiration for a whole civil rights movement in the US and the world. Martin Luther King's personal experience of discrimination fired him up and he went on to devote his life's work to civil rights. ↓
Remained a dream.	Became a vision that resulted in many social changes.
Visions and dreams have many things in common. Both are pictures, mental models of someone's imagination. Both do not represent current reality. However, a dream will remain a dream if we do not work toward realizing it by giving it our personal commitment and taking action. But with extra work (like Dr King) a dream can become a great vision inspiring millions of people!	

Vision without action is a dream
Action without vision is simply passing time
Action with vision is making a positive difference.
(Joel Barker's quote. Retrieved from www.thinkexists.com)

Vision and Action

Visions are essentially imaginative pictures of someone's idea and passion, a mental construct that points to a scenario in the future that is better, stronger, improved, more appealing, and so on. To accept someone's vision is a personal act of faith—why would we be willing to do that? Perhaps it is due to a basic human desire for change as a way to seek improvements in our lives. Therefore, you can't have a grand vision and not change fundamentally the way you do things. Because visions, by their very nature and intentions, demand change, big change! But how big should it be? The question is: how deeply do you care? Consider the following:

- Achieving any vision has a price. If stakeholders really want something, they must be willing to pay the price. Then, consider how much are you willing to change?

In view of the above, consider whether your vision should be floor-setting (what is the least we should aim for) ... or "going for the ceiling" (what we truly want "no matter what").

- How much can a person achieve? It is unlikely that a person will achieve more than his/her or her vision. We can turn things around and say, a vision limits what we can do! The only true limits are the ones that the mind accepts. For example, Abraham Lincoln lost 18 elections before he became the President of the US!

> Reflection: What are the limits of your achievement? Why?

Creating a Shared Vision

Many leaders seek to achieve the commitment and focus that comes with genuinely shared visions. Unfortunately, too many people still think that "vision" is the top person's responsibility. It may be true that many individual leaders' visions could succeed in carrying an organization through a crisis or transition. But there is a deeper challenge: creating a common sense of purpose that binds people together and propels them to fulfill their deepest aspirations within what the organization is trying to achieve.

Catalyzing people's aspirations doesn't happen by accident; it requires time, care, and strategy.

Thus, the discipline of building a shared vision is centered around a never-ending process—around vision, values, why their work matters, and how it fits in the larger world (see Figure 3.3).

Figure 3.3: *The Circle of Creating Shared Vision*

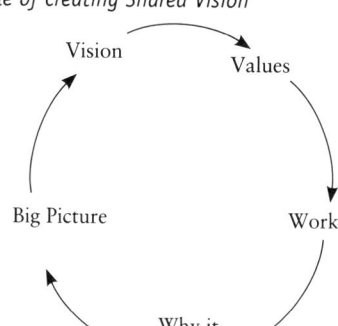

Source: Authors.

There is a need to get people to "buy-in" to the vision, to enlist others in the dream (see Box 3.8). Leaders need to communicate the purpose and build support for the direction. It is not enough for a leader to have a vision.

Box 3.8: *Positive Impact of Vision*

When a vision is well accepted, shared, and communicated, there is buy-in. The positive impact on staff could be

- Job satisfaction
- Motivation
- Commitment
- Loyalty
- Team spirit
- Clarity about organizational values
- Pride in organization
- Increase in productivity

Source: Adapted from several sources.

If this vision, however brilliant it may be, is not shared, it is of no use to anyone. Members of the organization (including outside stakeholders) must understand, accept, and commit to the vision. In other words, the hopes and dreams of the relevant parties are aligned. When they do, the organization's ability to change and reach its potential soars.

Leadership is not about one person's solo dreams; it is about developing a shared sense of destiny; it is about enrolling others so that they can see how their own interests and aspirations are aligned with the vision of the organization. They, thereby, mobilize to commit their individual energies to its realization.

Shared Vision: Precepts to Acceptance

A successful strategy for building a shared vision will be built around several key precepts:[17]

- *Every organization has a destiny*: A deep purpose that expresses the organization's reasons for its existence.
- Clues to understanding an organization's deeper purpose can often be found in its *founder's aspirations* and in the reasons why the whole sector came into being.
- Not all visions are equal. *Visions, which tap into an organization's deeper sense of purpose, and articulate specific goals* that represent making that purpose real, have unique power to engender aspiration and commitment.
- Many members of the organization, especially those who care deeply for it, have a *collective sense of its underlying purpose.*
- Thus, at the heart of building a shared vision is the task of designing and evolving ongoing processes in which people at every level of the organization, in every role, can *speak from the heart about what really matters to them* and be heard by senior management and others.
- Finally, there is the innate pull that emerges when we hold a *clear picture of our vision juxtaposed with current reality.*

[17] Senge, P. (1990). *The fifth discipline: The art and practice of learning organizations*. Retrieved from www.jerrit.msu.edu/pdf/Bulleting 1999Vol10-4.pdf/, accessed on January 5, 2013.

As the above precepts suggest, the shared vision is essentially focused around building shared meaning. Shared meaning is a collective sense of what is important and why.

In the following, we cite three examples of great health successes as documented by Center for Global Development.

EXAMPLE 1: *Creating a Shared Vision through Advocacy for Tobacco Control in Poland*

Tobacco is the second deadliest threat to adult health in the world and causes one in every 10 adult deaths. In the 1980s, Poland had the highest rate of smoking in the world. Nearly three-fourths of Polish men aged 20 to 60 smoked every day.

As the tobacco epidemic was escalating in the early 1990s, historic changes in Poland set in motion powerful influences that helped in amplifying anti-tobacco voices. Poland's scientific community laid the foundation of the anti-tobacco movement when they first established in-country scientific evidence illustrating the devastating health impact of smoking. Research conducted in the 1980s by the Marie Sklodowska-Curie Memorial Cancer Centre and Institute of Oncology contributed to the first Polish report on the health impact of smoking, highlighting, in particular, the link between smoking and the escalating cancer outbreak in Poland. The body of evidence about the harmful effects of smoking and the need for tobacco-control legislation were further strengthened through a series of international workshops and scientific conferences held in Poland.

With solid evidence in hand, Poland's budding civil society took up the call for tobacco-control measures. Health advocates in Poland were first brought together around the anti-smoking cause in the 1980s as civil society was experiencing a renewal. During this time, anti-tobacco groups, such as the Polish Anti-Tobacco Society, were formed which began to interact with the WHO, the International Union against Cancer, and other international groups.

Later, in the new political milieu, when NGOs could freely form, Poland's civil society had an even stronger voice. In 1990, Poland hosted "A Tobacco-Free New Europe" Conference of Western and Eastern European health advocates, which resulted in a set of policy recommendations that later proved instrumental in shaping Poland's anti-tobacco laws. Finally, the Health Promotion Foundation was established to lead health promotion and anti-tobacco education efforts.

The free media was essential to the success of the advocates' movement to control tobacco use. In the new democratic era, the Polish press could cover health issues, including the reporting of scientific studies illustrating the health consequences of smoking. The dissemination of this information raised awareness about the dangers of smoking and shaped public opinion about tobacco-control legislation. It also provided a venue for health advocates to broadcast special advertisements with health messages, such as how to take steps to quit smoking.

In 1995, the Polish Parliament passed groundbreaking tobacco-control legislation, which included the requirement of the largest health warnings on cigarette packs in the world, a ban on smoking in health centers and enclosed workspaces, a ban on electronic media advertising, and a ban on tobacco sales to minors. Health education campaigns and the "Great Polish Smoke-Out" have also raised awareness about the dangers of smoking and have encouraged Poles to quit. Cigarette consumption dropped by 10 percent between 1990 and 1998.

EXAMPLE 2: *Creating a Shared Vision for Reducing NTDs in Chile by Technical Experts as Champions*
In Chile, where folate supplements, fortified breakfast cereals, and other commercial products were out of reach for most income groups, it was necessary to develop a new method of reaching pregnant women with folic acid. Eva Hertrampf, one of the leading academics from the Institute, says:

> Aware of the effect of folic acid on the prevention of neural-tube defects, in 1997 a group of academics from Chile's Institute of Nutrition and Food Technology convinced authorities from the Ministry of Health to convene a working group to evaluate the feasibility of implementing folic acid fortification to prevent NTDs.

The working group, composed of academics (pediatricians, nutritionists, geneticists, food technologists), industry representatives (millers, premix vendors, pharmacists), and professionals from the Ministry of Health (representatives from the nutrition unit, monitoring, and primary child care programs), recommended that Chile should adopt the fortification of wheat flour with folic acid to prevent NTDs. Strong evidence was marshaled by the research community to support the government's decision to introduce an important nutrition intervention.

EXAMPLE 3: Acknowledged Leader Champions the Cause of Reducing Guinea Worm in Asia and Sub-Saharan Africa[18]
Progress was extremely slow until 1980s in addressing the guinea worm problem. Key events in the 1980s helped in overcoming these obstacles and turning the tide in the fight against guinea worm. In 1986, the World Health Assembly (WHA), the highest governing body of the WHO, passed a resolution that set the elimination of guinea worm as a goal of the organization and bestowed greater international legitimacy to the campaign. That same year, a meeting of public health leaders from 14 African countries helped to make important strides toward filling the gaps in data, awareness, and political commitment on the continent.

In 1986, US President Jimmy Carter began his personal involvement with the campaign which lasted nearly 20 years. By assuming the role of the lead NGO, providing both financial and technical support to these national eradication programs, the Carter Center became a powerful advocate which prompted a major turning point in the campaign.

With the technical and financial support of a global coalition of organizations led by the Carter Center, the United Nations Children's Fund, the US Centers for Disease Control and Prevention, and the WHO, 20 countries implemented national guinea worm eradication programs, run through their ministries of health. The primary interventions of the campaign included the provision of safe water (through deep well digging, applying larvicide, and purifying water through cloth filters); health education; and case containment, management, and surveillance. As a result, guinea worm prevalence dropped 99.7 percent. By 2005,

---

[18] Retrieved from http://cartercenter.org/health/guinea_worm/index.html/.

less than 11,000 cases were reported, a drastic change from the estimated 3.5 million people infected in 1986.

Sharing the vision statement met with skepticism at first, but as I kept coming back to parts of it over time, everyone bought into the idea. People began to see it as a statement about what we wanted to build together.
(Kevin Philbin, Solectron)[19]

A leader is best When people barely know he exists.
Not so good When people obey and acclaim him.
Worse when they despise him.
But of a good leader
Who talks little
When his work is done,
His aim fulfilled,
They will say "We did it ourselves." (Lao Tse)[20]

Building a Shared Vision

Shared vision strategies should be developmental. Every stage of the process should help to build both the listening capacity of the top leaders and the leadership capacities for the rest of the organization. There are four possible modes of the strategy for building a shared vision. Each organization uses a predominant mode. You can objectively assess which is the mode used in your organization and then plan to move to the next higher mode. The term "Boss" is used to mean a formal leader, executive manager, or somebody who has sufficient authority and autonomy to preside over a visioning process. Other participants are referred to as members.

Senge et al. (1994) identify four modes for creating a shared vision as follows:[21]

[19] Quoted in Kouzes & Posner, p. 141.
[20] Retrieved from www.motivatingquotes.com/leadership.htm/.
[21] Senge, P., Kleiner, A., Ross, R., Roberts, C., & Smith, B. (1994). *The fifth discipline fieldbook: Strategies and tools for building a learning organization.* New York: Doubleday.

1. *Telling* → Boss knows what the vision should be and the organization is going to have to follow it.
2. *Selling* → The boss knows what the vision should be but needs the organization to "buy-in" before proceeding.
3. *Testing/consulting* → The boss is putting together a vision and tests his/her ideas or consults to seek creative input from others.
4. *Cocreating* → The boss and members of the organization through a collaborative process build a shared vision together.

Telling: Although "telling" is a traditional and somewhat authoritarian form of instigating change, a "told" vision is still a vision, with power to galvanize activity. The boss could clearly describe the vision and say that we cannot afford otherwise. Leaders make full use of the power of language to communicate a shared identity and give life to visions. After a period of time, people will have to leave if they cannot support the new direction. There are limits to "telling." People often do not remember what they are told or interpret it differently. "Telling" often works when there is a crisis.

Selling: The leader, by "selling" his/her vision, tries to inspire or motivate people to join him/her, thereby trying to enlist as much commitment as possible. "This is the right thing to do and I believe in it," a chief executive may say, "but we can only do it if the organization comes on board with me." There are limits to selling. The boss wants to hear yes and the employees want to hear that they will keep their jobs. A compliant "yes" often seems like the safest course of action. If more commitment is needed then higher modes of testing/consulting or cocreating are needed.

Testing/Consulting: Testing is used when the leader "lays the vision for testing" but is prepared to revise it if necessary. It would not be possible for the boss to have all the answers so consulting could be a preferred mode. Consulting process may throw open many options and it may be difficult to reconcile them. This, therefore, requires a higher level of organizational capacity. If the organization is not ready then testing or selling may be the modes to use.

The first task in enlisting others is to identify constituents and find out what their aspirations are. By knowing their constituents, by listening to them, and by taking their advice, leaders are able to give voice to constituents' feelings.

Cocreating: It is an important day when people begin to work for something they want to build rather than just to please their boss. The organization whose leaders and members understand this is ready to benefit from a "cocreating" shared vision process. In this process, teams articulate their sense of common vision. They start with their personal visions and the organization becomes a tool for people's self-realization. Many leaders imagine that encouraging people to identify and express their personal vision would lead to anarchy and disarray. Experience shows that this assumption is ill founded. Most teams actually share a fundamental sense of alignment. If there is a deep lack of alignment, the leader should be concerned about it.

Thus, each higher mode of creating a shared vision involves a higher level of capacity on the part of the organization (see Figure 3.4). Telling has higher dependence on the boss's capacity for leadership and less dependence among the members of the organization. In contrast, cocreating has less dependence on the boss's leadership capacity and requires high level of capacity among members.

Figure 3.4: *Modes for Creating a Shared Vision*

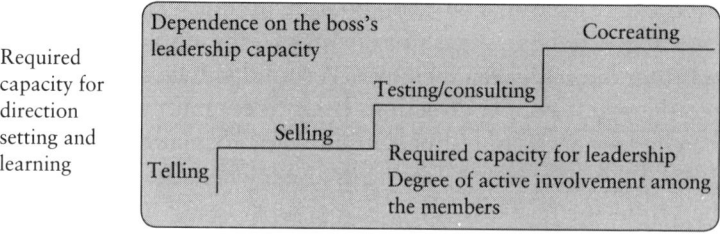

Degree of Active Involvement

Source: Senge, 1994.[22]

[22] Senge, P., Kleiner, A., Ross, R., Roberts, C., & Smith, B. *The fifth discipline fieldbook.*

Enlisting Others

Enlisting others in a common vision by appealing to shared aspirations is the key to leadership. Kouzes and Posner give the following advice, which uses a mix of the already discussed modes of creating a shared vision:

- Get to know your constituents
- Find the common ground
- Draft a collective vision statement
- Expand your communication skills
- Breathe life into your vision
- Speak from the heart
- Listen first and often
- Hang out

> *A blind man's world is bound by the limits of his touch;*
> *an ignorant man's world by the limits of his knowledge;*
> *a great man's world by the limits of his vision.* (E. Paul Hovey)[23]

Exercise | **What Do We Want to Create**[24]

There are two ways you can create a shared vision in your team:

1. Asking key questions
2. Seeking common motivators

Asking Key Questions: Asking key questions is an essential first step in the process of creating a vision. It can be done in two steps: (1) vision of the future and (2) current reality.

The team should spend time only with the questions which are meaningful to them. The words, phrases, and ideas that emerge from this exercise become the seed thoughts for a shared vision.

---

[23] Retrieved from www.goodreads.com/.
[24] Senge et al. *The fifth discipline fieldbook*.

Step 1: Vision of the Future
It is five years from today's date now. It is your job to describe it as if you were able to see it, realistically around you. Make sure each member of the team has an opportunity to comment on each of the following questions. You can do this exercise in a group within your team or organization.

- Who are the stakeholders of this organization that we have created (five years from now)?
- How do we work with them?
- How do we produce value for them?
- What are the most influential trends in our sector?
- What is our image among our clients and competitors?
- How do we compete?
- What is our organization's role in our community?
- What is our unique contribution to the world around us?
- What is the impact of our work?
- How do we raise our needed financial resources?
- What does our organization look like?
- How do we handle good times?
- In what ways is our organization a great place to work?
- How do we know that the future of our organization is secure?
- What are our values?
- How do people treat each other?
- How are people recognized?

Step 2: Current Reality
Now come back to the current year and look at the organization today.

- What are the critical forces in our systems?
- Who are the current stakeholders today—inside and outside?
- What change do we perceive taking place among our stakeholders?
- What are the most influential trends in our sector today?

- What aspects of our organization empower people?
- What aspects of our organization disempower people today?
- How is the strategic plan currently used?
- What major losses do we fear?
- What do we know (that we need to know)?
- What don't we know (that we need to know)?

Step 3: After a Vision Presentation

- For you, what are the keywords in this vision statement?
- Do you feel that it is a meaningful vision?
- Based on your own reactions and feelings, what implications do you see from this vision statement, about your organization's visioning process?

Seeking Common Motivators: You would need to identify those stakeholders you want your vision to inspire. Who are they? Be sure to include as many groups as you can identify. What motivates them? See the following example.

Stakeholder: Community

Motivators: Quality services, access to needed services, low cost, life-saving, respect from service providers.

1. Step 1: Identify each stakeholder group and list their motivators.
2. Step 2: Now review what you have written with one objective in mind: To identify what these stakeholders have in common? What can you do to appeal to their overlapping interests?

Complete below:

What they have in common?	How I can appeal to this motivator?

Step 3: Now complete the following:

Stakeholder: _____

Motivators: _____

Stakeholder: _____

Motivators: _____

Group Exercise   Creating and Sharing a Vision

Guidelines

You will be assigned to one of the four groups: organization, community, program development, and policy stakeholders (for details of the work of each group, please see the following paragraphs in this exercise). Your task is to create a shared vision. Please select a role for each of the members. A member from each group would make a three-minute presentation on their "shared vision." An observer will be assigned to each group who will give his/her observations on the process in about two minutes (40 minutes is the total time allocated for the exercise).

1. Organization

Mr S, the founder of an NGO Urban Slum Trust (UST), recently retired as executive director and Ms Y, a recently retired corporate executive, has taken over.

> **Characters for Organization Group**
> 1. Ms Y: Executive Director
> 2. Doctor
> 3. Head of Finance/Administration
> 4. Program manager
> 5. Supervisor 1
> 6. Supervisor 2
> 7. Midwife
> 8. Community worker

UST was funded by Mr S when he retired from government service seven years ago. He was very concerned about reproductive health conditions in urban slums in his city and was able to secure some funding from a donor to start this NGO. Subsequently, the NGO had earned credibility for its clinic and community-based work. Its staff comprised a finance and administration head (FA), a program manager (PM), two supervisors (S1 and S2), a doctor (Doc), a midwife (MW), and 10 community workers (see Box: Characters for Organization Group).

Ms Y felt that the organization should have a definite vision which can guide its work, now that it was well established in the community. She called a meeting of selected staff and posed the question: What are we?
Task: Create a shared vision for UST.

2. Community

Your rural village community of 10,000 population has never given any importance to women's health. However, in a recent local government election, a woman (Mrs Margo) has been elected as its head. She is very keen to improve women's health, particularly their reproductive health. There is a nurse-midwife posted in this village. The health center is about

> Characters for Community Group
> 1. Mrs Margo: Head of LGU (a feisty lady)
> 2. Mr M1: Member of LGU (businessman)
> 3. Mr M2: Member of LGU (teacher at local school)
> 4. Father X: Head of local churches
> 5. Ms NM: Nurse-midwife

20 km away and shared taxis are available to reach this town. She feels that a common vision should be developed.

She called a meeting of the local government unit (LGU) members (Mrs Margo and two male members), leader of the local churches, and the nurse-midwife to develop a shared vision (see Box: Characters for Community Group).
Task: To create a shared reproductive health vision for the community.

3. Program Development

The government has decided to launch an Adolescent Reproductive Health (ARH) Program. However, there is considerable concern in many circles that ARH will actually increase sexual activity and is not good for government to do. Mr YP has recently been appointed to

> Characters for Program Development Group
> 1. Mr YP: Head of ARH
> 2. Mr EO: Education Director
> 3. Ms NG: Head of NGO active in ARH
> 4. Mr RL: Local religious leader
> 5. Mr TP: Head of TV division of Ministry of Information and Broadcasting

develop this program. He felt that program development should be guided by a shared vision. Therefore, he convened a meeting for himself and a group of local leaders from various sectors (see Box: Characters for Program Development Group).

Mr YP began by asking the question: What do we want to create?

4. Policy Stakeholders

The health minister of your country recently visited an international conference where it was recommended that each country should formulate its reproductive health policy.

Characters for Policy Stakeholders Group
1. Ms AB: P. Secretary, MOH
2. Ms YZ: Commissioner, Maternal Health
3. Mr PD: Director, Population Board
4. Ms XT: Commissioner, STI/ HIV/AIDS
5. Ms NM: Head of local NGO

Upon her return, she has asked you, the Permanent Secretary, MOH, to convene a small group to develop a shared vision to guide the policy. You have convened a meeting of the various government and local leaders (see Box: Characters for Policy Stakeholders Group). Task: Create a shared vision to guide the reproductive health policy.

It is not what the vision is but what it does...
(Kazuo Inamori, Kyocera Inc.)[25]

Benefits of Developing a Shared Vision

There are several benefits of developing a shared vision, which is the key to visionary leadership.

- Shared vision provides focus and energy in a learning organization. You cannot have a learning organization without a shared vision.

[25] As cited in Senge (1990), p. 207.

- Generative learning occurs only when people are trying to do something that matters deeply to them.
- Shared vision clarifies what is important and what is not.
- Shared vision makes our work much more meaningful.
- Shared vision fosters risk-taking and innovation.

On the other hand, what happens when we don't have a vision at all or when we have a vision and it is not shared? The organization suffers from

- Confusion
- Low effectiveness
- Inefficiencies
- Loss of time and opportunities
- Pettiness prevails

Thus, where there is no shared vision, people go in different directions and confusion prevails. Cynicism arises when there is a divergence between talk and actions leading to a false vision.

> *In the presence of a shared vision, pettiness disappears. In the absence of a great dream, pettiness prevails.* (Peter Senge)[26]

CASE STUDY 1: Creating a Shared Vision Requires Persistence: Mechai Viravaidya and Leadership for HIV and AIDS in Thailand

Dr Mechai Viravaidya, one of the early leaders for HIV and AIDS, mounted a campaign in 1987 to educate the public about AIDS through the Population and Community Development Association (PDA), an NGO he founded. Despite official denial, Viravaidya knew that AIDS was a problem for Thailand. The campaign used mass media extensively, including IEC materials (audio tapes, videocassettes, books, pamphlets, etc.), lectures, and discussions at public and private

---

[26] Ibid.

institutions, to explain modes of HIV transmission and how it could be prevented.

If promiscuous behavior was the norm among Thai men, then once HIV infection reached a critical mass among sex workers, it would spread rapidly into the general population. However, there were powerful vested interests: brothel owners, police, and politicians who had financial interest in propagating and expanding the sex industry.

Viravaidya took his message to the two most powerful men: the Prime Minister and the Army Chief General. The Prime Minister did not agree to chair the National Committee on AIDS. However, the General considered the proposal and agreed that Army would spearhead the mobilization of a national effort to combat the growing AIDS menace. Army TV and radio channel launched a three-year nationwide education campaign to prevent further spread of HIV.

For about a year, Viravaidya personally campaigned assiduously for concerted action against HIV/AIDS. He urged businesses to take care of their own workers rather than waiting for the government. More than 100 companies enrolled in PDA's Corporate Education Programme on HIV/AIDS.

Viravaidya knew he needed reliable data to quantify the economic implications of HIV if he wanted to convince the government. He assembled a team of economists and social scientists to research and compile the data; the findings presented at 1990 International Congress on AIDS in Bangkok were startling. The then Prime Minister immediately created a National Advisory Committee and appointed Viravaidya as the chairman; the Committee was responsible for developing a National Plan for the Prevention and Control of HIV/AIDS. Even with a change of government and a new position as Minister of Tourism, Public Information, and Mass Communication, Viravaidya continued to be involved with HIV and AIDS; he asked and got responsibility for coordinating the National AIDS Prevention and Control Programme.

Later in the 1990s, under another Prime Minister, a multisectoral HIV/AIDS program was launched that was based on many of Mechai Viravaidya's initiatives. A multi-sectoral National AIDS Committee chaired by the Prime Minister was established, which implemented a massive educational program and instituted the now famous 100 percent condom policy for commercial sex workers. A convincing body of evidence indicates that the number of new HIV cases had declined and the incidence of STDs had fallen in Thailand. Thailand, today, has one of the most effective programmes for HIV and AIDS in Asia Pacific. For that, Mechai Viravaidya bears much of the responsibility (see Box 3.9).

Box 3.9: *Creating Shared Vision for HIV/AIDS in Thailand*

Leadership Lessons
1. _____
2. _____
3. _____
Source: Authors.

CASE STUDY 2: People Buy into the Leader, Then the Vision Story of Mahatma Gandhi[27]

The Law of Buy-In
Today, people take for granted that Gandhi was a great leader. But the story of his leadership is a marvelous study of the Law of Buy-In.

Mohandas Karamchand Gandhi, called Mahatma (which means "great soul"), was educated in London. After finishing his education in law, he traveled back to India and then to South Africa. There he worked for 20 years as a barrister and political activist. During that time he developed himself as a leader, fighting for the rights of Indians and other minorities who were oppressed and discriminated against by South Africa's apartheid government.

[27] Maxwell, J. *The 21 irrefutable laws of leadership*. California, USA: Thomas Nelson, p. 143.

By the time he returned to India in 1914, Gandhi was well-known and highly respected among his countrymen. Over the next several years, as he led protests and strikes around the country, people rallied to him and looked to him more and more for leadership. In 1920, a mere six years after returning to India, he was elected president of the All India Home Rule League.

The most remarkable thing about Gandhi isn't that he became their leader, but that he was able to change the people's vision for obtaining freedom. Before he began leading them, the people used violence in an effort to achieve their goals. For years riots against the British establishment had been common. But Gandhi's vision for change in India was based on nonviolent civil disobedience. He once said, "Non-violence is the greatest force at the disposal of mankind. It is mightier than the mightiest weapon of destruction devised by the ingenuity of man."

Gandhi challenged the people to meet oppression with peaceful disobedience and noncooperation. Even when the British military massacred more than 1,000 people at Amritsar in 1919, Gandhi called the people to stand, but without fighting back. Rallying everyone to his way of thinking wasn't easy. But because the people had come to buy him as their leader, they embraced his vision. And then they followed him faithfully. He asked them not to fight and eventually they stopped fighting. When he called for everyone to burn foreign-made clothes and start wearing nothing but home-spun materials, millions of people started doing it. When he decided that a March to the Sea to protest the Salt Act would be their rallying point for civil disobedience against the British, the nation's leaders followed him the two hundred miles to the city of Dandi, where they were arrested by government representatives.

Their struggle for Independence was slow and painful but Gandhi's leadership was strong enough to deliver on the promise of his vision. In 1947, India gained Independence. Because the people had accepted Gandhi, they accepted his vision.

And once they had embraced the vision, they were able to carry it out. The leader finds the dream and then the people. The people find the leader and then the dream (see Box 3.10).

Box 3.10: *Creating Shared Vision on Non-violence Movement by Gandhi*

Leadership Lessons
1. _____
2. _____
3. _____
Source: Authors.

All men dream; but not equally.
Those who dream by night in the dusty recesses of their minds
Awake to find that it was vanity;
But the dreamers of the day are dangerous men,
That they may act their dreams with open eyes to make it possible.
(T. E. Lawrence)[28]

[28] Retrieved from www.goodreads.com/.

Four

Analyzing Vision–Reality Gap

Without imagination we would never venture outside the box. Our reality would only exist within the confines of the status quo.... For your dreams to become your reality, you need only bridge the gap ...
—Jonathan Wells[1]

Introduction: What Is Vision–Reality Gap?

A visionary leader would have developed a compelling shared vision and generated the necessary drive and energy to translate that vision into reality. However, with time, there are chances that the current reality may differ from the existing vision. Therefore, to direct the drive and energy, the leader needs to analyze the vision–reality gap. A visionary leader assesses the gap between the vision and reality, and then identifies the root causes that need to be addressed for devising a path.

A vision is a picture of the desired future. Therefore, the first step in analyzing vision–reality gap would be to understand the picture of current reality and identify the essential respects in which these two pictures differ. However, to be able to analyze these differences and assess their magnitude, it is necessary to identify the indicators that can be used to assess the gap between vision and current reality. For instance, MMR is one of the associated indicators for the vision of "healthy mothers." One could

---

[1] Wells, J. *Advanced life skills*. Self published. Retrieved from www.advancedlifeskills.com.

compare the current MMR with the one that prevails in, say, developed countries to assess vision–reality gap.

In the following section of this chapter, we present some possible visions and the associated indicators. However, it is not enough to assess the current situation. Things are never what they seem or appear on the surface. As the only constant in life is change, a leader must constantly see and think beyond the obvious. An important item in the basket of skills necessary to be a visionary leader is the ability to "envision" the future, to see beyond the obvious, to analyze events or activities beyond the superficial level. Therefore, the leader would need to understand temporal and spatial trends to assess how the situation is most likely to change in the future without any action. We call this "seeing the big picture."

It is not enough to identify gaps but to also understand these gaps from a leadership perspective and analyze them using systems thinking. By thinking of system as a whole, a visionary leader starts seeing things differently when he/she starts thinking of them differently. Systems thinking would lead to understanding cause-effect relationship. This is discussed in the third section (Systems Thinking).

There is a need to identify root causes for vision–reality gap. Only then a path can be devised to bridge the gap between vision and the reality. The fourth section (How to Think in an Organized Way in a Complex Situation?) presents two ways to identify root causes: why-why tree and root cause analysis tree. The path chosen would need to address root causes so that the gap between vision and reality can be narrowed. Finding a path is the subject matter of next chapter.

Analyzing Vision–Reality Gap

As mentioned earlier, we need to identify indicators to describe the vision in quantitative terms so that the magnitude of gap between vision and reality can be assessed. In Table 4.1, we show some illustrative indicators used in defining a few societal visions.

Table 4.1: *Illustrative Indicators for Assessing Vision–Reality Gap*

Vision	Illustrative Indicator
Make poverty history	Proportion of people whose income is less than $1 a day
No hunger	Proportion of people who are undernourished
Healthy children	Under-five mortality
Healthy mothers	MMR

Source: Authors.

These indicators may not capture the vision in its all ramifications. For instance, the indicator for "healthy child" vision is under-five mortality rate. However, the vision also means not merely absence of morbidities (mortality is an extreme form of morbidity) but also physical, mental, and social well-being, and other indicators need to be devised to fully assess vision–reality gap.

It is not enough to assess current vision–reality gap by using appropriate indicators. One also needs to ascertain what the gap is likely to be in future, if the current trends continue, and where the gap is likely to be more.

Therefore, leaders see the "big picture" when they assess the vision–reality gap.

- Trends over time and projections
- Trends over geographic space and differential in gap
- Results from different levels of administration and how they would be perceived
- From different level of objectives

In the following paragraphs, we discuss ways to analyze vision–reality gap using MMR as an indicator.

See the Big Picture: Trends over Time

Trends over time are an important indication of both reality on the ground and effectiveness of program interventions for maternal health. For instance, Tamil Nadu state in India, an improved reporting system could explain the big increase in maternal deaths between 1994 (640) and 2001 (1,636).[2] Then, in three years, maternal deaths decreased to 1,219 (2004) perhaps indicating that the high figure that emerged from better reporting in 2001 prompted quick effective actions by the authorities to improve maternal health. One would now need to ascertain whether such decline would continue with current program interventions or new actions would be needed.

See the Big Picture: Trends over Geographic Areas

The National Maternal Mortality Survey in 1992–1993 revealed that the metropolitan areas and Upper Egypt had a higher MMR than Lower Egypt (see Table 4.2). In response to these results, the Egyptian Ministry of Health and Population intensified the efforts of Safe Motherhood Programs in Upper Egypt. The result is that the regional situation had reversed in 2000. Clearly the gains in reducing MMR have been limited in the Lower Egypt region and efforts may also have to be directed there for further success.

Table 4.2: *MMR Comparisons between Geographic Areas in Egypt*

Regions	MMR 1992	MMR 2000
Metropolitan	233	48
Lower Egypt	132	93
Upper Egypt	217	89
Frontier	*	120
National	174	82

Source: Campbell et al. (2005).[3]
Note: * Not included in project.

[2] Dasgupta, J. (ed.) (2009). Maternal death and disability in India: welcome kit for parliamentarians. SAHAYOG. Available at http://www.clraindia.org/include/Final.pdf%20maternal.pdf (accessed on March 13, 2014).
[3] Campbell, O., Gipson, R., Issa, A. H., Matta, N., El Deeb, B., El Mohandes, A., Manosur, E. (2005). National maternal mortality ratio in

See the Big Picture: Results from Different Levels of Administration

The overall situation of maternal deaths should be seen from different levels. Maternal deaths could be a rare event (may be once in two years) in a village, say, with a population of 5,000, a 25 per thousand birth rate, and MMR of 40 per 100,000 live births. Therefore, residents of this village may not perceive maternal mortality as a serious issue. However, an international comparison at the state or national level may show that there is considerable avoidable maternal mortality. Also for some other village, it could be a different picture. So, to better understand the issue, we need to look from different levels, from village to district to state to region, and so on.

See the Big Picture: From Different Level of Objectives

A high MMR not only symbolizes an individual death or a calamity for the surviving child and family but is also an indicator of gender values in the society where women's health may be undervalued. Therefore, a vision of gender equality could use MMR as an indicator of progress in reducing the gap between this vision and reality.

Systems Thinking

It has often been said that when you start thinking differently, you see things differently, and then your actions start to change. For a visionary leader to effectively deal with changes and challenges, he/she must constantly think and see things beyond what is obvious and within their sphere of influence or control.

Egypt halved between 1992–1993 and 2002. Bulletin of the World Health Organization, *83*(6), 462–472.

Visionary leaders need to promote systems thinking because this will foster greater appreciation and understanding of shared vision, better coordination, and teamwork. This is a vital leadership trait for greater personal and organizational effectiveness.

Everything around us exists in a world of its own, that is, everything has its own "system." In this regard, because it is necessary to deal with systems—what to "think" of them or how to analyze them and hence what action to take—it is imperative that leaders understand systems thinking.

What Is Systems Thinking?

A system is a group of interacting, interrelated, or independent elements forming a complex whole.[4] A system is something that maintains its existence and functions as a whole through the interactions of its parts. It has properties above and beyond the properties of the parts that comprise it. These interactions and changes in behavior of one may influence the other parts of the system. Change in one part of the system causes change in other parts of the system and vice versa. The component parts are all cause-and-effect linked. Some of these may be unintended. So, if a leader wishes to take action to bridge the gap between vision and reality, there is a need to think of the underlying system which is creating the gap.

Our modern life both dictates and reinforces our dependency on systems, on assemblages of people or technology or both; however, among our greatest difficulties is making "systems" work where and when we want them to. Gawande says that we are obsessed in medicine with having great components—the best drugs, the best devices, the best specialists—but pay little attention on how to make them fit well together. He quotes Berwick, President of the Institute for Health Care Improvement in Boston as noting how wrong-headed this approach is: "Anyone who

---

[4] Answers.com.

understands systems will know immediately that optimizing parts is not a good route to system excellence."[5]

Figure 4.1: *A Country's Health System*

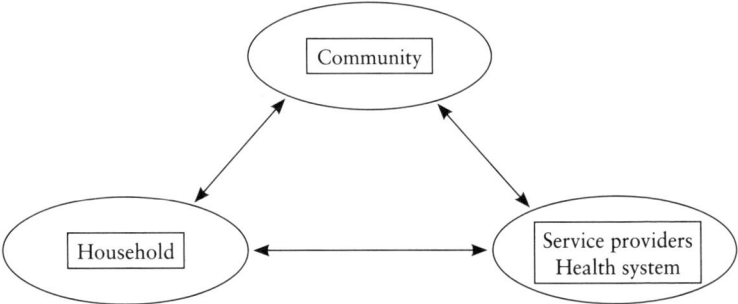

Source: Johns Hopkins Bloomberg School of Public Health, Center for Communication Programs. www.benandhenryleadership.blogspot.com (accessed on March 18, 2014).

The health system comprises individuals/households, communities, and government/private service providers (see Figure 4.1). To understand a country's health system, we need to ask: who are the primary producers of health and how do they interact? The primary producers of health are households or families including the individuals, community groups, and health service delivery systems including government and private sector. Their interaction produces health. However, the households may be the producers of health as their decisions have the most impact.

According to Senge (1990), systems thinking can be regarded as a discipline on how to look at things as a whole and finding appropriate solutions. It thus provides a framework from which interrelationships can be examined for patterns of change, and not as static snapshots. Put simply, in systems thinking, every picture tells a story.[6] Because systems have links and connections, and because nothing exists in isolation within an organization,

[5] Gawande, A. (2009). *The checklist manifesto: How to get things right.* Metropolitan Books, New York: USA.

[6] Goodman, M., Kemeny, J., & Roberts, C. (1994). The language of systems thinking: Links and loops, in P. Senge (ed.), *The fifth discipline fieldbook: Strategies and tools for building a learning organization*, p. 113. New York: Doubleday/ Currency.

there is always a cause and an effect. The key elements in systems thinking are interdependent, and linkages can be weak or strong, and thus they determine the capacity and resilience of your "systems."

Systems thinking can be manifested in four main ways:

1. *Spatial perspective*: To see components or parts in terms of a whole package
2. *Temporal perspective*: To see the present in terms of the past and future
3. *Relational perspective*: To see how events and variables are related
4. *Process perspective*: To see how processes or patterns unfold and how they affect the whole

Systems are *dynamic and organic* mechanisms, often demonstrating complex and unpredictable behavior. Smooth functioning of systems depends on a lack of friction or constraints between and among these mechanisms. Peter Senge's Laws of the Fifth Discipline[7] identify the usual failures in the absence of system thinking as:

- Today's problems come from yesterday's solution
- The harder you push, the harder the system pushes you back
- Behavior grows better before it gets worse
- The easy way out usually leads back in
- The cure can be worse than the disease (shifting the burden)
- Faster is slower
- Cause and effect are not closely related in time and space
- Small changes can produce big results but areas of highest leverage are often the least obvious
- You can have your cake and eat it too, but not at once
- Dividing an elephant in half does not produce two small elephants

---

[7] Senge, P. (1990). *The fifth discipline: The art and practice of the learning organization*. New York: Doubleday/Currency.

Why Think of a System When Analyzing Vision–Reality Gap?

Visionary leaders could more effectively develop and achieve results if they can use the system to their advantage. Greater appreciation and understanding of a shared vision can be fostered and better coordination and teamwork can be achieved through promoting systems thinking within an organization.

Improving a part may not improve the system as a whole. As a system is made up of component parts, the behavior and actions of each part have an impact on the performance of the others. Therefore, one needs to find what is constraining the performance of the system. In other words, a constraint is something that limits or restricts a system's performance.

A straightforward and simple way to see the effect of this is the Boy Scout troop illustration. A Boy Scout troop takes a hike up to a mountain. The distance is 10 km, and they estimate that by walking at 2 km per hour, they can reach the top in five hours. But as different troop members walk at different pace, the time to reach the top is determined by the slowest person. Suppose the slowest person walks at 1 km per hour, it may take 10 hours for the whole troop to reach the mountain. Thus, we need to address a key constraint affecting the performance of the system, in this case the slowest person. The key constraints would change as the speed of the slowest person is increased; some other person may become the slowest.

EXAMPLE: Reducing Unmet Need for Contraception
The unmet need for contraception arises when women who do not want a child or do not want one for two years or more do not practice contraception. It depends upon

- Access to information on contraception
- Access to family planning services
- Quality of family planning services
- Sociocultural influences that mediate between the individual and health service delivery system

For instance, out of women in the group with need for contraception either for limiting or spacing birth, only 90 percent have the information, of whom only 85 percent have access to services. Of these women, only 80 percent feel that the quality is adequate and 85 percent of them are able to utilize the services because of the socioeconomic constraints. Therefore, the need for contraception that will be met is calculated at only 52 percent (= $0.90 \times 0.85 \times 0.80 \times 0.85$) women will be met. Increasing knowledge to 95 percent will increase the met need to only 55 percent.

EXAMPLE: Better Resource Allocation in Reducing Maternal Mortality
The following factors determine the possibility of death when there is a complication in delivery (see Figure 4.2):

- Delay in decision to seek medical attention (lack of knowledge of danger signs, complicated decision-making, etc.)
- Delay in transport of patients (availability of transport, distance, etc.)
- Delay in delivery of needed emergency care (needed staff, supplies, medicines, blood, equipments, etc., not available)

Figure 4.2: *Components of the Three Delays*

Source: www.maternityworldwide.org (accessed on March 18, 2014).

Reduction in any one of these delays will reduce overall delays. However, the death may still not be averted if there is considerable delay in providing needed emergency care. Avoiding maternal deaths is possible, but programs must be designed using the right kind of information.

The MMR in Tami Nadu in India reduced from 380 in 1993 to 90 in 2007 maternal deaths per 100,000 births, thus nearly achieving MDG 4.[8] A variety of innovations in maternal health service delivery coupled with improvements in socioeconomic conditions led to this accomplishment. However, the state wishes to reduce MMR further and, therefore, it looks for causes of vision–reality gap. The investigation of causes of maternal deaths through maternal death audit was launched as a concurrent activity of identification and reporting process and intensified over a period of time. The following methods for investigation are often used to find answers on what should be done to reduce MMR:[9]

- *Community-Based Maternal Death Reviews (Verbal Autopsy)*: This investigation has helped in finding out the medical and non-medical causes of death and ascertaining the personal, family, or community factors that may have contributed to the deaths of pregnant women which occurred outside of a health facility.
- *Facility-Based Maternal Death Reviews*: A qualitative in-depth investigation of the causes and circumstances surrounding maternal deaths occurring at health facilities.
- *Surveys of Severe Morbidity* (Near Miss Cases Audit): The review of cases of severe morbidity identifies "Near Miss Case" as "any pregnant or recently delivered woman (within six weeks after termination of pregnancy or delivery), in whom immediate survival is threatened and who survives by chance or because of the hospital care she receives."
- *Clinical Audit*: Clinical audit is a "quality improvement process" that seeks to improve patient care and outcomes by the systemic review of care against explicit criteria and implementation of change.

[8] Padmanaban, P., & Desikachari, B. R. (2005). Averting maternal deaths and disabilities: Rights-based approach towards reduction of maternal mortality ratio in Tamil Nadu. Retrieved from www.searo.who.int/Regional Health Forum_Volume 9_No_1_Reviewing Maternal Deaths.pdf.

[9] WHO. Reviewing maternal deaths and complications. Retrieved from www.who.int/reproductive-health.

In Tamil Nadu, key findings from Investigation of Maternal Deaths (Verbal Autopsy) in a year were found to be as follows:[10]

- Misdistribution of First Referral Units (FRUs) and shortage of specialists
- Substandard care in the existing institutions
- Unnecessary referrals
- Majority of the patients visited more than two institutions before death
- Delay in accessing emergency transport
- Underutilization of PHCs resulted in the overcrowding of FRUs for normal deliveries
- Unmet need for abortion or tubectomy services
- Obstetric first aid not provided before referral
- No birth preparedness

Several solutions were then implemented including the following:

- Comprehensive emergency obstetric care centers with contractual appointments of staff
- Emergency transportation
- Blood storage facilities in 385 PHCs
- Capacity building of staff nurses and village health nurses
- Emergency obstetric management protocols in place
- Strengthening of FRUs
- Marketing of PHCs as places for delivery

In summary, we need to think of the system as a whole because:

- Improving a part may not improve the system performance as a whole
- Obvious solution could be wrong
- Leaders need to know what needs to be corrected and how much attention and resources are needed to do it.

---

[10] Retrieved from www.similima.com 20.

One could change the system functioning, get better performance by reallocating resources and/or utilizing new resources well.

Assumption: Inference Ladder

One of the reasons for misdiagnosing causes of vision–reality gap is the role assumptions play in interpreting reality.[11] The argument runs as follows (see Figure 4.3). We observe the reality based on observable facts. What we observe, however, may be biased by our beliefs and experiences. As it is said, we often see what we want to see. We interpret this reality and analyze it based upon our assumptions, sometimes without making them explicit. Conclusions are then drawn on the causes based on some beliefs, and actions are taken to address only these causes.

Figure 4.3: *Assumption–Inference Ladder*

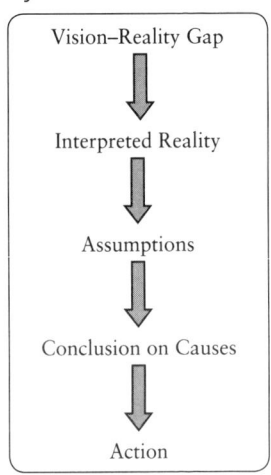

Source: Senge, 1994.[12]

By consciously using the ladder of inference, the leader can learn to get back to the facts and use beliefs and experiences to remove biases leading to selectivity. By explicitly examining assumptions, the step-by-step analysis can lead to better results avoiding unnecessary mistakes. It is often said that conflicting conclusions arise because of different assumptions underlying them. In summary, the following are needed:

- Becoming more aware of your own thinking and reasoning (reflection).

[11] Senge, P. M., Kleiner, A., Roberts, C., Ross, R. B., & Smith, B. J. (1994). *The fifth discipline handbook*. New York, USA: Crown Publishing Group.
[12] Ibid.

- Making your thinking and reasoning more visible to others (advocacy).
- Inquiry into others' thinking and reasoning (inquiry).

Let us apply this reasoning to a group participating in leadership development program. The group was reviewing the contraceptive prevalence rate in a region and observed that the rate was low because of the large population of Muslims in the region, as many of them see the use of contraception against their religious beliefs. So, the action identified was to request local religious leader to issue a fatwa. However, survey and focus group discussions revealed that the non-users of contraception were concerned about side effects of contraception and poor quality of care. Therefore, the action needed was to improve the quality of care of RH services including family planning.

How to Analyze Systems?

A system could be analyzed in terms of its functioning and cost. There are many ways to analyze functioning of a health system. One can use performance metric to see if the system is functioning at a desired level of performance or not. For instance, one way is to use equity metric and analyze how well the health system provides services to the poor. A variety of tools, such as cost-benefit analysis and cost-effectiveness, are used for analyzing the cost of the system. One can also analyze the impact of potential interventions to identify the most cost-effective intervention.

How to Think in an Organized Way in a Complex Situation?

Clearly when we think of the systems, we need to think of the links and linkages among them. This often leads to complexity and dynamic behavior. An important feature of complex systems is that they are very often stable and resistant to change. Often dynamic behavior of systems is determined by feedback linkages. Some feedback linkages are reinforcing and in that, good things become better (virtuous cycle) or bad things become worse (vicious cycle). A mix of reinforcing feedback linkages often keeps the system in a stable state. When changes do occur, however, these can be very sudden and dramatic. Changes may be easy if a leader knows where to intervene or apply leverage.

Often, in human organizations, the best leverage points are how people think or the mental models supporting the system. For instance, the progress in improving adolescent RH may be constrained because community may believe that providing information about sexuality and contraception will make adolescents more promiscuous.

Usually the gap leader will see only the surface of an iceberg with the real system structure and causes submerged. The big picture comprising seeing trends and patterns provides a deeper level of understanding and leads to looking at underlying causes in other parts of the system. For instance, among the multiple causes of why women may deliver at home, one could be the rude behavior of health service providers at the institution (see Box 4.1).

Box 4.1: *Know Your Vision–Reality Gap*

Leadership Checklist

Do you have the big picture of vision–reality gap?
Do you know the causes of vision–reality gap in systems?

Source: Authors.

Identifying Key Constraint

One of the key tools we have to gain understanding of the cause-effect and to identify the key constraint is to ask the "why" questions. The technique basically requires asking "why" and repeating it at each level. Some people say that at least five levels may need to be analyzed to find the root cause of the vision–reality gap.

EXAMPLE: The Why Tree: Analyzing Low Coverage of Postinor in Mongolia

In the following paragraphs, we discuss the use of "Why Tree" as a tool to analyze why there was low coverage of Postinor, an emergency contraceptive pill, in spite of it being available. The question raised was: "Why is the rate of abortion so high for young people in Mongolia, particularly those of university-going age? Why is Postinor not used more widely?"

To understand the key constraint, one sought answers to the series of "why" questions.

Why do young persons in Mongolia not use Postinor?

It is because they cannot get access to it; they may not know about it. Even if they know, they may not be able to access it. In Mongolia, Postinor is supplied by doctors who have to serve a large geographical area. They go from village to village, carrying a very limited (and maybe old) supply of Postinor. These doctors are not likely to be available when young people need this emergency contraceptive pill.

Why is Postinor only available from doctors?

Postinor supplies are sent by a foreign donor to the Mongolia Ministry of Health at the central level. The supplies are divided up into various districts and then a small quantity is further allocated to individual doctors. These doctors are, in fact, "traveling" doctors as they have to go from settlement to settlement in the rural areas of Mongolia to provide health services.

Why are doctors not being reached by young people?

Government doctors' geographical coverage is wide, they are never in one place for long or they will appear at a particular area after a long time. Thus most likely, they are never there when needed.

Why is Postinor not made available to pharmacists?

Pharmacies only exist in urban areas in Mongolia. Even, if Postinor is made available through pharmacies, it would be sold, rather than given free of charge. Only young people living in urban areas with some money would get access to it, which due to widespread poverty is not a likely situation.

Why do many young people not know about Postinor?

Because it is not a contraceptive method that is promoted among young people.

Why are young persons in colleges and universities not reached? It is because the current government program practice is to teach what amounts to "sex education" only in secondary schools. Mostly this falls on the biology teachers who don't generally feel comfortable teaching it, so they teach "life skills" instead. So, the quality of information on RH is low to nil. After secondary school, there are basically no programs on RH for young people, when they actually need them.

Two chains of causes as seen in the diagram help to explain why the performance of Postinor fell short of expectations where young people were concerned (see Figure 4.4).

The rate of abortion is high for university-age young people because they have no easy access to family planning methods and information. It is found that, at their age, they are mostly experimenting with casual sex and not in any stable long-term relationship to warrant regular or consistent usage of contraceptives. Postinor would be an ideal emergency measure, but unfortunately, the Why-Tree analysis shows that this is not the situation. Abortion then becomes the easiest solution to unwanted pregnancies (see Figure 4.5).

Finding the new path involves identifying and addressing root causes of vision–reality gap and core cause, if it accounts for several root causes. Goldratt,[13] in his theory of constraint management, provides a methodology to identify root causes that constrain the achievement of vision. A constraint at a point in time in the system is the one that limits performance of the current path in the system. It is the weakest link between input and outcome.

---

[13] Goldratt, E. Y. M. (1999). *Theory of constraints*. Great Barrington, Massachusetts: North River Press.

Figure 4.4: *The Why Tree*

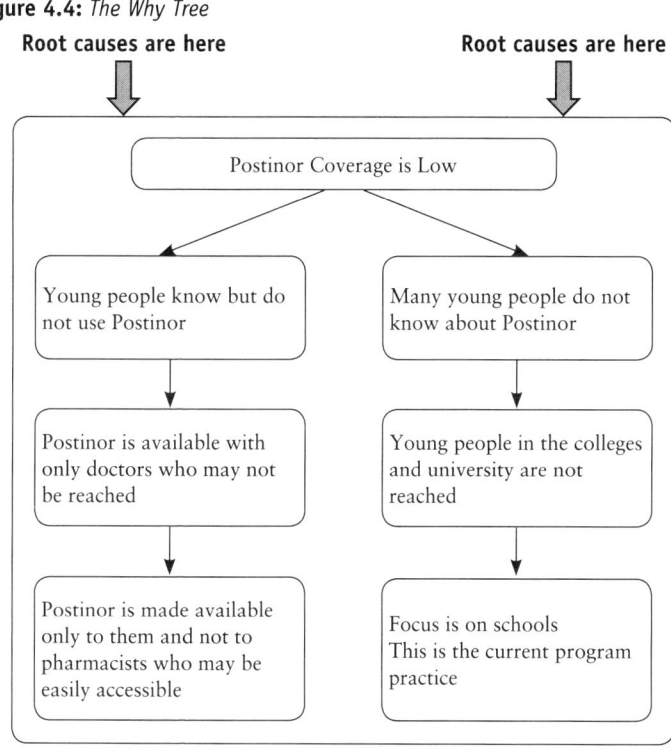

Source: Authors.

Figure 4.5: *Reality-Tree Analysis: Why Abortion Rate Is High among Young People in Mongolia*

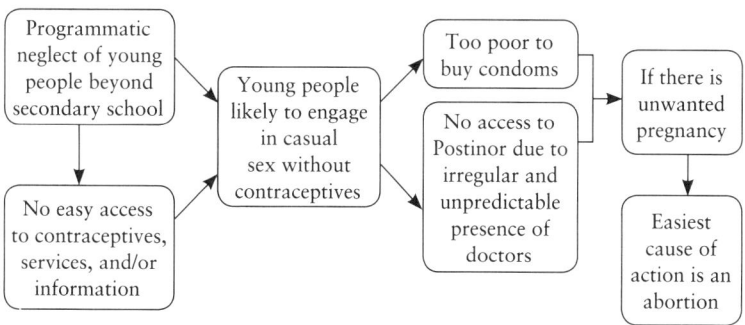

Source : Authors.

An in-depth analysis is needed to find out the core or root causes. Goldratt has developed a tool called "current tree analysis" to highlight the constraint in the existing reality that constrains reaching the vision and to identify the root causes of these constraints and not just the symptoms of vision–reality gap.

The team developing the current reality tree should (i) have an intimate and intuitive knowledge of the system based upon experience and data; (ii) be able to recognize and understand the pattern and connections between different parts of the system, and (iii) be ready for an in-depth discussion about the causes.

Constructing the current reality tree

The team starts by listing all the "undesirable effects" (UDEs) in the current situation pertaining to the vision. The UDEs are the undesirable realities such as women not accessing skilled birth attendant for improved maternal health, unsafe sex when considering reduction in HIV, patients not completing the treatment when addressing tuberculosis, etc. To keep this exercise manageable, it is recommended that this listing may be limited to about 10. Sometimes, tendency is to list the UDEs as "people are poor" or "education levels are low." While these may be true, it does not help identify the system constraints. It may be that the poor do not access services because they cannot afford them and improving affordability could be a way to address this constraint. It is to be noted that UDEs are effects caused by something else. One needs to ensure that UDEs are clearly and completely defined. Index cards or post-it-notes may be used to move UDEs around or add new UDEs.

The team then proceeds to examine causalities by asking whether one UDE is the cause of another UDE either directly or through some missing connections or intermediate steps. Current reality tree is organized by placing the cause underneath the effect and connecting them. This process needs to be repeated until all such connections have been made. In this process, it may be needed to clarify assumptions, beliefs, policies, and practices. For instance, illiterate often do not access services because the information and communication efforts are not appropriate for them.

The team now needs to review to ensure that all the UDEs and their connections have been identified. The connected UDEs can then be clustered and UDEs which are not the result of any other UDE are the root causes. If any one of them accounts for more than 70 percent of all the UDEs then it could be considered a core cause.

For changes in path to address core or root causes, one needs to ask what needs to be changed, to what and how. One should first investigate whether activities can be effectively reorganized to address the root cause. For instance, service providers may be rewarded on the number of malaria cases they have treated rather than reducing new cases of malaria. One should then consider redesigning the system. For instance, health promotion resources may be reallocated between media and interpersonal activities. Only if these two measures—reorganizing or redesigning—do not suffice, possibilities for further investments should be considered.

CASE STUDY 1. Inspiring and Empowering Communities on HIV/AIDS: Seeing the Big Picture through Mobilizing for Active Participation (MAP) in Tanzania[14]

Tanzania is not only one of the poorest countries in the world, but also among the countries with the highest HIV/AIDS prevalence in the world and the rate of infection is rising rapidly. It is one of the countries experiencing a reversal in human development due to the HIV/AIDS pandemic, and the cost of care for a person living with HIV/AIDS (PLWHA) is about twice the Tanzanian GDP per capita. There are glimmers of hope however: (1) Tanzania has begun very meaningful work in mobilizing a community-level response to the epidemic and (2) prevalence rates of HIV infection have been declining consistently for three years in two regions, where prevention and care interventions have been implemented in a comprehensive package.

---

[14] Swai, Ronald. 2003. Country presentation on *Inspiring and Empowering Communities on HIV/AIDS*. At the ICOMP International Seminar on strategic leadership of HIV/AIDS programs, May 5–8, 2003, Uganda. Adapted for this publication.

> *National responses cannot attain much success in scope, continuity and quality by acting alone without the support of communities.*
> (Dr Ronald O Swai, Head, National AIDS Control Program, Tanzania)

There is no doubt that communities are the source of all successful health programs, they are the direct link between those needing services and service providers. Communities' natural coping structures and mechanisms must be used as the starting point for coordination and strengthening of community initiatives. Too often many communities are relegated to being beneficiaries rather than producers, and their voices are left unheeded. The exclusion of communities will lead to weak responses to HIV/AIDS. Experience has shown however, that in combating HIV/AIDS, local communities can be empowered to implement their own programs. The essential ingredient is giving communities the needed "push"—the opportunity for input and then ongoing support to move forward—in short, inspiring, and empowering communities, see Box 4.2.

Box 4.2: *Three Phases of National Response*

1983–1990: Medical response (first National Task Force in 1985)

1990–1995: Public health response

1995 to present: Multi-sectoral response (an official multi-sectoral strategy prepared only in 2002)

Source: Authors.

Shifting the National Response toward Communities

Community mobilization and empowerment, and creation of a supportive social and cultural environment have now become cardinal elements of Tanzania's response to HIV/AIDS.

After nearly 20 years of providing information and a wide range of biomedical services, Tanzania's focus has shifted from "top-down" to "people strategies," where partnerships are formed and ownership of problems and their solutions lies with the stakeholders. This approach is expressed in the National Multi-Sectoral Strategy Framework for HIV/AIDS, with a vision of a Tanzania free from the threat of HIV/AIDS and which cares for and supports all those who are infected and affected by HIV/AIDS.

Mapping: A Tool for Community Mobilization

A community in Tanzania has implemented a donor-funded pilot program on community mobilization called "Mapping" which has been used with great success. The word MAP means "Mobilizing for Active Participation," and it involves drawing a map of "risky areas," where risky behavior takes place in a community. The goal is to create a participatory process of community empowerment; the program is planned so as to avoid top-down approaches and instead build partnership through decentralized actions with clear roles for all.

In Tanzania, the concept of mapping has been used as an entry point to community participation in problem identification, planning, and implementation of HIV/AIDS prevention and control activities. Through mapping, the community members come up with their own position on what must be done to solve the problem of HIV/AIDS at their community level. In fact, participants are separated by gender and subgroup (that is, PLWHAs, youth, etc.) to better understand the different problems that each group faces (see Figure 4.6).

As a result, communities have proposed several initiatives:

- Restricting youth from drinking establishments
- Increasing condom accessibility
- Presenting the mapping findings at community meetings to stimulate discussion about HIV/AIDS between men and women and among youth

Figure 4.6: *From Mapping to Action*

In the mapping process, participants:	These mapping findings are then used to support communities to
• Visualize and identify where people socialize for sex and where risky behavior takes place • Discuss barriers to avoiding/preventing risky behaviors • Propose actions for behavior changes • Identify opportunities for action • Identify community responses and impacts	• Initiate group discussions on topics related to HIV/AIDS • Develop "AIDS competency" in communities accepting that AIDS exists and is causing serious problems in the lives of people • Support other communities in mapping out the HIV/AIDS problem in terms of high-risk activities and areas

Source: Author.

Efforts such as these will be supported by the newly created District HIV/AIDS Committees, which are beginning to assume a leadership role in coordinating the multi-sectoral health-based HIV/AIDS interventions at the district, ward, and community levels, see Box 4.3.

Box 4.3: *Visionary Leadership Challenges in Inspiring and Empowering Communities*

Communities are the direct link between those needing services and the service providers, and therefore, it is essential that they should be given authority and be empowered. The visionary leadership challenges are

- How to create mechanisms for community institutions to participate in HIV/AIDS programs?
- What are the effective ways to strengthen and sustain community leadership for HIV/AIDS?
- How to involve religious leadership at the community level?
- How to enhance community leadership capabilities to address HIV/AIDS issues?

Source: Authors.

In community mapping sessions, communities have found a way to generate solutions to their own problems. Elements of successful community empowerment include ownership and inclusiveness.

The overall challenge for the Tanzanian government then is to mobilize resources and design mechanisms to scale up successful interventions and make them accessible to all populations at risk. This calls for a strong partnership between the government and communities, and it is mandatory to create a synergy of efforts and increase coverage. Neither can do it alone.

A starting point for strengthening the coordination of community initiatives is taking a thorough inventory of all actors involved in HIV/AIDS prevention, care, and support, including the health sector, NGOs, government at all levels, and community groups. The goal is for these various sectors to become both advocates and leaders, and use the Community AIDS Action Committee as a facilitator in creating a successful, multi-sectoral response with community empowerment as its base.

Discussion of the Case

A visionary leader would be able to see that:

At the first and immediate level, HIV/AIDS affects the individual and the family and loved ones. Not much action can be effected as the concern here is mainly with the personal experience of the infected person—with getting treatment, living positively, and modifying behavior.

At the second level, HIV/AIDS goes on to affect the community impacting on the resources of its health system and socioeconomic conditions such as stigma suffered by PLWHAs and their families or availability of personnel for work. The community can take action such as the MAP approach in Tanzania. Here a lot can be done by the communities taking ownership of such initiatives as MAP and action through specific activities such as increasing condom access, encouraging more open discussions on HIV/AIDS, etc.

At the third level, policymakers at the national level can see the clear benefits of giving ownership of HIV/AIDS prevention and care to the communities (such as the MAP approach in Tanzania). They can capitalize on the efficacy of this model by duplicating it throughout the country. The challenges would be on how to energize the communities and how to mobilize resources for this to be achieved.

In other words, one needs to step back and see whether the benefits and actions are doing well, and think how then to implement more (see Box 4.4).

Box 4.4: *Conclusion*

Through the mapping process, several lessons have been learned.

- A response that excludes communities will not work
- Communities need to develop the capacity to analyze the causes of vulnerability to HIV infection and to propose their own actions
- Successful community empowerment requires leadership and political commitment
- Ownership by the community is key in creating a supportive environment for behavior-change interventions
- Alliances create a synergistic effect of efforts
- Community empowerment activities need to be integrated into other ongoing community services
- Involvement of PLWHAs strengthens the responses to HIV/AIDS
- Community support is effective when it is provided at several levels

Source: Adapted by authors.

CASE STUDY 2: Eradicating Female Genital Mutilation (FGM) in Upper Appia[15]

One-third (33 percent) of the women population in Upper Appia has undergone female genital mutilation (FGM). This is

---

[15] The health of a nation: A case study for strategic thinking, planning and action. Prepared for the Africa Regional Workshop on the WHO Strategic Approach to Improving the Quality of Reproductive Health Care Services held in Nyeri, Kenya, November 5–8, 2002.

primarily in the eastern provinces of the country. While almost three-fourth (74 percent) of the women population in the East is circumcised, only 10 percent in the West undergo this practice. The immediate and long-term negative health consequences of FGM have been well documented in Upper Appia and there have been increasing efforts to address this issue.

In order to bring together some of the small-scale efforts undertaken to address FGM, a local women's NGO called Women's Rights and Protection (WRAP) organized a meeting called "No More Cutting!" The purpose was to develop coordinated activities to more effectively meet their goal of addressing FGM. They brought together all the key players involved in FGM work in Upper Appia, including women's groups, health representatives, and Muslim leaders and groups. The meeting opened with a passionate speech by the executive director of WRAP arguing for the elimination of violence against women, of which FGM was one example. She concluded by stating the goal of the meeting: to end FGM now and completely in Upper Appia. This goal statement brought immediate reactions from the audience. Some representatives from the health field said that the goal should be to reduce the negative health consequences of the practice by making sure it was done under safe conditions. A representative of one of the Muslim groups argued that FGM was an important rite of passage, and that instead of trying to get rid of it completely, they should work to create alternate rites with fewer health risks. The leader of another women's group disagreed strongly, saying that these approaches just legitimized the practice and treated the symptoms without getting at the real cause of the problem. The meeting ran over time as this debate raged on for much of the morning, forcing the presenters to significantly cut short their talks, leaving no time to develop a group plan of action. The organizers of the meeting met afterwards, feeling quite discouraged about the outcome and complaining about the fact that the participants did not agree with their goal. Some wanted to just give up on the coordination idea, but one member suggested that they should bring in an experienced facilitator to try and bring the different groups together.

A few months later, after emotions had cooled down, another meeting was held. The facilitator began by asking participants to talk about the issues that they focused on in their work. She made a list of these issues and the group worked together to cluster the different issues in categories. In spite of the differences among the groups, they all saw the many common areas of interest. The facilitator then had participants describe the activities they undertook to address some of these issues. As the group worked together during the day, they saw the strong potential for collaboration in many areas. They concluded the day with a new goal statement: to improve women's status in Upper Appia through education and empowerment activities. The activities included addressing FGM as well as many other issues affecting women's lives. The WRAP organizers were pleased to see the participants continue to talk amongst themselves after the meeting ended, exchanging business cards, and making plans to meet again.

Case discussion

The meeting was called by WRAP to address the problem of FGM. It invited all the key players—women's groups, health representatives, and Muslim leaders and groups—to address the problem of FGM as violence against women. The goal of the meeting was clear—to end FGM once and for all now. However, instead of getting a consensus, the meeting aroused heated reactions and arguments from the various groups present. Why?

WRAP's intentions and arguments were good. It even had a catchy slogan for the meeting: "No More Cutting!" But in addressing a well-entrenched traditional practice, WRAP cannot expect to get agreement at one go or at the first try. Furthermore, it did not see the "big picture" at the first meeting. Heifetz and Linsky,[16] in their book *Leadership on the*

---

[16] Heifetz, R. A., & Linsky, M. (2002). *Leadership on the line: Staying alive through the dangers of leading*. Boston: Harvard Business School Press.

Line, suggested that leaders should occasionally go out to the balcony and take a look at the room from there. From this vantage point, they believed leaders would see the behavior and actions of people inside in a different light. After getting a refreshing and new perspective, they could go back into the room and resume whatever they were doing.

WRAP took a break—and possibly got this balcony perspective—and organized a second meeting a few months later because FGM was too important an issue to give up on at one try.

There were a couple of new actions taken at the second meeting:

1. *Addressing FGM as both a health risk and a way to improve women's status*: Tempers are generally more subdued when it comes to more practical concerns such as women's health and status. Everyone wants to be a part of this. The way the earlier meeting addressed FGM, it was an assault on religion and ancient practices.
2. *The use of a facilitator*: A facilitator acted as a neutral third party and, therefore, it was easier to solicit more open responses calmly.

The outcome was that positive dialogue and networking were initiated. Everyone agreed to "talk" and that could be the start of effective collaborations and actions.

Seeing the "big picture" occurred when WRAP was able to see FGM in the wide context of Upper Appia society and saw the need to change its strategy. While WRAP's vision was "Beyond Imagination," calling for an ancient traditional practice to be stopped immediately was something "Not Easy to Do." It achieved something positive ("Looks Difficult") at its second meeting and will surely go on to "Not Possible."

Five

Finding the Path and Formulating Strategies

Two roads diverged in a road, and I took the one less travelled by,
and that has made all the difference.
—Robert Frost[1]

Introduction

A leader's role in taking people to a future they have not seen before is to find a path—a route along which people should travel—to achieve the vision by bridging the vision–reality gap. The need to find a new path has gained urgency because of rapid changes in technologies, increased competition, changes in socioeconomic conditions, and rapidly rising expectations due to increased communications. While the pressure for and hazards of new paths have increased, so have the opportunities for radically improved performance.

Leaders choose new paths when they find that following or retaining the current path constrains progress either because there are too many obstacles in the path or strategic changes within the confines of a path are not resulting in a large difference. Socialism and capitalism are the two major paths chosen by countries to manage their economies. In each of these systems, strategies may vary among countries. One of the famous examples of a change in path is by Deng Xiaoping,[2] the chief of the Communist Party's

---

[1] Frost, R. The road not taken. Retrieved from www. Poemhunter.com/poem/the-road-not-taken, accessed in March 2014.

[2] Retrieved from www.en.wikipedia.org/wiki/Deng_Xiaoping, accessed on March 12, 2012.

Central Military Commission. He famously said, in the early 1960s, when discussing economic policy, "It doesn't matter if the cat is black or white, so long as it catches mice." When implemented, this reduced the role of ideology in economic decision-making and enhanced the role of policies of proven effectiveness, leading China on the path of "socialist market economy."

Often change in strategy is contemplated for bridging the gap between vision and reality. However, strategic changes within the confines of the current path may not suffice and changes in path may be needed. In the second section of this chapter (A Taxonomy of New Paths), we present several examples of new paths that have proven successful.

Finding the path is actually a simple practical skill that is often a matter of asking questions, a trait that we expect of leaders; a matter of challenging the status quo, another trait we expect of leaders; a matter of achieving something unexpected out of a situation. However, it also requires thinking "big." In Dr Ben Lozare's[3] concentric circle model (in the third section), he shows that most people operate at the lowest level (smallest circle— "easy to do") for many reasons. As you move to the next level and the next, there are fewer and fewer people. True leaders with the compelling vision and the necessary drive and energy would operate at the sphere of the "beyond imagination." Only at this level can big dreams and grand plans be achieved. Visionary leaders have to practice the art of thinking big constantly because achieving their vision depends on it. The third section (Finding the new path) discusses approaches to finding new paths: revising the reality tree discussed in the previous chapter, piloting the new path, and Steven Covey's Third Alternative.

Strategies indicate how journey along the chosen path would be undertaken including prioritization of services and target groups, and ways by which demand, services, and resources will be mobilized. Formulating and implementing strategies for progress on the path is discussed in the fourth section (Formulating and Implementing Strategies for Progress on the Path).

---

[3] Dr Benjamin Lozare is Head of Training at Johns Hopkins University Center for Communications.

Changes in path generally involve major changes in policies, health service delivery, role of public and private sector, health financing, or human resource configurations. Strategic changes would generally be within the confines of current policies and may involve smaller changes. Orchestrating process of change is a major challenge for leaders and is the subject of the fifth section (Orchestrating Process of Change). It presents Kotter's eight steps for successful change. Nevertheless, risks are involved in any process of change and the sixth section summarizes Heifetz and Linsky's advise on staying alive through the dangers of leading (Addressing Risks Involved in Implementing New Path).

A Taxonomy of New Paths

There are several examples of new paths that have led to significant success. We have analyzed the 20 cases of successes documented by Center for Global Development[4] in "Millions Saved: Proven Successes in Global Health" and have drawn upon from other literature. Broadly, they could be classified as follows:

- Program innovations in service delivery: These involve changes in mix of services delivered, how they are delivered, and who delivers them.
- Program innovations for behavior change: Strategies for changing behavior are almost always a key to health improvement.
- Utilizing new technologies: Discovery of new techniques or medicines often results in new paths.
- Delivering micronutrients through fortifying food: Deficiency in micronutrients can cause several diseases and providing them through fortifying foods has often proven to significantly improve health.

---

[4] Center for Global Development. (2004). Millions saved: Proven success in global health. Retrieved from www.cgdev.org.

- Financial innovations have been recently used both for shaping demand and modifying health-care seeking behavior.

In the following paragraphs, we discuss selected examples of these proven successes in global health through each of these paths.

Program Innovations in Service Delivery

Program innovations can make a significant difference and are generally directed toward improving access, coverage, and quality of services or adherence to treatment as the following examples show.

Controlling Tuberculosis in China

In the mid 1990s, WHO developed the DOTS (directly observed treatment-short course system) strategy.[5] Within a decade, almost all countries adopted this strategy. China was one of the earliest to adopt it through which trained health workers watched patients take their treatment at local tuberculosis county dispensaries. It achieved a 95 percent cure rate for new cases within two years of adopting DOTS. Between 1990 and 2000, the number of people with tuberculosis declined by over 37 percent in project areas. The MDG target to halt and reverse the tuberculosis epidemic by 2015 has already been achieved. The tuberculosis mortality rate has decreased by 41 percent since 1990. Nevertheless, the global burden of tuberculosis is high and 1.4 million people died from tuberculosis in 2011.

Controlling Trachoma in Morocco

Trachoma is the number one cause of preventable blindness. In 1992, a national survey found that just over 5 percent of

[5] WHO. (2012). Global tuberculosis report. Geneva.

Morocco's population had the blinding disease trachoma. Between 1997 and 1999, the National Blindness Control Program implemented a new strategy called SAFE (surgery, antibiotics, face washing, and environmental change). Mobile teams performed simple, inexpensive surgeries in small towns across the provinces, 4.3 million treatments of the antibiotic azithromycin were distributed, health education efforts promoting face washing and hygiene were conducted, latrines were constructed, and safe drinking water supplied. Overall, the prevalence of active disease in children under 10 was reduced by 99 percent since 1997.

Indonesian Midwifery Program to provide a skilled attendant at birth

Concerned by high MMR in Indonesia, the Ministry of Health initiated midwifery education program from 1989 to 1996 that trained 54,000 community-based midwives. Due to this program, the proportion of deliveries assisted by a skilled attendant throughout Indonesia rose from 25 percent in early 1990s to 76 percent in 2006.[6] The national MMR in 2006 was estimated to be 230 per 100,000 births[7] compared to about 400 per 100,000 live births in 1989 and neonatal mortality rate was 20 per 1,000 live births. Thus, progress was made by the new path for coverage by skilled birth attendants, but why was it not greater? Shankar et al. argue that several factors affected performance:[8] (1) rapid deployment of midwives compromised candidate selection and quality of training, (2) supervision and mentoring of midwives was not adequate in all areas, and (3) there was limited access and financial support for referral to emergency obstetric-care centers. These issues were addressed as implementation progressed. The above example shows that while a new path may result in progress, careful strategies and their execution is needed to realize its full benefit.

[6] Retrieved from www.who.inst/ bulletin/Volume 85/10/07-031007/en/.

[7] World health statistics. Retrieved from www.who.int.

[8] Shankar, A., Sebayang, S., Guarenti, L., Utomo, B., Islama, M., Fauveau, V., & Jalal, F. (2008). The village-based midwife programme in Indonesia. *The Lancet*, 371, 1226–1229.

Eliminating Polio in Latin America and the Caribbean

Although the oral polio vaccine was introduced in 1977, it was 1985 when the Pan American Health Organization (PAHO) began a polio eradication campaign in Latin America. To increase immunization coverage in areas with weak routine health services, all endemic countries in the region implemented national vaccine days twice a year to immunize every child under-five, regardless of vaccination status. In the final stages of the campaign, "Operation Mop-Up" was launched to locate children missed by the campaign with house-to-house vaccinations in communities reporting polio cases and with low coverage. In 1991, the last case of polio was reported in Latin America. Today, the world is on the verge of eradicating polio.

The above examples show that changes in service delivery strategies can increase coverage and reduce mortality as well as morbidity.

Program Innovations for Behavior Change

Healthy behaviors by people can have a significant impact on health. However, it is not easy to bring about large-scale change in behaviors. There has been some success in reducing prevalence of smoking tobacco over the years. However, a quicker response was realized in the oral rehydration therapy (ORT), as the examples of Egypt and Bangladesh show.

Egypt: A pioneer in ORT

In 1977, diarrhea caused at least half of the large number of infant deaths in Egypt. Although the efficacy of ORT was proven and the Egyptian Ministry of Health had introduced packets of oral rehydration salts (ORS), only a small proportion used them. A national program to promote ORT was launched to produce, promote, and explain ORT by strengthening the capacity of the health service delivery units. The four main components of the program included product design and branding, production and distribution, training, and promotion and marketing. The program was guided by research and evaluated; it used a successful nation-wide media campaign which included television.

Reaching Bangladeshi children with ORT

Bangladesh had high prevalence of diarrhea but logistics of ORS distribution and poor media reach meant that it had to develop its own strategy. Beginning in 1980, the Bangladesh Rural Advancement Committee (BRAC), a large NGO, began a program to promote ORT in rural Bangladesh. The program trained tens of thousands of female health workers. They went door-to-door training mothers about dehydration and ORT. The health workers visited each household in the program area and taught at least one woman in the household the "10 points to remember," including what diarrhea and dehydration is and looks like, how to rehydrate through ORT, how to make the solution at home and when to use it, when to call the doctor, and when to continue feeding. They also demonstrated how to make a homemade oral solution by mixing a three-finger pinch of salt, a fistful of sugar, and a liter of water. The workers were paid based on their performance in terms of how accurately and thoroughly they taught mothers the 10 points. Because men in Bangladesh are the key decision-makers, the program also tried to reach men. Male workers at bazaars, mosques, and schools helped influence the attitudes of men toward ORT. Between 1980 and 1990, 13 million mothers were taught to make oral rehydration mixtures in their homes. Today, the usage rate of ORT in Bangladesh is 80 percent, one of the highest in the world, and packaged oral rehydration salts are widely available in most of the country, including the rural areas.

Utilizing New Technologies

Availability of new or improved technology, when appropriately delivered, can have a significant impact on health, as the following examples show.

Development of safe strategy for controlling Trachoma in Morocco

The SAFE strategy discussed earlier for controlling trachoma in Morocco became highly effective with the discovery of a much more potent new antibiotic. Studies showed that a single dose of the antibiotic azithromycin was as effective as (or even more effective than) the six-week regimen of the widely used tetracycline antibiotic. Pfizer, the global pharmaceutical giant, and the Clark Foundation formed the International Trachoma Initiative and Pfizer pledged to contribute $60 million worth of the new antibiotic. The International Trachoma Initiative aimed at eliminating blinding trachoma worldwide got a start in Morocco.

Onchocerciasis or "River Blindness" in Africa

River blindness afflicts approximately 42 million people worldwide, almost all residing in sub-Saharan Africa. Many abandoned their fertile land due to a threat of this disease. Aerial spraying worked in the 11 designated West African countries during the 1970s and 1980s. However, this was not feasible in 19 central, east, and southern African countries given the area's longer distances and thick forests. In 1978, Merck discovered that the new antiparasitic agent (Mectizan) they had developed to treat gastrointestinal worms in cattle and horses was also effective against the family of worms responsible for onchocerciasis. A single dose of Mectizan (ivermectin) could kill up to 95 percent of the tiny worms—offspring of the adult worm—for up to a full year. The Carter Center, affiliated to the Emory University, agreed to distribute the medicine donated by Merck. Since 1988, the program has provided more than 472 million annual treatments.

Fortifying Food: Delivering Micronutrients

Micronutrient deficiencies can result in severe health problems and supplementation, often, is difficult to organize and adhere to. Therefore, food fortification is sometimes an efficient way to provide necessary micronutrients, as the following examples show. However, legislation is needed, supply chain needs to either exist or be organized, initial investment costs may need to be subsidized, quality has to be monitored, and incremental cost of fortification needs to be affordable.

Preventing iodine deficiency disease in China

Iodine deficiency—a range of disorders including goiter (enlarged thyroids), stillbirths, stunted growth, thyroid deficiency, and mental defects—affects 13 percent of the world's population. Globally, iodine-fortified salt has been a major strategy to prevent iodine deficiency. In 1993, China launched the programs which raised awareness of the health impact of iodine deficiency; strengthened the capacity of the salt industry to iodize and package salt; monitored and enforced the quality of the salt; and promoted compliance among the salt industry through enforcement of licensing regulations and legislation banning non-iodized salt. By 1999, iodized salt was reaching 94 percent of the country, up from 80 percent in 1995, and salt quality had improved markedly. As a result, total goiter rates for children aged eight to 10 fell from 20.4 percent in 1995 to 8.8 percent in 1999.

Prevention of neural-tube defects in Chile

Each year, neural-tube defects (NTDs) affect more than 300,000 newborns worldwide. Anencephaly and spina bifida, the two most common NTDs, are important contributors to infant and fetal mortality: all infants with anencephaly are stillborn or die shortly after birth, and those born with spina bifida suffer lifelong disabilities and require extensive medical care. The NTD rate had stagnated at 17.2 per 10,000 live births in Chile from 1967 to 1999. Aware of the effect of folic acid on the prevention of NTDs and encouraged by public health experts, the Chilean Ministry of Health introduced a new legislation in early 2000 stipulating that all domestically produced wheat flour must be fortified with folic acid. Flour mills began producing, distributing, and marketing wheat flour in compliance with the new legislation, and the government helped to regulate and monitor the quality of fortified flour. Shortly after the fortification legislation was passed, 91 percent of wheat bread was being produced with fortified flour. Chile's fortification intervention produced a significant decrease in the NTD rate, a reduction of approximately 51 percent for spina bifida and 46 percent for anencephaly.

Preventing dental caries in Jamaica

In the early 1980s, dental caries in Jamaica was widespread. On an average, fewer than three in every 100 children were free of caries. Untreated caries is painful and may affect diet, school attendance, and sleep. In 1987, at the encouragement of a dentist from the country's Ministry of Health, Jamaica's only salt producer began producing and selling fluoridated salt. The Ministry of Health and the Jamaican Parliament passed the necessary legislation and regulatory framework for its implementation. The government provided biological and chemical monitoring of the salt. The health of children's teeth in Jamaica improved dramatically due to fortification. In both six-year-olds and twelve-year-olds, the index of the severity of caries had fallen by more than 80 percent by 1995.

Financial Innovations

Public–private partnership for increasing institutional deliveries in Gujarat state, India

The MMR was high and unchanging in Gujarat, India. The Commissioner of Family Welfare identified three issues constraining progress: (a) package of services for mothers and newborn babies was not available to the poorest, (b) government health facilities had significant shortage of qualified health-care providers, particularly at the district level, and (c) three-fourth of the gynecologists worked in the private sector and were not affordable for most women. Therefore, a new public–private partnership was introduced at the state level between district government and private providers, initially in a few districts and subsequently expanded to cover the whole state. The private providers are paid by the government for any maternity care they provide to women below the poverty line. As of November 2007, in the pilot areas there were more than 131,000 deliveries. About 40 percent of eligible poor pregnant women benefited from the scheme in just two years. Available data show that the proportion of deliveries in institutions has risen to 76 percent in November 2008 from 54 percent in 2005.[9]

Health of the poor in Mexico: Conditional cash transfer

Financial incentives to promote behavior change have been used in many health programs. However, Mexico's experience of large-scale cash transfer provided a fillip to the use of this instrument. In 1997, Mexico launched *Progresa* program with the goal of increasing the basic capabilities of extremely poor people in rural Mexico. Unlike most health programs which focus on supply side, this program was principally designed to affect the "demand side." It provided monetary incentives directly to families to help overcome the financial barriers to health services use and schooling as well as to induce parents to make decisions that would bring their children more education and better health. The government provided significant levels of financial support directly to households only if the beneficiaries did their part by sending children to school and taking them to clinics for immunizations and other services. *Progresa* also sought to simultaneously influence behavior on education, health, and nutrition as they are mutually reinforcing. This would also bring pressure for coordinated service delivery in these three sectors.

The conditional cash transfer involved the following:

- In the health component, cash transfers were given if (and only if) every member of the family accepted preventive health services delivered through the Ministry of Health

[9] Mavalankar, D., Singh, A., Bhat, R., Desai, A., & Patel, S. R. (2008). Indian public–private partnership for skilled birth-attendance. *The Lancet*, 371, 631–632.

and IMSS-Solidaridad, a branch of the Mexican Social Security Institute.

- In the nutrition component, the cash transfer was given to the household if (and only if) children (aged five years and under) and breastfeeding mothers attended nutrition monitoring clinics where growth was measured, and if pregnant women visited clinics for prenatal care, nutritional supplements, and health education. A fixed monetary transfer of $11 per month was provided for improved food consumption. Nutritional supplements were also provided to a level of 20 percent of daily calorie intake and 100 percent of the micronutrient requirements of children and pregnant and lactating women.
- In the education component, monetary education grants were given for each child under 18 who was enrolled in school between the third grade of primary school and the third grade of secondary school, the period when risk of school dropout was the greatest. Monthly grants ranged from $7 for a child in the third grade of primary school to around $24 for a boy in the third grade of secondary school.

The monthly income transfers were provided through wire transfer that could be cashed immediately. The transfers constituted about 22 percent of household income, on an average. This significantly increased the monthly income of poor families and their purchasing power which fed financial resources into the local economy. In addition to a striking impact on health, nutritional status was also better for *Progresa* children than for those outside the program. As a result of the favorable evaluation findings, the program not only survived the political change from the Zedillo administration to the Fox administration but was also extended to urban areas.

Janani Suraksha Yojana (JSY) scheme in India to increase demand for institutional deliveries

In 2005, with the goal of reducing the numbers of maternal deaths, the Government of India launched *Janani Suraksha*

Yojana (JSY), a conditional cash transfer scheme, under which poor women delivering at a health facility receive a cash amount of about US$28.[10] According to government reports, the number of women receiving JSY benefits in the year 2009–2010 stood at 9.3 million. JSY is, thus, one of the largest in the world in terms of the number of beneficiaries and represents a major Indian health program. Although uptake of JSY varied among districts, receipt of financial assistance from JSY was associated with a significantly increased probability of receiving antenatal care, giving birth in a health facility, and either giving birth in a facility or having a skilled attendant present at the time of delivery. Lim et al. note that JSY has probably contributed to reductions in the number of perinatal and neonatal deaths.

Finding the New Path

A path should essentially address root cause of the vision–reality gap problem or of inadequate progress toward the vision, as discussed in the previous chapter. Finding the path, therefore, is a creative process requiring thinking "out of the box" or "breaking the box." It will require deep understanding of the situation, root causes, the reasons for persistence of root causes, and ways of addressing them. One would have to fight this sort of view: "we have always done things this way." Finally, it will also require looking beyond the "zone of control" to "zone of influence" or even creating new zones of influence as some of our earlier examples of new paths show.

---

[10] Lim, S. S., Dandona, L., Hoisington, J. A., James, S. L., Hogan, M. C., & Gakidou, E. (2010). India's Janani Suraksha Yojana, a conditional cash transfer programme to increase births in health facilities: An impact evaluation. *The Lancet, 375,* 2009–2023.

Future Reality Tree Analysis

The theory of constraints by Goldratt[11] provides a way of thinking and a set of tools to find answers to questions of what to change, what to change to, and how to change. In Chapter Four, we had discussed use of current reality tree for logically thinking about identifying key constraints or root causes for the vision–reality gap. This is what needs to be changed. A constraint at a point in time in the system is the one that limits performance of the current path in the system. It is the weakest link between input and outcome.

To further strengthen the logical thinking process for finding the path, the above analysis has been extended by the following: Cloud analysis helps reveal various assumptions that underlie the connections among the UDEs in the current reality tree. It brings out the beliefs and values that have led to current policies and practices, in turn, resulting in these UDEs. Usually the constraint persists because of two opposing wants that represent the conflict and the need that both are trying to satisfy. Instead of compromising between these two wants, a breakthrough solution needs to be created by examining the assumptions behind the wants. Once a solution (called injection) has been identified, the team that constructed the current reality tree can proceed to develop a future reality tree which is the answer to question "what to change to." Future reality tree is a representation of how desirable realities will look if some changes are injected leading to desirable realities. It is constructed by tracing the effect of "injections" or planned changes in the path on the UDEs which will then be replaced by desirable realities. Thus, it helps in looking at effect of changes in a systematic way. Sometimes application of injection may result in possible side effects—favorable or adverse—on the system as a whole. The negative consequences would need to be addressed.

If there is insufficient clarity about "how to change" then obstacles in implementation need to be identified. These are called prerequisites which uncover obstacles to implementation

[11] Goldratt, E.M. (1997). *Critical chain*. Great Barrington, Massachusetts: North River Press Publishing Corporation.

of changes in the path and helps ways to address these obstacles. The implementation plan needs to be developed, called transition tree—transition from the current reality tree to future reality tree.

The Third Alternative

Stephen Covey[12] suggests that transformational leaders, faced with a lack of progress or conflict, should seek to find a third alternative. He suggests two steps to achieving the synergy through third alternative.

> Would you be willing to search for a solution that is better than what either one of you (us) have proposed?
>
> Would you agree to a simple ground rule: No one can make his/her point until they have restated the other person's point to his/her satisfaction?

The above implies that mode of communication has to become Win-Win by mutual understanding and caring for the different points of view.

The third alternative is created by a process of synergy. Synergy is not the same as compromise. In compromise everyone loses something. However, process of synergy would lead to a fresh promise and transform the future. This would result in moving from "my way" and "your way" to "our way." The third alternative thinking requires change in paradigm. It requires: (a) seeing yourself as independent of your position, (b) seeing the other side as having legitimate view, and (c) willing to synergize to create an amazing future that no one could have foreseen. The process of creating synergy requires both parties to agree to go for a solution that is better than the one currently available on agreed criteria

---

[12] Covey, S. R. (2011). *The 3rd alternative: Solving life's most difficult problems*. New York, USA: Simon and Schuster.

of success, creating the third alternative and getting the synergy or third alternative.

Collins and Porras[13] in their book *Built to Last* talk about genius of the word "AND." Those companies that last long embrace both extremes on a number of dimensions at the same time and figure out a way to have both choices. Visionary companies find ways to do well in the short term and long term, rather than sacrifice one for the other. They don't look for a balance— rather, acquiring both to the maximum. Instead of choosing A OR B, we should figure out how to have A AND B—continuity AND change, freedom AND responsibility, and so on. They are able to find a path that addresses these seeming contradictions through a core ideology and guiding vision. So, while practices and path may change, the core ideology provides consistency.

Role of Pilot

When there are uncertainties regarding the efficacy of the new path, it is often advisable to pilot test to assess its impact and ways to implement it. Examples of pilot projects abound in the literature and in the following paragraph we present one such example.

Preventing Hib disease in Chile[14]

Two Hib conjugate vaccines were licensed in Chile in 1992 based on their proven efficacy in controlled trials in the industrialized countries. However, the Ministry of Health in Chile did not introduce them into the country's routine immunization system because it was not convinced that the high costs of the vaccine would justify its routine use. Researchers in Chile estimated that the incidence of *Haemophilus influenzae* type b (Hib) disease

---

[13] Collins, J., & Porras, J. (1997). *Built to last: Successful habits of visionary companies.* New York, USA: HarperCollins.

[14] Center for Global Development. (2004). Millions saved: Proven success in global health. Retrieved from www.cgdev.org.

in Santiago during the late 1980s was 32 per 100,000 infants below six months of age, and 63 per 100,000 in infants aged six to 11 months. Once the disease burden had been shown to be significant, the ministry agreed in 1994 that researchers should further explore the use of the Hib vaccine. Rather than performing a randomized clinical trial, the researchers did what is known as an "intent-to-vaccinate" study. This observed the *effectiveness* of the vaccine—its impact on a large population of infants receiving it in the normal conditions of a routine immunization service. Thirty-six PHCs in Santiago were enrolled for the study and administered the vaccine with other routine immunizations for a year. To minimize the number of shots for children and to increase cost-effectiveness, the researchers tested a combination of Hib conjugate vaccine and the established Diphtheria, Tetanus, and Pertussis (DTP) antigens in the same syringe. For a comparison group, they observed children in 35 additional centers in the city where Hib vaccine would not be offered but would receive only DTP as usual. The total number of children involved was more than 70,000. The results of the study were dramatic. Among the children in the health centers where Hib vaccine was available, the number of meningitis cases was reduced by 91, and the number of cases of pneumonia and other forms of Hib disease was reduced by 80 percent, compared with children in the DTP-only centers. Based upon these results, Chile's Ministry of Health introduced the Hib vaccine into the routine immunization program for infants in 1996.

Path finding and shared vision

Sometimes, path findings can result in creating shared vision among different stakeholders. For instance, the public–private partnership created a shared vision of reducing maternal mortality statewide among private practitioners in Gujarat, India. Similarly, in Indonesia, provision of midwives strengthened the vision of skilled attendant at the delivery among general population. Inspiring and empowering stakeholders involved in a new path is a key to success and requires special efforts.

Formulating and Implementing Strategies for Progress on the Path

While a new path will involve a large-scale change in direction, a strategy is a way to progress along the path. Even when the current path is to be followed, the leader would need to formulate/validate current strategies. Strategy implies choice of which services to provide, to whom, and in what sequence and includes ways to mobilize demand, services, and resources for that purpose.

There is a voluminous literature on strategy formulation. In the following paragraphs, we briefly mention the methodologies for formulating strategies.

- SWOT Analysis: First, one needs to identify strengths, weaknesses, opportunities, and threats (SWOT) to progress on the path chosen. The basic options for strategy are to (a) build on strengths, (b) address weaknesses, (c) exploit opportunities, and (d) protect from threats. After identifying all feasible options, one can prioritize the strategic interventions depending upon their potential impact, feasibility of implementation, and congruence with the path.
- Stakeholder Perspectives: First, one needs to identify all the key stakeholders affected by moving on the path. Then current stakeholder perspectives on the new path, desired perspectives, and strategies needed to realize the desired perspectives would need to be identified.
- Strategic Issues: Several strategic issues would need to be addressed to progress on the path. The strategic issues may change as progress is made and strategies to address them would also change.
- Brainstorming: First step is to collect as many ideas as possible for making progress on the path and not reject any idea encouraging participants to think "out of the box." In the second step, these ideas would need to be evaluated. Those that could have high potential impact, are feasible and are within the path desired would be selected.

- Operational Improvements: Sometimes it is enough to improve implementation of strategies—what services are provided by whom and where—for progress on the path.

Implementing Paths/Strategies

Convincing people to traverse a new path will involve exercising influence in all directions: up towards higher levels (typically the planning and finance departments or even the head of the state), laterally towards peers in the organization, down to direct reports as well as service providers, and to the individuals/households and communities as it will generally involve a change in their behavior. It may also involve private or civil society actors.

It is said that you cannot change others without changing yourself. So, leaders would need to look at themselves on whether they have the credibility and passion to move along a new path. It may also involve consciously building relationships with others whom they may normally not be in contact with. Traversing a new path may also involve higher level of risks of failure which need to be handled carefully.

Hughes and Beatty[15] provide a framework for strategic influence. Stakeholders can be influenced in two ways: (1) involving them in the process or (2) by connecting them at an emotional level. Direct involvement will not only ultimately create ownership but also bring about diverse and critical perspectives so as to mitigate the risks and increase the chances of success. When people are party to the ultimate decision, they are more likely to champion the cause and assist in overcoming "bumps" which invariably would arise during the journey on the new path. A wider group, however, can generally be influenced by connecting with them at an emotional level. This would require a leader to learn "what is important to others." For instance, in the Indonesian example above, it was important to households that

---

[15] Hughes, R. L., & Beatty, K. C. (2005). *Becoming a strategic leader: Your role in your organization's enduring success*. Jossey-Baas, John Wiley and Sons and Center for Creative Leadership.

deliveries took place at home but rather than relying on traditional birth attendants they needed access to a midwife who was based in the community rather than at a facility which might be at some distance. They also had to feel that a maternal death was not acceptable, and as households and communities they should have low or zero tolerance to maternal deaths.

The language used to convey the need for change is critical for establishing the emotional connection. There are several examples of this. For instance, the advocates for reducing poverty used the slogan "make poverty history"—a phrase which is likely to connect with a large group of people at an emotional level.

Thus, the process of finding the path is just as important as implementing the journey along the path. This process could involve creating a widespread consensus on the need for change. A carefully crafted communication strategy would be needed for this purpose.

Orchestrating Process of Change

Implementation of any new path/strategy will involve changes. Some organizations have been able to make successful changes and have improved their performance. However, most changes meet with some level of resistance from those who must implement the change. People resist not only change that is bad for them, but also change that will benefit them in the long run. Any change involves some pain. Therefore, it is not surprising that many change efforts have failed.

The probability of change being successful depends upon the degree of dissatisfaction with the status quo, a clear statement of the desired end state after the change, and agreement on concrete first steps toward the goal.

Most alterations in norms and shared values come at the end of the transformation process. New approaches usually sink into a culture only after it is clear that they work and are superior to old methods. Sometimes, the only way to change a culture is to change key people.

Box 5.1: *Eight Steps to Transform Your Organization*

1. Establishing a sense of urgency
2. Forming a powerful coalition
3. Creating a vision
4. Communicating the vision
5. Empowering others to act on the vision
6. Planning for and creating short term wins
7. Consolidating improvements and producing still more change
8. Institutionalizing new approaches

Source: Kotter, 1999.[16]

Kotter (1999) in his book *What Leaders Really Do* provides eight steps for successful change (see Box 5.1).

1. Creating Urgency: Leaders have to create a feeling of urgency in the stakeholders for change so that they would be willing to participate in the process of change. Unless a high sense of urgency is felt, the change effort is not likely to succeed and transformation efforts would fail to achieve their objectives.
2. Forming a Powerful Team: A team would need to be formed which will have the capability to guide the change process. Major change is often impossible unless the head of the organization is an active supporter. However, this is not enough for a successful transformation unless senior managers and other people, who have a commitment to improved performance, come together as a team. In the most successful cases, the coalition-seeking change would be sufficiently powerful to overcome the inertia for change.
3. Get the Right Vision: Transformation effort should lead to a different future and unless that future can be visualized, change is not likely to occur. Therefore, leaders need to "create" the right vision and strategies to guide action in all of the remaining stages of change. Of the remaining elements listed below for successful transformations, none

[16] Kotter, J. P. (1999). *What leaders really do.* Boston, USA: Harvard Business Press.

is more important than a sensible vision. Vision plays a key role in producing useful change by helping to direct, align, or inspire actions on the part of organizations of people (see Chapter Three). Vision is an imaginable picture of the future. Effective visions are those which are desirable, feasible, focused, flexible, and communicable. An ineffective vision may be worse than no vision at all. Without an appropriate vision, the transformation effort may lead to incompatible actions and become very confusing.

4. Communicate for Buy-in: Leaders need to communicate change visions and strategies effectively so as to create both understanding and buy-in. Major change is impossible unless most employees are willing to help, often to the point of making short-term sacrifices. But people will not make sacrifices if they are unhappy with the status quo, unless they think the potential benefits of change are attractive and they really believe that a transformation is possible. Without credible and sufficient communication, employees' hearts and minds are never captured. The success of communication effort depends upon the clarity and simplicity of the message, use of multiple forms and channels, and intensity of communication. Behavior from important people that is consistent with the vision can support other forms of communication.

5. Empower Action: Employees need to be empowered to participate in the necessary action required for the change process. Lack of information, non-supportive performance measurement and reward systems, lack of self-confidence, and hindering organization structure can create obstacles to action and they need to be overcome. These barriers may be real or only perceived. Unless employees are empowered to overcome these obstacles, change process may be undermined.

6. Plan for and Create Short-Term Wins: The transformation process often takes time and unless people see some tangible short-term progress, they may be disheartened. Therefore, leaders need to plan the transformation effort in such a way that short-term goals are set and their achievement is

celebrated. Such short-term wins would encourage employees to continue with the transformation effort.
7. Don't Let up: The leader cannot pause with just some short-term gains or performance improvement. Persistence over a long period is needed to realize the vision. Until changes are internalized and become a part of the organization culture, the organization may revert to its old ways.
8. Institutionalize the Change in the Organization Culture: The organization structure, systems, style, and skills should support creating the organization culture where the changed behaviors are institutionalized. Until new behaviors are rooted in the organization's social norms and shared values, they are always subject to degradation as soon as the pressures associated with a change effort are removed.

Addressing Risks Involved in Implementing the New Path

Heifetz and Linsky[17] suggest that anyone who has stepped out on the line, leading part of an organization, a community, or a family, knows the personal and professional vulnerabilities. However gentle your style, however careful your strategy, however sure you may be that you are on the right track, leading change is a risky business.

However, leadership is worth the risk because the goals extend beyond material gain or personal advancement. By making the lives of people around you better, leadership provides a meaning in life. It creates purpose.

And it ought to be remembered that there is nothing more difficult to take in hand, more perilous to conduct, or more

---

[17] Heifetz, R., & Linsky, M. (2002). *Leadership on the line. Staying alive through the dangers of leading.* Boston,USA: Harvard Business School Press.

uncertain in its success, than to take the lead in the introduction
of a new order of things.
(Niccolo Machiavelli, The Prince. Retrieved from
www.constitution.org)

They propose that there are two kinds of problems. When the organizations or communities face problems for which solutions are known then these could be called technical problems. As the paths to solve such problems are known, leadership entails little risk. However, there are many problems where solutions need to be found. Such problems require adaptive changes for the organization or the communities to discover new paths through experimentation, discoveries, and adjustments. The adaptive changes are risky because people may not be confident about their outcomes and cannot see at the beginning of the adaptive process that the new situation will be any better than the current condition. While the gains would still be uncertain, those likely to lose out because of such changes will see their losses clearly. For instance, in the earlier Indonesian midwives example, the traditional birth attendants faced a risk to their livelihood as midwives took over their work.

Adaptive changes require modifications in behaviors and well-established habit patterns. As habits provide stability, people resist such changes being introduced by the leader even though they may have the potential for a better future. Leaders need to address dangers arising from such resistance to change.

Heifetz and Linsky (2002) provide the following guidance on ways to respond to these dangers.

Get a "Balcony" Perspective: Often one gets into a change process with many opposing it and forgets the overall perspective. It is, therefore, useful to occasionally step back and remember the overall perspective; perspective from the balcony, so to say. Visionary leadership is an improvisational art. The leader may have an overarching vision, clear orienting values, and even a strategic plan, but what the leader needs to actually do from moment to moment cannot be scripted. To be effective, a leader should respond to what is happening. Therefore, it is useful to watch out for an authority figure's words and behavior as it will provide a critical signal about the impact of change actions on the organization or community as a whole.

Think Politically: Any change is a political process with gains for some and losses for others. Therefore, it is important to have personal relationships with those who may oppose changes. However, one also needs to keep a watch on the behavior of those who support change so that their actions do not enhance resistance to change.

Orchestrate the Conflict: There will be differences, passions, and conflicts along the way of an adaptive change. The leader should work with them in a way that diminishes their destructive potential and constructively harnesses their energy.

Put the Responsibility on Those Who Need to Make the Change: To meet the adaptive challenge, people must change their hearts as well as their behavior. The leader should put the issue back to the team and to those who need to make the changes so that it is placed where it could be resolved. Too often leaders tend to take everything on their own shoulders. Exercising leadership necessarily involves interventions in the change process. Four types of interventions constitute the tactics of leadership: making observations, asking questions, offering interpretations, and taking actions.

Hold Steady: Finally, the leader will have to learn to take the heat and receive people's anger in a way that does not undermine the change process. This is one of the toughest tasks of leadership. The leader should not get too far ahead of the others, otherwise there is a risk of being sidelined. One needs to wait until the issue is ripe. Leader should be steadfast and focused on the change that is being sought and for the reasons why it is sought. The eye should be on the better future that would result while addressing the painful issues involved.

Six

Inspiring and Empowering Stakeholders

Without inspiration the best powers of the mind remain dormant.
There is a fuel in us which needs to be ignited with sparks.
—Johann Gottfried Von Herder[1]

Introduction

Inspiring and empowering stakeholders to pursue the path for achieving a shared vision is the essence of visionary leadership. It is even more important for the health sector as the results of prevention are not immediately visible and will only be seen over a long period. Therefore, people need to be inspired by a shared vision. Some issues, such as RH, are also culturally sensitive. For instance, provision of adolescent sexual and reproductive health information and services is not accepted in many cultures. Therefore, people would need to be empowered through commitment to common values.

"Leaders take the initiative in mobilizing people for participation in the process of change, encouraging a sense of collective identity and collective efficacy," says Burns in his classic book on leadership.[2] This, in turn, brings stronger feelings of self-worth and self-efficacy as an enhanced sense of "meaningfulness" in their work and lives. The word for this process is *empowerment*.

---

[1] Retrieved from www.searchquotes.com/quotes/author/Johann_Gottfried_Von_Herder, accessed on January 5, 2013.
[2] Burns, J. McG. (1978). *Leadership*. New York, USA: Harper Collins.

Instead of exercising power over people, transformative leaders champion and inspire followers.

Covey[3] says that leadership is communicating to people their worth and potential so clearly that they come to see it in themselves. It is this that would inspire people to a shared vision and empower them to journey on the chosen path. One has to address the whole person—body, mind, heart, and spirit. Neglecting them will lead to four chronic problems in an organization—low trust, no shared vision and values, misalignment, and disempowerment.

Kouzes and Posner[4] identify the following five practices of exemplary leadership:

- Model the Way: To effectively model the way they expect of others, a leader's behavior is important. "Exemplary leaders go first," say Kouzes and Posner. Modeling the way is essentially about earning the right and respect to lead.

- Inspire a Shared Vision: Leaders have a clear vision of the future that pulls them forward. However, as mentioned in Chapter Two, visions seen only by leaders are insufficient to create an organized movement. People will not be inspired to follow until they accept that vision as their own.

- Challenge the Process: Leaders are pioneers. They realize well that taking people to a future would require challenging the current process and experimentation with attendant risks of failure.

- Enable Others to Act: Leadership is a team effort. Leaders make possible for others to do good work. Therefore, empowerment is crucial to achieve results.

- Encourage the Heart: Realizing the desired vision requires considerable efforts and often involves ups and downs. Leaders encourage the heart of their constituents to carry on a path to the vision.

[3] Covey, S. R. (2006). *The 8th habit: From effectiveness to greatness.* New York, USA: Free Press.

[4] Kouzes, J., & Posner, B. Z. (1995, updated 2003, 2008). *The leadership challenge. How to keep getting extraordinary things done in organizations.* San Francisco, USA: Jossey-Bass, A Wiley Imprint.

Except for challenging the process, all the other four practices relate to inspiring and empowering constituents.

In the second section (Inspiring), we describe how leaders could inspire people to follow them. There is considerable confusion on what distinguishes motivation and inspiration and this is discussed in the third section (Inspiration versus Motivation). The fourth section (Empowerment) addresses ways the leaders can empower others and systems that disempower people. Finally, the fifth section (Combining Inspiration, Motivation, and Empowerment) concludes this chapter by discussing how an effective leader can combine actions for inspiration, motivation, and empowerment.

Inspiring

The word inspiration comes from the Latin *inspirare* and means "to breathe life into others." It implies to be *in spirit*. It is something that fills us with a purpose or calling higher than ourselves. Inspirational leadership can move people to act on a compelling shared vision. Thus, inspiring has an animated or exalted effect. It appeals more to our "heart" than to our "head."

To inspire, leaders must do two things: create resonance with a compelling vision which has been articulated in ways that move people to act. And the leader must embody what he/she asks of others and/or offer a sense of common destiny or purpose over and above the ordinary.[5] Thus, leaders inspire others through three main ways:[6]

- Communicating shared vision
- Being a role model
- Aligning systems and structures that reinforce the core values and strategic priorities identified in the path-finding process

[5] Retrieved from www.1000advice.com/guru/; www.1000ventures.com/.
[6] Covey, S. R. (2006). *The 8th habit: From effectiveness to greatness.*

A visionary leader who has created a shared vision creates energy and passion which inspires others to achieve more than they may have ever dreamt possible. The inspiring leader is able to articulate and communicate a shared vision that inspires others to act. Thus, communicating shared vision is a key to inspire others (Box 6.1).

Communicating means holding conversations focused on vision/values and results; clarify assumptions, beliefs, and feelings within yourself and others. It requires balancing advocacy and enquiry.[7]

Storytelling

Storytelling is one of the oldest ways to communicate the vision and values. Stories have more of an impact than simply stating facts and are remembered longer. The story captures our attention while entertaining us. Therefore, storytelling can influence behavior. For instance, story of how a young woman suffered because of unintended pregnancy and possibly fatal abortion effort can have more impact than all the statistics about adolescent RH.

In *Encouraging the Heart*, Kouzes and Posner[8] say that stories teach, mobilize, and motivate. As storytelling has been found so crucial to learning and inspiring, effective storytelling is a leadership tool. Tichy points out that storytelling is crucial to leading organizations into the future.[9]

[7] Management Sciences for Health (2005). Managers who lead: A handbook for improving health services. Retrieved from http://www.msh.org/resource-center/managers-who-lead.cfm, accessed in March 2014.

[8] Kouzes, J., & Posner, B. Z. (2003). The leadership challenge. How to keep getting extraordinary things done in organizations. San Francisco, USA: Jossey-Bass, A Wiley Imprint.

[9] Tichy, N. M. & Cohen, E. (2002). *The leadership engine*. New York, USA: Harper Business Essentials.

Box 6.1: *Interview with an Inspiring Leader*

"Results are the inspiration," says Mr Fazle Hasan Abed. More than three decades ago, Fazle Hasan Abed left a lucrative career in a prestigious oil company to dedicate himself entirely to development of Bangladesh by founding the Bangladesh Rural Advancement Committee (BRAC). Since its founding in 1972, BRAC has grown to be one of the largest NGOs in the world and its work has contributed immensely to the country's development.

To be a good leader, Mr Abed emphasizes the need to devote oneself entirely to one's work, "Your commitment has to be total." He says,

> The way you live and the way you think also affect your leadership. If you are not hardworking, then you will not be able to inspire others to be hard working. A leader's lifestyle inspires others. So, I would not say that BRAC would be a hardworking organization if I had not been hardworking myself. Leaders cannot really inspire others by word of mouth. They have to live a life that inspires others.

In response to a question, "What do you do to align your commitment with that of your colleagues, coworkers?" he responds as follows.

> Whenever I have a chance to meet my coworkers, I try to give them a broader vision of things rather than operational ideas alone. I try to give them a Big Picture of what needs to be done in Bangladesh. I think the best way is to transmit your values to your coworkers and thus make them share the same enthusiasm and commitment towards their work. After all, the kind of work we do is values-driven and not profit-driven. So continuously instilling in people the principles of development and changes that we want to see in our society is always helpful and seems to inspire them to action....The most important thing is to be able to transmit a vision and values.

Mr Abed has remained focused on the cause of empowering the poor and helping them to become empowered members of the society. "I also think that it is impossible to empower the poor without empowering our staff. Empowerment is not something disempowered people can do. It is important for your staff to feel that they are empowered to do things to empower others."

Bangladesh was a lot poorer when BRAC was started, with lots of people going hungry. Things have much improved since then and there is a huge difference between then and now. So, the challenges have also changed. BRAC is now trying to provide more services and technologies than before.

Source: ICOMP.

Role Modeling

Inspiring requires that leaders model the role they expect from their followers. The famous quote of Gandhi, "be the change you want to see," applies here. Role modeling to inspire requires:[10]

- Match deeds to words
- Demonstrate honesty in interactions
- Show trust and confidence in staff, acknowledge the contribution of others
- Provide staff with challenges, feedback, and support
- Be a model of creativity, innovation, and learning

The followers of a leader as role model would show commitment in pursuit of higher goals even when setbacks occur.

Perhaps role modeling is best illustrated by servant leadership. Servant leaders primarily lead by serving others. The phrase "servant leadership" was coined by Robert K. Greenleaf in "The Servant as Leader," an essay that he first published in 1970. In that essay, he said:

> The servant-leader *is* servant first…. It begins with the natural feeling that one wants to serve, to serve *first*. Then conscious choice brings one to aspire to lead…. The difference manifests itself in the care taken by the servant-first to make sure that other people's highest priority needs are being served. The best test, and difficult to administer, is: Do those served grow as persons? Do they, *while being served*, become healthier, wiser, freer, more autonomous, more likely themselves to become servants? *And*, what is the effect on the least privileged in society? Will they benefit or at least not be further deprived?[11]

Aligning Goals and Systems for Results

Role modeling alone may not suffice to inspire others. It could be supplemented by continuously communicating the vision, path,

---

[10] Management Sciences for Health. (2005). Managers who lead: A handbook for improving health services.

[11] Retrieved from www.greenleaf.org/whatissl/.

and strategy. However, these would need to be supplemented by aligning goals and systems for results.[12] Aligning requires designing and executing systems and structures that reinforce the vision and core values as well as the path and strategies. It requires creating institutional capacity to consistently produce quality. Organizations need to develop trusting relationships with various stakeholders. Aligning work needs to be continuously reinforced. Therefore, alignment requires feedback on how these relationships are. Also, the key to the principle of alignment is to always begin with results.

Sometimes there may be a trade-off in achieving goals and being honest to values. Clearly, a leader would need to reward behavior of adherence to values. However, in the long term, such adherence is likely to pay off in terms of trust of stakeholders and their support.

Aligning should enable the stakeholders to devote time and energy to support the vision, values, and strategies. It would require:

- Ensuring congruence of values, vision, path/strategy, and daily actions
- Uniting key stakeholders around an inspiring vision
- Facilitating team work
- Linking goals with reward and recognition
- Enlisting stakeholders to commit resources

To lead an organization through adaptive change a leader would need the ability to inspire. A combination of idealism of shared vision and a realistic path would inspire people. John Baldoni argues that often when people seek inspiration, they are really seeking hope.[13] A leader who is confident of the path chosen can provide hope to followers. Communicating the shared vision and chosen path through a variety of media—meeting, one-on-one conversations, print, video, etc.—could inspire people.

---

[12] Covey, S. R. (2006). *The 8th habit: From effectiveness to greatness.*
[13] Retrieved from www.johnbaldoni.com, accessed March 2012.

Inspiration versus Motivation

It is often said that leaders inspire, managers motivate. However, inspiration and motivation are seen by many as synonymous. At other times they are used interchangeably and often the word "motivation" is used in a variety of shades of emphases on motivation and inspiration.

However, there are differences between the two. Motivation comes from *Motivere* (Latin word for "to move"). It is a psychological need for a behavior usually driving toward a goal or incentive. A motivated person will be dedicated to the task with a drive, energy, and commitment to achieve.

There are several theories of motivation. Maslow in his theory of Hierarchy of Needs (see Figure 6.1) argues that we are motivated by needs which are at different levels. As one level of needs is satisfied, people are no longer motivated by them and seek to satisfy the next higher level of needs. The first level consists of *physiological* needs such as shelter, hunger, etc. Once these physiological needs are satisfied, the next higher level is *safety* needs such as security and protection from danger. The need for job security is at this level. Then there are *social* needs such as belonging, acceptance, and social life.

Figure 6.1: *Maslow's Theory of Hierarchy of Needs*

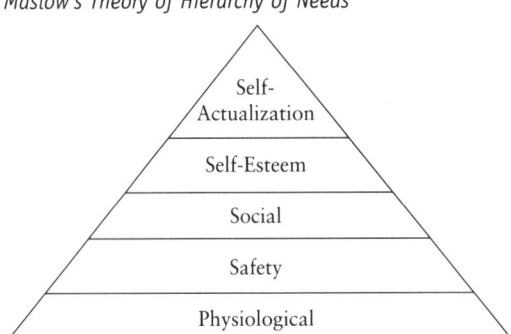

Source: Maslow (1999).[14]

---

[14] Maslow, A. H. (1999). *Toward a psychology of being.* John Wiley and Sons. Retrieved from www.abraham-maslow.com/.

After this are the self-esteem needs which relate to achievement, status, and recognition. Rewards and recognition motivate people at this level. Finally, the highest need is for *self-actualization* including realization of one's potential and personal development. Continuing to learn and facing challenges on the job will motivate the person at this level.

Herzberg[15] classified motivation factors in two parts: (1) hygiene factors and (2) motivators. Absence of hygiene factors such as money, status, treatment, and security result in dissatisfaction with the job. These need to be assured first. The motivators include feeling of achievement, recognition for accomplishment, challenging work, increased responsibility, personal growth and development. While extrinsic rewards such as increased pay and perks may motivate employees for some time, it is the intrinsic rewards through interesting and challenging work and the opportunity to achieve and grow that will lead to sustained motivation. These rewards can be had by

- Increasing accountability and responsibility
- Making information available to employees
- Challenging people to new, more difficult tasks
- Becoming experts at some specialized tasks

Thus, motivation is assured through an external system of incentives and disincentives. It appeals more to the head than to the heart.[16] Therefore, motivating people requires:

- Treating people with respect
- Making work interesting
- Giving public recognition for good work
- Creating opportunities to develop skills
- Encouraging or facilitating participation in decisions

---

[15] Herzberg, F. (2003). One more time: How do you motivate employees? Boston, USA: Harvard Business Review.

[16] Cohen, W.A. (2002). *The new art of the leader.* New Jersey, USA: Prentice Hall.

Often the role of fear in motivation is debated. Some emphasize power of the positive but often fear combined with a path for the way forward and a goal to reach can motivate people to change.

Nohria et al.[17] say that new cross-disciplinary research in fields such as neuroscience, biology, and evolutionary psychology shows four basic drivers of motivation:

1. Acquire: Obtain scarce goods, including intangibles such as social status
2. Bond: Form connections with individuals and groups
3. Comprehend: Satisfy our curiosity and master the world around us
4. Defend: Protect against external threats and promote justice

They found that employee commitment is most affected by the bond they have or feel about something which provides an understanding of employee engagement. However, they advise that an organization can best improve motivation of its employees by satisfying all four drivers in concert.

Is Inspiration Different from Motivation?

From the previous description, we may conclude that inspiration is different from motivation as the following Table 6.1 shows.

It is said that people do what they have to do when they are motivated by a manager *but* they do their best or do much more for a leader who inspires them.

It would, however, be wrong to conclude that inspiration is higher than motivation. Both are needed for success, as can be seen in the visionary leadership framework with leadership and management being complementary. A more recent trend is, therefore, to combine the two.

---

[17] Noharia, N., Grogsberg, B., & Lee, L-E. (2008). Employee motivation: A powerful new model. Harvard Business Review. Retrieved from www.hrb.org/2008/07.employee-motivation-a-powerful-new-model/ar/1/.

Table 6.1: *Key Differences between Inspiration and Motivation*

	Inspiration	*Motivation*
Role	Leaders inspire	Managers motivate
Source	Comes from within	Externally influenced
Result of	Service to a great cause higher than self	Incentives and disincentives
Appeals to	Heart	Head
Concerned with	To a value or purpose that stands higher than the person	To self's well-being
Provides	Meaning in life	Livelihood with some satisfaction

Source: Authors.

For instance, Kouzes and Posner[18] in their book *Encouraging the Heart* argue that even though people may be inspired and are doing their best, they could perform even better with encouragement. They identify seven elements of encouragement:

1. Set clear standards
2. Expect the best
3. Pay attention
4. Personalize recognition
5. Tell the story
6. Celebrate together
7. Set the example

Elements 1, 3, and 6 are more toward motivational drivers and the remaining elements emphasize inspirational generators.

Daniel Goleman[19] in his work, "What Makes a Leader," says that most effective leaders are alike in one critical area—they have some level of well-defined emotional intelligence (EQ). EQ comprises, according to Goleman, a group of five skills.

[18] Kouzes, J., & Posner, B. Z. (2003). *Encouraging the heart: A leader's guide to rewarding and recognizing others.* San Francisco, USA: Jossey-Bass, A Wiley Imprint.
[19] Goleman, D. (1996). What makes a leader? Harvard Business Review. Retrieved from www.hbr.org/2004/01/what-makes-a-leader/ar/1/.

- Self-awareness: Knowing one self
- Self-regulation: Controlling or redirecting one's undesirable impulses and moods
- Motivation: Relishing achievement for its own sake
- Empathy: Understanding other people's emotional makeup
- Social skill: Building rapport with others to move them in desired directions

The word "motivation" is used here to imply both organizational commitment and a passion to work for reasons that go beyond money or status or be inspired by a higher cause. Such inspired people seek out creative challenges, love to learn, and take great pride in a job well done. Inspiration allows people to be optimistic even when they are faced with failures.

John Kotter, while describing what leaders really do,[20] suggests that good leaders motivate in a variety of ways. First, they articulate the organization's vision to align it with the audience's values system to the extent that the objectives, goals, or work become important to them. Second, leaders then provide the necessary support (coaching, feedback, role modeling, for example) to enable them to realize this vision. Finally, they recognize and reward success. Kotter argues that when all this is done then work itself becomes intrinsically motivating.

George et al. argue that every leader should discover his/her authentic leadership as there is no unique formula for an effective leader.[21] In this they distinguish between two types of motivations: extrinsic and intrinsic. Leaders are themselves motivated or even propelled to achieve this vision by benchmarking what is success to parameters set by the outside world. Some such parameters are recognition and status that are linked to promotions and financial rewards. Intrinsic motivation, on the other hand, is derived from their sense of meaning in their life. Authentic leaders need to balance extrinsic and intrinsic motivations, or as discussed in this section, motivation and inspiration.

---

[20] Kotter, J. P. (1990). What leaders really do? Harvard Business Review, May 1990.
[21] George, B., Sims, P., McLean, A. N., & Mayer, D. (2007). *Discovering your authentic leadership*. Harvard Business Review, February 2007.

EXAMPLE[22]

Three stone masons in the middle ages were hard at work when a visitor came along and asked them what they were doing.

The first stone mason was hard at work, sweat beading his brow. "I am cutting this stone," he grumbled.

The second stone mason, though less distraught, responded with a deep sigh, "I'm building a parapet."

The third stone mason, replied with a radiant face, "I am building a beautiful cathedral that will glorify God for centuries to come."

In the story, who is inspired, who is managing, and who is just performing a task?

Thus, in the world of business, often, the word "inspiration" is underemphasized and the word "motivation" is used to subsume both, externally induced motivation and internally generated inspiration. In the health sector, we assign a separate role to each of them explicitly in a mutually reinforcing way. Health service providers get motivated when they receive praise from their clients and see their patients improve. However, they would be inspired by a big humanitarian vision and see how they are a part of realizing that vision.

Empowerment

A leader empowers followers to produce profound and fundamental change. Empowering people implies that they have responsibility with authority and accountability. Transformative leaders focus on the collective organization, or group of people, utilizing their own unique personal values that empower them to transform the organization.

Inspiration itself empowers as it results in discovering inner strengths and resources in pursuit of a vision. However, if such strengths/resources are inadequate, it may result in frustration and dilution of inspiration.

[22] Overview of vision and the visioning process. Page 1, March 2005. Retrieved from www.uwcc.wisc.edu/coopcare/docs/vision.pdf/.

How Do Systems Disempower People?

Leaders seek out ways to empower others by having a belief in their abilities and by providing greater decentralization in decision-making. However, simultaneously they strengthen accountability.

Sharing power to empower others is not like sharing money or knowledge. Money given away reduces one's own store of money whereas knowledge shared increases knowledge of both the provider and receiver. However, results are more complex when power is shared with others to empower them. Power shared is power multiplied only if the provider and receiver have shared vision and values. Otherwise power shared may detract from the chosen path and compromise ability to realize the vision.

Maxwell[23] lists "empowerment" as one of the 21 irrefutable laws of leadership. Many successful leaders do not empower others in their organization or among their followers and, thereby, put their organization or cause at risk. Only secure leaders can empower others. There are several barriers why some leaders do not empower others: desire for job security, resistance to change, and lack of self-worth. Maxwell says, "I believe the greatest things happen only when you give others the credit. That is the law of empowerment in action." (see Box 6.2).

Leadership analysts—Lynne J. McFarland, Larry Sen, and John Childress[24]—affirm that the empowerment leadership model shifts away from position power, where all people are given leadership roles so they can contribute to their fullest capacity.

Values are a key to empowerment, just as vision is important for inspiration. The stronger the value system, the more strongly leaders can be empowered and more deeply leaders can empower followers both during competition and conflict.[25] Values strengthen leaders' capacity to reach out to wider audiences and

[23] Maxwell, J. C. (1998 and 2007). The 21 irrefutable laws of leadership: Follow them and people will follow you. Thomas Nelson Inc., 12th law of empowerment.

[24] McFarland, L. J., Senn, L. E., & Childress, J. (1994). *21st century leadership: Dialogues with 100 top leaders*. California: Leadership Press, SAGE Publications.

[25] Burns, J. McG. (1978). *Leadership*.

Box 6.2: *Empowering Communities for Behavior Change*

The strategy to address Female Genital Mutilation/Cutting (FGM/C) in Kenya recognizes that real change needs to come from within communities themselves, through a process of dialogue and debate, in which individuals, empowered with information, have an opportunity to challenge social norms. The aim is to leverage social dynamics, which are constantly in flux.

Information about the medical and psychological harm, caused by this practice, can help inform such dialogues, as can discussions of human rights. These discussions often take place over weeks or months and address FGM/C not as a standalone issue—which can create suspicion and resistance—but within a broader context of health, human rights, and gender-based violence. The Joint Program, in partnership with the Ministry of Gender, Children and Social Development and other partners, has trained more than 400 community facilitators on how to carry out dialogues that eventually encourage communities to recognize that FGM/C violates a girl's rights.

Source: Retrieved from www.unfpa.org/public/site/global/lang/en/pid/5409, accessed on March 22, 2011.

to gain support for broader arrays of values and value system. In sum, values are power resources for a leadership that would transform society or an organization for the fuller realization of the higher moral purposes.

As personal values are critical to self-leadership, shared values empower others. Therefore, leaders need to examine their own values. Covey[26] suggests that 90 percent of all leadership failures are character failures. Empowering role of the leader requires that the leader is trustworthy. Trust comes from three sources: the personal, the institutional, and a person consciously chooses to give it to another. Trust comes from the potential trustworthiness of the one receiving the trust and the clear trustworthiness of one giving the trust. Trustworthiness comes from character and competence. Three facets of personal character are

- Integrity: Integrated around principles that ultimately govern the consequences of our behavior. It is the number one quality people expect in their leader.

[26] Covey, S. R. (2006). *The 8th habit: From effectiveness to greatness.*

- Maturity: When the person pays the price of integrity after it has been tested.
- Abundance mentality: Person sees life as an ever-enlarging opportunity, resources, and wealth.

Competence includes technical competence, conceptual knowledge, and awareness of interdependency.

Results can only be achieved when all the key stakeholders are together. For instance, maternal mortality can only be reduced by addressing the three delays:

- Households recognize the need for emergency obstetric care during complications of pregnancy
- Communities are organized to provide transport
- Emergency obstetric care facilities are prepared to provide services without delay

Thus, information and skills are empowering at the household level. The visionary leaders need to empower others by fostering collaboration and trust among all stakeholders. Finally, all those who are involved need to work together to achieve the desired vision.

For others to be empowered to follow the path, they must first find a sense of personal power and ownership. Therefore, there is a need for leaders to invest in capability and commitment of all stakeholders.

Combining Inspiration, Motivation, and Empowerment

Teamwork, trust, and empowerment are essential for journey on any path chosen to improve health. Leaders have to learn to combine inspiration with motivation to create buy-in and to empower followers with alignment of values, public recognition, and encouragement to get superior results.

For this combination of competencies, a leader must be able to:[27]

- Provide an inspiring vision and strategic alignment
- Help people connect their personal goals to organizational goals
- Make relentless innovation a religion
- Encourage entrepreneurial creativity and experimentation
- Involve everyone, empower and trust employees
- Coach and train people to greatness
- Build teams and promote teamwork, leverage diversity
- Motivate, inspire, and energize people, recognize achievements
- Encourage risk-taking
- Make business fun

By applying these actions, the leader would be able to expand his/her sphere of influence beyond the zone of control and bridge the gap with the circle of concern (see Figure 6.2).

Figure 6.2: *Control, Influence, and Concern*

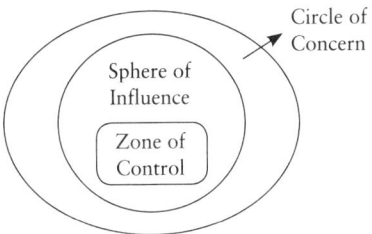

Source: Authors.

---

[27] Retrieved from www.1000advice.com/guru; www.stt.co.za/Inspirationalleadership.htm/.

Seven

Doing it Right: Results-Based Management

Effective leadership is putting first things first. Effective management is discipline, carrying it out.
—Stephen Covey

Introduction to Management

The classical definition of management is *"the act of getting people together to accomplish desired results with efficient and effective use of physical, human, financial and entrepreneurial resources."*

Henri Foyel[1] proposed a functional approach to management. In this approach, the process of management involves implementation of strategies through a process of planning, organizing, execution, and monitoring and evaluation with optimal use of resources.

- *Planning*: Planning is a process of converting goals into specific measurable and time-bound objectives using the strategy. Work plans need to be prepared to identify the needed activities—who will do what and when—to achieve the objectives. Finally, needed inputs—human (staff and skills), physical (facilities, supplies, and equipment), and financial—and ways to mobilize these inputs would need to be identified.
- *Organizing*: It involves aligning strategies to structure, systems, and style of decision-making to implement the plans.

[1] Retrieved from http://www.managetrainlearn.com/page/henri-fayol/.

- *Executing*: It is often neglected because of the belief that once plans are made and the work organized, it will get done. This is not necessarily so. Continuing supervision would be needed to ensure that obstacles to implementation are resolved. This means bringing congruence among processes of people, operations, and strategies (discussed in the following). Foyel classified execution to comprise commanding and coordinating.
- *Monitoring and Evaluation*: This function was referred by Foyel as controlling. Monitoring is to detect deviations between plans and actual implementation in terms of inputs, activities, and outputs. Clearly, a good management information system is needed to support monitoring. Evaluation is to assess what outcomes/impact—intended and unintended—have been achieved. Strategy mediates between outcomes and outputs. If the outputs were according to the plan and the strategy was appropriate then outcomes should have been achieved. If not, the strategy would need to be reviewed. Thus, monitoring is a routine assessment of ongoing activities and progress in outputs; looks at what is being done; tracks changes in inputs, activities, and outputs; and takes corrective actions. On the other hand, evaluation is an episodic assessment of outcomes/impact, examines what results have been achieved and why.

Mintzberg[2] studied management roles, a complete set of behaviors that will be needed to perform the above-mentioned functions. He categorized them as follows:

1. Interpersonal

- *Figurehead*: All social, inspirational, legal, and ceremonial obligations serving as a symbol of status and authority.
- *Leader*: Although classified as leader role, it is basically a human resources management role comprising

[2] Mintzberg, H. (1973). *The nature of managerial work*. New York, USA: Harper & Row.

recruitment and selection, structuring and motivating subordinates, overseeing their progress, and promoting and encouraging their development.

- *Liaison*: Manager must network and engage in information exchange to gain access to needed knowledge.

2. Informational

- *Monitor*: Manager needs to assess deviations between plans and actual operations in terms of inputs, activities, and outputs, also investigating reasons to implement the needed corrective actions.
- *Disseminator*: This role is related to filtering external views about the organization and conveying them to the right staff in the organization.
- *Spokesperson*: Manager serves in a public relations role with key stakeholders to support the operations of the organization.

3. Decisional

- *Entrepreneur*: Managers work toward improvement in the performance of the organization through teams of staff.
- *Disturbance handler*: Manager needs to take charge when an organization is unexpectedly upset or transformed due to external disturbances.
- *Resource Allocator*: Describes the responsibility of allocating and overseeing financial, material, and personnel resources.
- *Negotiator*: Managers need to negotiate with both external and internal stakeholders in performing their functions.

Skills

Three types of managerial skills can be distinguished—conceptual, technical, and interpersonal—although the mix of using these skills will vary as one rises to higher management levels. For instance, at the lowest level considerable focus will be on technical skills. However, this focus will decline in importance at the highest level of management.

Thus, we can view management as utilizing managerial skills to perform management roles for carrying out management functions to accomplish the desired results (see Figure 7.1).

Figure 7.1: *What Is Management?*

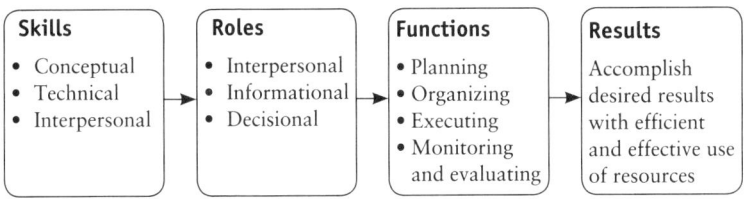

Source: Authors.

Evolution of Management Thought

Management must have been practiced for long in the history wherever people were organized to accomplish desired results. However, we can say that modern management, as we know, began in the 19th century. In the following paragraphs, we highlight a few milestones in the development of modern management.

Scientific Management School

Frederic W. Taylor is credited with coining the term "scientific management."[3] He was a supervisor in Bethlehem Steel Company in USA and was responsible for supervising the loading of pig iron on trolleys for their transport to furnaces. This required shoveling pig iron from heaps on to trolleys. As he observed this work, he was puzzled that every person did this work differently in terms

[3] Taylor, F. W. (1913). *The principles of scientific management*. New York, USA: Harper and Row Publishers.

of load lifted on shovel, speed of movement, etc. He then hypothesized that there must be a best way of shoveling and proceeded to discover it by experimenting with different elements of work. He found that a workman could load 47 tons a day compared to the current output of 12.5 tons if the best procedure was used (see Figure 7.2).

Figure 7.2: *A Comparison of Current vs Best Practice*

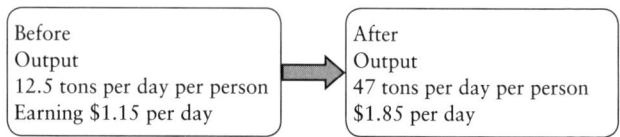

Before
Output
12.5 tons per day per person
Earning $1.15 per day

After
Output
47 tons per day per person
$1.85 per day

Source: Authors.

The implementation of the best way of shoveling or "science of shoveling" required changes in processes of selection, training, planning, tool room, monitoring, and feedback. Despite the extra costs involved in these processes, there was an estimated saving of US$75,000 per year.

He wrote a book in 1913 and postulated that managers have the following four duties under scientific management:

1. Develop a science of work, namely best way of doing the work
2. Scientifically select, train, teach, and develop the workmen in science of work
3. Heartily cooperate with workmen in implementing the science of work
4. Have a division of responsibilities between management and workers

Currently, the same principles are applied through benchmarking and looking for best practices.

Behavioral School of Management

As principles of scientific management took hold despite criticism that it reduced humans to machines, research teams from Harvard

University conducted field studies on worker productivity at the Western Electric Hawthorne plant near Chicago, one of the most advanced manufacturing facilities that employed 29,000 workers to produce telephones and telecommunications equipment for AT&T between 1924 and 1933. The experiments initially concentrated on the relationship between productivity and workplace lighting. Groups of six workers were removed from the production line to perform their normal work in an enclosed space where researchers changed the intensity of the electric lighting. As lighting was improved, productivity increased. However, to the researchers' surprise, it continued to increase as lighting was reduced. Sociologist Mayo joined the experiments in early 1928 and realized that the workers chosen for the experiment were accorded higher status by their coworkers.[4] The increased performance was due to their increased motivation. Productivity was related to social effects, not the level of lighting. Mayo called such social behavior the "Hawthorne Effect." He expanded the research to look at pay and incentives, rest periods, hours of work, supervision, and work pace. Again, he recorded remarkable increases that had little relation to these variables. Mayo concluded that the workplace was above all, a social system of interdependent actors in which workers are influenced more by the social demands of the workplace, by their need for recognition, security, and a sense of belonging, than by their physical working environment.

He also concluded that:

- Job satisfaction leads to higher productivity
- Pay is a relatively low motivator
- Management is only one factor affecting behavior
- The informal group exerts a strong influence on motivation

This led to behavioral or human relations school of management.

---

[4] Elton, M. (1933). *The human problems of an industrial citizen*. USA: MacMillan.

Quantitative Methods School

In 1941, an Operational Research (OR) Section was established in Coastal Command of UK which was to carry out some of the most well-known OR work in World War II.[5] The responsibility of Coastal Command was, to a large extent, the flying of long-range sorties by single aircraft with the object of sighting and attacking surfaced U-boats (German submarines). The operations involved organization of flying maintenance and inspection and comparison of aircraft type. Experience showed that it required some 170 man-hours by maintenance and ground staff to produce one hour of operational flying and more than 200 hours of flying to produce one attack on a surfaced U-boat. Hence, over 34,000 man-hours of effort were necessary just to attack a U-boat. In early 1941, the attack kill probability was 2 percent to 3 percent (i.e., between 1.1 million and 1.7 million man-hours were needed by Coastal Command to destroy one U-boat). Six variables were considered as influencing the kill probability: depth (time) setting for depth charge explosion; lethal radius; aiming errors in dropping the stick; orientation of the stick with respect to the U-boat; spacing between successive depth charges in the stick; and low level bombsights. Each of these variables was studied and optimal measures found. The overall effect of all the measures discussed above was such that by 1945 the attack kill probability had risen to over 40 percent.

Such successes in war effort led to a formal discipline of OR. In the decades after the war, the techniques began to be applied more widely to problems in business, industry, and society. Since that time, OR has expanded into a field widely used in industries moving to a focus on the development of mathematical models that can be used to analyze and optimize complex systems, and has become an area of active academic and industrial research. OR, when applied to managerial decision-making, became the management science which provides managers with a scientific basis for solving problems and making decisions.

[5] Retrieved from http://people.brunel.ac.uk, accessed on April 15, 2012.

During the last 30 years, there have been attempts to achieve integration of the above three approaches to management. One of these attempts, the systems approach, stresses that the organizations must be viewed as total systems. It is based on the concept that an organization is a system. A system is defined as a number of interdependent parts functioning as a whole for some purpose (see Chapter Four). Another, the contingency approach, stresses that the correctness of a managerial practice is contingent upon how it fits the practical situation in which it is applied.

Strategic Management School

In the 1960s, researchers questioned why some companies were successful whereas others were not. Nearly 500 years ago, Machiavelli[6] had asked a similar question, "Why some princes are successful and others are not?" and concluded that those princes who matched their actions to circumstances succeeded and others did not. The researchers analyzing reasons for success of companies also concluded that it was the right strategies that led to success. However, it was not enough to formulate strategies but they also needed to be implemented well. This led to the strategic management school of thought:[7]

- Strategy Formulation: How the organization responds to changes in environment (social, political, and economic context; changes in customer expectations, competitors' actions, and the organization itself) through well-formulated strategies—which services/products to provide to whom and in what sequence; how to mobilize demand, supply, and resources. Strategy will direct energies of the whole organization and use resources optimally toward achieving those goals.

---

[6] Machiavelli, N. (1961). *The prince.* London: Penguin.
[7] Ansoff, H. I. (1979). *Strategic management.* New York: Wiley.

- Implementation of Strategy: Changes in strategy would require corresponding changes in one or more of the following: structure, staff, systems, skills, style, and shared values.
- Change Management: The above-mentioned changes would have to be brought about through a carefully orchestrated process of change.

However, as environment changes, organizations would have to change their strategies. The researchers then asked the question why is it that some organizations are able to do this and deliver superior performance over time. In their bestseller book on America's best-run companies, *In Search of Excellence*, Peter and Waterman[8] found eight basic principles that reflected these companies, management value, and corporate culture. The eight principles of excellent companies are

- *Bias toward action*: Successful companies value action, doing, and implementation.
- *Closeness to the customer*: Successful companies are customer driven; a dominant value is customer need satisfaction.
- *Autonomy and entrepreneurship*: Organization structure in excellent corporations is designed to encourage innovation and change.
- *Productivity through people*: Staff are encouraged to participate in production, marketing, and new product decisions.
- *Hands on, value driven*: Excellent companies are clear about their value system.
- *Sticking to the knitting*: Successful firms are highly focused. They do what they know best.
- *Simple form, lean staff*: The structural form and systems of excellent companies are elegantly simple and few personnel are employed in staff positions.

[8] Peters, T. J., & Waterman, R. H. (1982). *In search of excellence: Lessons from America's best-run companies*. New York, USA: Harper Collins.

- *Simultaneous loose-tight properties*: Excellent companies use tight controls on core values and loose controls in others areas where they can innovate.

Unfortunately, several of the companies that Peters and Waterman had classified as excellent did not deliver superior performance soon after the study was completed. This showed how difficult it is to be and continue to remain excellent. More recently, Jim Collins[9] has studied this issue in his famous book *Good to Great*. He put forward the following practices of the companies which transformed themselves from just being "good" companies to becoming "great" companies.

1. *Level 5 leadership*: The leaders combined personal humility with strong professional will.
2. *First who...then what*: They found the right people and let go of the wrong people.
3. *Confront the brutal facts*: While having the unwavering faith that you will succeed you confront the most brutal facts about the current reality.
4. *Hedgehog concept*: Work at the intersections of what is your passion, what you can be best in the world at, and what is the revenue engine.
5. *Culture of discipline*: Have disciplined people, thought, and action combined with entrepreneurship.
6. *Use technology as accelerators*: Use technology as a primary means of igniting a transformation.

Managing for Implementation

Thus, the management process will convert inputs into desired outputs leading to outcomes and impact to realize the vision (see Figure 7.3).

---

[9] Collins, J. (2001). *Good to great*. New York, USA: Harper Collins.

Figure 7.3: *Systems Diagram for Converting Inputs to Outcomes*

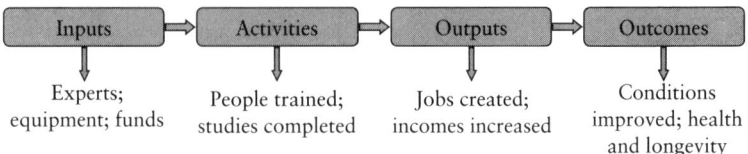

Inputs	Activities	Outputs	Outcomes
Experts; equipment; funds	People trained; studies completed	Jobs created; incomes increased	Conditions improved; health and longevity

Source: Authors.

Often there is a confusion between outputs and outcomes.

- *Outputs* are the specific products and services which emerge from processing inputs through program or non-program activities. Outputs, therefore, come from the *completion* (rather than the conduct) of activities and are the type of result over which managers have a high degree of influence.

- *Outcomes* are actual or intended changes in development conditions that interventions are seeking to support. They describe a change in development conditions between the completion of outputs and the achievement of impact.

The Execution Gap

Bossidy and Charan[10] discuss execution as the discipline of getting things done and identify it (or lack of it) as one of the key factors for leadership failure. Effective execution depends upon interaction between three processes: People, Strategy, and Operations.

1. *People* process is the most important as it is people who will participate in formulating strategies and translating these strategies into realities. The people process should involve: (a) evaluating individuals accurately and in-depth analysis and (b) providing a framework for identifying

---

[10] Bossidy, L., & Charan, R. (2002). *Execution: The discipline of getting things done.* New York, USA: Crown Business.

and developing the leadership talent at all levels and of all kinds—the organization will need to execute its strategies down the road.

2. *Strategy* process should not only identify what services will be provided to whom but also the question of how the strategy will be implemented. It should also ask: are the right people available to execute the strategy? Finally, the strategic plan should be linked to the operational plans.

3. *Operations* process. While the strategic process defines where organization wants to go and the people process defines who is going to take it there, it is the operations plan that provides the road map with the necessary details for the people to enact the vision and mission.

Results-Based Management

Results-based management (RBM) differs from the above description of the management view. It begins with the results or outcomes desired rather than the inputs, from right to left in Figure 7.3 rather than from left to right. The objective of RBM[11] is to "provide a coherent framework for strategic planning and management based on learning and accountability in a decentralized environment." Introducing a results-based approach aims to improve management effectiveness and accountability by "defining realistic expected results, monitoring progress toward the achievement of expected results, integrating lessons learned into management decisions, and reporting on performance."

Beginning with inputs often leads to a sense of helplessness when inputs are inadequate. On the other hand, application of RBM would lead to a sequence of questions such as:

1. What outcomes are being achieved compared to goals?

---

[11] UNDP (2002). Results-based management. Retrieved from http://web.undp.org/eveluationdocuments/RBMconceptsmethodologyjuly 2002.pdf /.

2. Is there a shortfall in outcomes? If so, then is it due to short-falls in outputs? Or, if the outputs do not lead to desired outcomes, the strategies being pursued need to be reviewed.
3. Are the activities leading to desired outputs? (the execution/implementation gap)
4. Are inputs being converted into activities which reflect efficient use of available inputs?
5. Finally, are the inputs adequate? If not, then there is a need to mobilize resources.

RBM is, therefore, a system to improve management performance by comparing and analyzing actual versus planned results. Usually a logframe is used to support RBM in projects as discussed in the following paragraphs.

Logical Framework

A Logical Framework (Logframe) is:

- A set of interlocking concepts which must be used together in a dynamic fashion to permit the elaboration of a *well-designed, objectively described*, and available project.
- To provide a *clear structure* which will allow project planners and evaluators to specify the components of their activities and identify the *logical linkages* between a set of means and ends.
- A *planning tool* that allows a proposal writer to determine whether the different elements of the project proposal make sense and have logic.
- To clarify the relationships which underlie judgments about likely efficiency and effectiveness of projects for *evaluation*.
- To provide a practical summary to inform project staff, donors, beneficiaries, and other stakeholders, which they can refer to throughout the project life cycle. Most international donors now require a Logframe in the proposal.

This practical summary will explain to the stakeholders:

- What the project is going to achieve?
- What activities will be carried out to achieve its outputs, objectives, and goal?
- What inputs (resources) are required?
- What are the potential problems which could affect the success of the project?
- How will the progress and ultimate success of the project be measured and verified?

Logical Framework Matrix

The structure of the Logframe is very simple. It consists of a 4 × 4 matrix as shown in Table 7.1.

Logframe tips

- It should be concise. Generally, it should take up no more than two pages.
- It should be comprehensible to a first-timer. Acronyms should best be avoided.
- Beneficiaries should also take part to help design it. The inputs should be a team effort.
- It will provide a basis for later on monitoring and evaluation. Therefore, it must be reviewed and amended regularly whenever the project changes its course.

The Vertical Logic

The vertical logic

- Clarifies the causal relationships between different levels in the Summary of Objectives (column 1)

Table 7.1: *Logframe Matrix Structure and Content*

Summary of Objectives	Objectively Verifiable Indicators (OVIs)	Means of Verification (MOV)	Assumptions/ Risks
Goal The ultimate end which the specific project will contribute to.	How the achievement of the Goal will be measured?	Sources of information on the Goal indicators.	Assumptions affecting Objectives– Goal linkage.
Objectives What the project is expected to achieve in development terms once it is completed within the allocated time. It is the motivation behind the production of Outputs.	How the achievement of the Objectives will be measured?	Sources of information on the Objectives indicators.	Assumptions affecting Outputs– Objectives linkage.
Outputs The specific results to be produced by the management of Inputs.	How the achievement of the Outputs will be measured?	Sources of information on the Outputs indicators.	Assumptions affecting Activities– Outputs linkage.
Activities The tasks to be undertaken and the resources available to produce Outputs.	**Inputs** E.g., teaching material, transportation, teaching staff, training space, accommodation. **Budget** E.g., summary of the project budget.	Financial out-turn report as agreed in the grant agreement.	Assumptions affecting inception of the project.

Source: AusAid. (2005). 3.3 The Logical Framework Approach. AusGuideline. Activity design: Commonwealth of Australia. Retrieved from http://www.sswm.info/ sites/default/files/reference_attachments/AUSAID%20.

Note: The two colored boxes in the **Activities** row are not used for the OVIs and the MOV. Since the **Activities** are undertaken to achieve the **Outputs**, its success is measured at the **Outputs** level. The two boxes are normally used to provide useful additional information such as inputs and budget.

- Specifies the important Assumptions/Risks (column 4) at each level in the Summary of Objectives (see Table 7.2)
- Major components involved are given in Table 7.3.

Table 7.2: *Assumptions/Risks and Summary of Objectives*

Summary of Objectives (1)	OVIs (2)	MOV (3)	Assumptions/Risks (4)

Goal — Assumptions affecting Objectives–Goal linkage

Objectives — Assumptions affecting Outputs–Objectives linkage

Outputs — Assumptions affecting Activities–Outputs linkage

Activities

Source: Authors.

Table 7.3: *Clarifying the Major Components of Vertical Logic*

Components	Clarifications
Goal	The reason for undertaking the project, that is, the ultimate end of the program to which the specific project will contribute to.
Objectives	What the project is expected to achieve in development terms once it is completed within the allocated time. It is the motivation behind the production of Outputs.
Outputs	The specific results to be produced by the management of Inputs.
Activities	The tasks to be undertaken and the resources available to produce Outputs.
Assumptions and Risks	Some Logframe users prefer using the term **Risks** in column 4 instead of **Assumptions**. The difference between these two terms is that **Risks** are negative statements about what might go wrong, emphasizing on external factors which the project manager does not have control over. On the other hand, **Assumptions** are positive statements about the conditions that need to be met in order to achieve the next level in the Summary of Objectives. Whichever term is used, the purpose is to assess and address external impacts and improve where possible to achieve the Outputs, Objectives, and Goal of the project.

Source: Authors.

How, then, do you decide which potential **Assumptions/Risks** to include in column 4?

The Assumption Decision Tree (see Figure 7.4) will help you to evaluate the importance of each potential assumption/risk and decide whether it should be included or omitted from the Logframe matrix.

Figure 7.4: *Assumption Decision Tree*

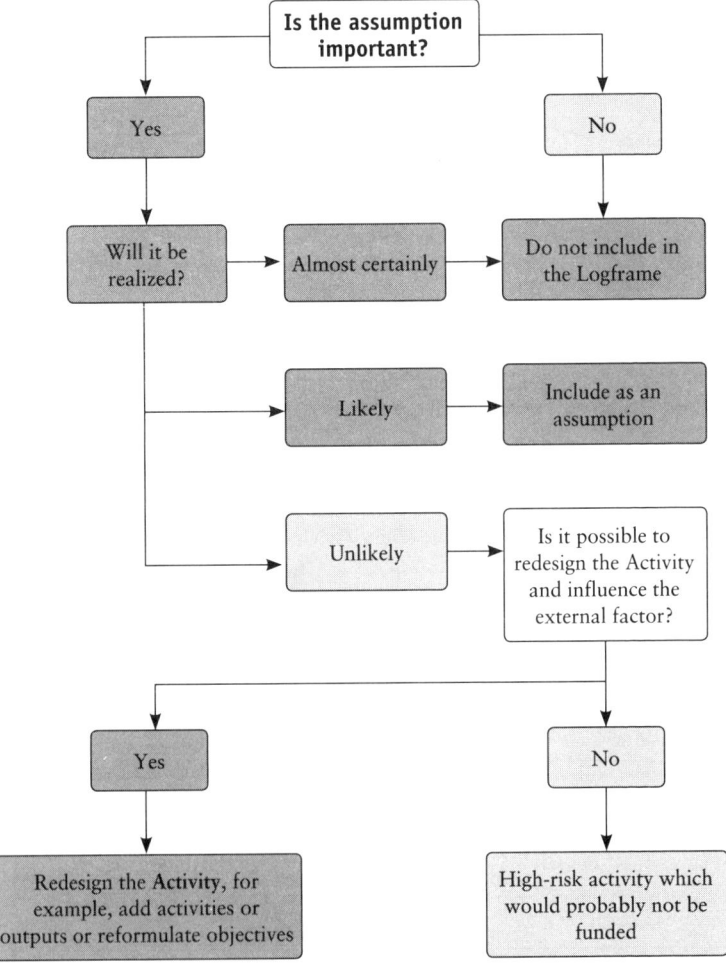

Source: AusAID. (2005). AusGuideline, 3.3 the Logical Framework Approach, p.19.

The Horizontal Logic

The horizontal logic defines (see Table 7.4)

- How the Summary of Objectives specified in column 1 of the Logframe (Goal, Objectives, and Outputs) will be measured (column 2)
- The means by which the measurement will be verified (column 3)

Table 7.4: *Clarifying the Major Components of Horizontal Logic*

Summary of Objectives	OVIs	MOV	Assumptions/ Risks
Goal ⟶	OVIs ⟶	MOV	
Objectives ⟶	OVIs ⟶	MOV	
Outputs ⟶	OVIs ⟶	MOV	
Activities			

Source: Authors.

The horizontal logic provides a framework for activity monitoring and evaluation.

Major components involved are as given in Table 7.5.

A useful guideline on developing good indicators is the SMART analysis.

- Specific: Must be specific and related to the conditions each level of the Summary of Objectives (Goal, Objectives, and Outputs) seeks
- Measurable: Must be quantifiable so that the information/data can be aggregated and analyzed statistically
- Attainable: The information/data can be collected using appropriate collection method at a reasonable cost
- Relevant: Should be relevant to the management information needs of the person who will be using the information/data
- Timely: The information/data must be collected and reported at the right time to influence many management decisions

Table 7.5: *Objectively Verifiable Indicators (OVIs)*

Component	What	Define or Clarify
OVIs	Represent a set of criteria which will indicate in concrete terms whether expected Outputs, Objectives, and Goal have been achieved.	• Who? (target group/s) • How much? (quantify) • How well? (qualify) • By when? (set deadlines) • Where? (location)
Means of Verification	Are a set of methods used to measure, assess, and evaluate the process.	• Ensure that OVIs can be measured effectively by identifying • What information to collect? • Who will collect it? • How often should it be collected? • Confirm that the indicators chosen are realistic, since they specify how the indicators can be verified. • Facilitate project evaluation by establishing in advance how the criteria for success should be verified.

Source: Authors; AusAID.

How can you be confident that your MOVs are up to the mark? You need to ask yourself some important questions when selecting the sources of information such as:

- How frequent is the information available/updated?
- How reliable is the information?
- How much will it cost to collect the information?
- How should the information be collected (e.g., survey, focus groups, national statistics, administrative records)?
- How should the information collected be recorded/ analyzed?

Five Steps to Preparing a Logical Framework Matrix

It is rather difficult to see the relationships of the different levels of a Logframe if you are to write them immediately on the Logframe matrix. A simple process to help you prepare a Logframe matrix involves the following steps:

- Step 1

    o Draw a simple flowchart showing the different levels in the Summary of Objectives.
    o You can use the following template as given in Figure 7.5.

- Step 2
  Write Goal, Objectives, Outputs and Activities inside the boxes in the flow chart

- Step 3
  Once the boxes are filled, check the logical interconnectedness from bottom to top by using the "if_____, then _____" deductive reasoning as follows:

Figure 7.5: *Hierarchy of Objectives*

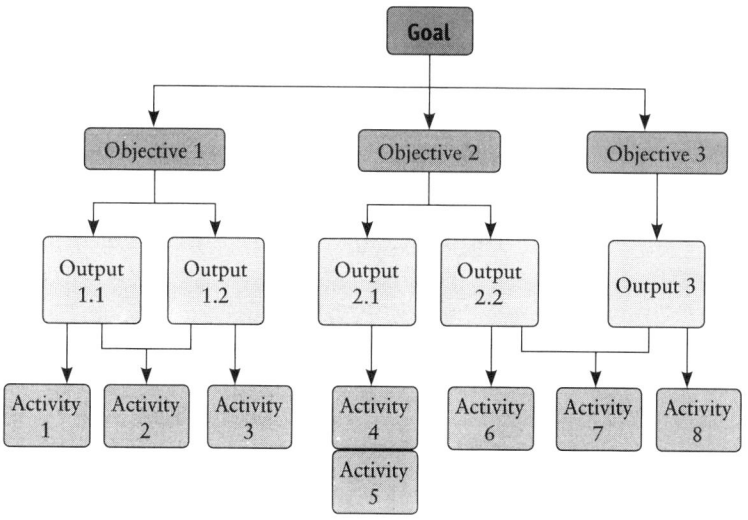

Source: Authors.

o If the *activity/activities* is/are implemented, it will result in the identified *Output/s*.

o If the *Output/s* is/are generated, it will result in the achievement of the stated *Objective/s*.

o If the *objective/s* is/are achieved, it will contribute to the realization of the stated *Goal*.

Following is an example of adolescent RH program in a city. However, some of the boxes in *activities* are left blank. Do try to complete it by adding on activity/activities you think will contribute to the achievement of the respective *outputs* (see Figure 7.6).

Figure 7.6: *Hierarchy of Objectives for Adolescent Reproductive Health in La Carlota City*

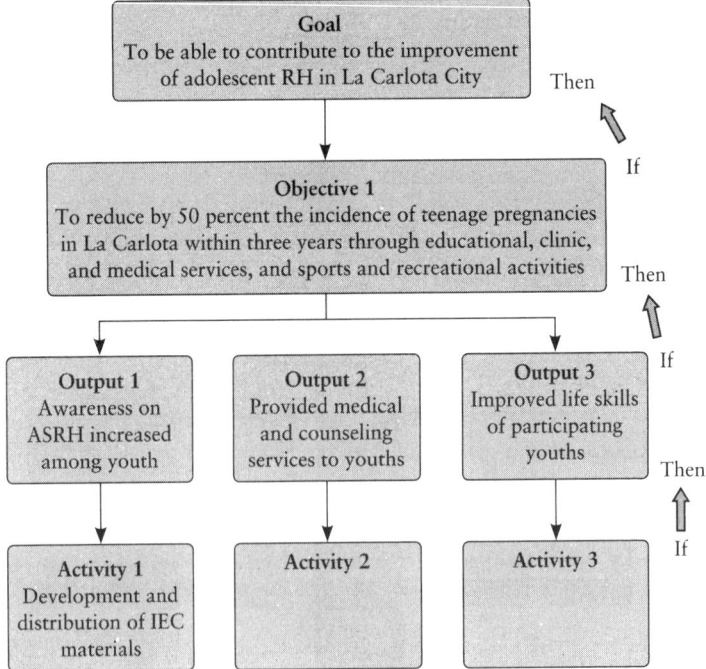

Source: Authors.

Possible Answer (see Figure 7.7).

Figure 7.7: *Use of Logframe to Determine Activities*

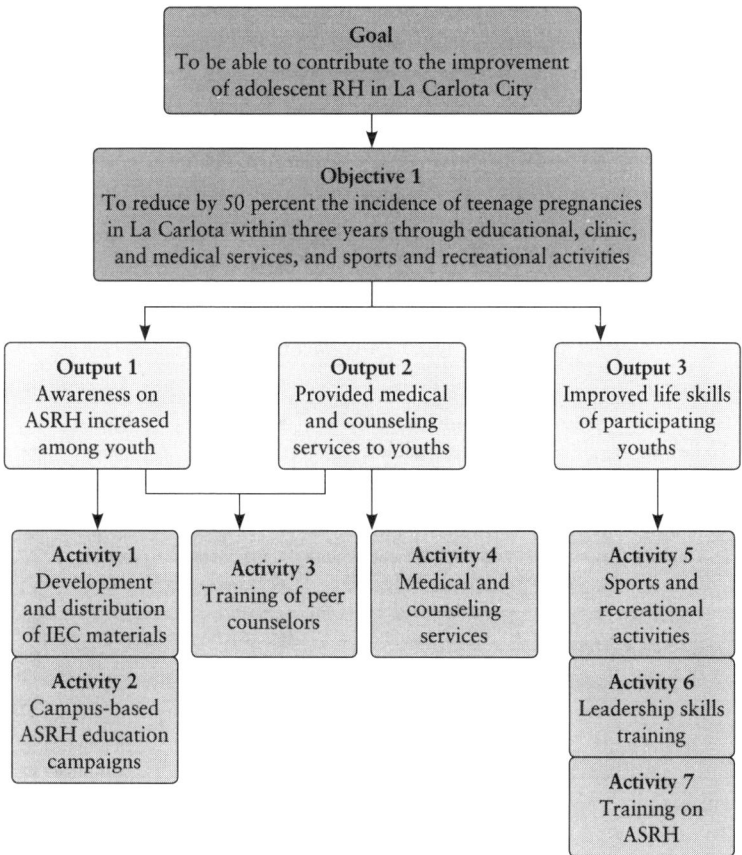

Source: Authors.

- Step 5

    o   Once the logic is established, you may then proceed and complete the Logframe matrix.
    o   You may want to try preparing a Logframe matrix based on the above flowchart. Use the following template as given in Table 7.6. Compare it to that given in Table 7.7.

Table 7.6: *Template for Logframe Matrix*

Summary of Objectives	OVIs	MOV	Assumptions/Risks
Goal			
Objectives			
Outputs			
Activities			

Source: Authors.

o   Answer (using the case study):

Table 7.7: *Designing a Program Plan for Adolescent Reproductive Health in La Carlota Using Logframe*

Objectives	OVIs	MOV	Assumptions
Goals To be able to contribute to the improvement of adolescent RH in La Carlota City	• Improvement in overall adolescent RH status of youth in La Carlota • Increased awareness on adolescent sexual and reproductive health (ASRH) • Reduction in abortion incidence • Reduction in teenage pregnancy	• Baseline and end of project surveys • Progress reports • Interviews with teachers, health providers, counselors, youths	Various stakeholders (e.g., government agencies, school authorities, health providers, local leaders) maintain their commitment
Objective To reduce by 50 percent the incidence of teenage pregnancies in La Carlota within three years through educational, clinic, and medical services, and sports and recreational activities	• Percentage reduction in teenage pregnancy in La Carlota	• Baseline and end of project surveys • Progress reports • Interview with health providers, counselors, youths	A majority of the target youths participate in the process

(Table 7.7 Contd)

(Table 7.7 Contd)

Objectives	OVIs	MOV	Assumptions
Outputs • Awareness on ASRH increased among youth • Provided medical and counseling services to youths • Improved life skills of participating youths	• New knowledge acquired from IEC materials, life skills courses, and counseling • New skills acquired from life skills workshops • Ability to apply skills and knowledge acquired	• Interviews with counselors, trainers, teachers, youths • Workshop report and evaluation	
Activities • Development and distribution of IEC materials • Campus-based ASRH education campaigns • Training of peer counselors • Medical and counseling services • Sports and recreational activities • Leadership skills training • Training on ASRH	**Inputs** • Technical assistance • Campaign organizers • Trainers of peer educators • Medical personnel • Medical equipments • Rooms for counseling • Transport • Training space • Community centers/ school field • Trainers on leadership skills, etc. **Budget** • Cost for Developing IEC materials • Organizing campaigns/trainings • Trainers • Health-care providers, etc.	Financial out-turn report	• Government support is maintained

Source: Authors.

Eight

Delivering Superior Results: Applying the Visionary Leadership Framework

If your actions inspire others to dream more, learn more, do more and become more, you are a leader.
—John Quincy Adams

Introduction

There is a massive amount of literature on ways leaders can deliver superior results. For instance, Malcolm Gladwell discusses personal excellence as "outliers" in his book[1] *Outlier: The Story of Success.* "Outliers" is a scientific term used to describe things or phenomena that lie outside normal experience. People who are outliers, for one reason or another, are so accomplished and so extraordinary and so outside of the ordinary experience, that we think they are "outliers." He attributes such excellence to hard work and opportunities presented by external circumstances. He postulates the 10,000-hour rule—that practice of 10,000 hours is needed to build an expertise in any field. In addition, the fact is that some people also get an extraordinary set of opportunities so that they become outliers. The latter is considered "luck."

Does one have to be lucky to deliver superior results? Jim Collins in his book[2] *Great by Choice* argues that almost all

---

[1] Gladwell, M. (2008). *Outliers: The story of success.* New York, USA: Little, Brown and Company.

[2] Collins, J., & Hansen, M. T. (2011). *Great by choice: Uncertainty, chaos and luck—Why some thrive despite them all.* New York, USA: Harper Collins.

organizations get favorable external opportunities but what they do with it that determines how great they become. He discusses two teams of adventurers who wanted to reach the South Pole:

> In October 1911, two teams of adventurers made their final preparations in their quest to be the first people in modern history to reach the South Pole. For one team, it would be a race to victory and a safe return home. For the second team, it would be a devastating defeat, reaching the Pole only to find the wind-whipped flags of their rivals planted 34 days earlier, followed by a race for their lives—a race that they lost in the end, as the advancing winter swallowed them up. All five members of the second Pole team perished, staggering from exhaustion, suffering the dead-black pain of frostbite, and then freezing to death as some wrote in their final journal entries and notes to loved ones back home.
>
> Here we have two expedition leaders—Ronald Amundsen, the winner, and Robert Falcon Scott, the loser—of similar ages (39 and 43) and with comparable experience. Amundsen and Scott started their respective journeys for the Pole within days of each other. One leader led his team to victory and safety. The other led his team to defeat and death. What separated these two men? Amundsen and Scott achieved dramatically different outcomes not because they faced dramatically different circumstances. In the first 34 days of their respective expeditions, Amundsen and Scott had exactly the same ratio, 56 percent, of good days to bad days of weather. If they faced the same environment in the same year with the same goal, the cause of their respective success and failure simply cannot be the environment. They had divergent outcomes principally because they displayed very different behaviors.

We believe that leaders intuitively apply the visionary leadership framework. However, a systematic application of the framework will improve your odds of delivering superior results. In Chapters Three through Seven, we have discussed specific components of the framework. We now discuss specific issues that may arise when the framework is systematically applied in a situation in the second section (Applying the Framework). We then conclude the discussion in the third section. It is followed by two examples—gender violence against women and youth's access to reproductive health care.

Applying the Framework

In applying the visionary leadership framework, a leader needs to decide from where he should begin the process. The first question is—is there a shared vision for the issue at hand? Often leaders realize that the first step they should take is to create a shared vision. For instance, a team from a district in Gujarat, India, which had gone through a leadership development program, wanted to reduce maternal mortality in their district and found that there was no shared vision on maternal mortality among the staff. Upon discussion, it was realized that maternal health was almost always last in the agenda for quarterly review meetings and, consequently, the discussion was often shortened for want of time, creating an impression that maternal health was not as important as other areas such as family planning or malaria. So this review process was changed and the sequence of topics for quarterly review was altered to begin the discussion with a different program each quarter. Thus, at least in one quarter maternal health was reviewed first and this provided a communication opportunity for creating a shared vision for maternal health.

If there is a shared vision, the leader needs to assess—why there is a gap between vision and reality? What are the key constraints or root causes holding up progress? This would require a thorough understanding of the situation. Often, the leaders in this situation consult a wide range of stakeholders and hold dialogue with them. It would also involve reviewing of all the documents. Sometimes, it may happen that adequate information is not available and some operations research may need to be commissioned. Several agencies have also developed methodologies for situation analysis to assist in this process.

The above analysis will also identify whether the path currently followed is appropriate. If not, the challenge is to review/change path and/or strategies, and inspire/empower the relevant stakeholders as well as strengthen RBM. Often, however, it may be that there are no actions being taken to address the issue. Therefore, a new path is needed. This is a much bigger challenge as the quantum of change involved is large. On the other hand, there may be no vested interest opposing the new path.

Having identified a path, there would be a need to orchestrate its implementation. Often a constraint exists because the incentives for implementers either do not reward for or there is a disincentive for addressing that constraint. Therefore, there will be a need to look at both overt and covert incentives/disincentives for implementers and to adapt them for progress toward the desired path.

If a careful process of creating a shared vision has been followed then many implementers may already be inspired. However, this may have to be supplemented by a communication strategy. The leader would also need to see what will be needed to empower the providers or individuals/households/communities. Often these include necessary facilities, supplies, equipment, information, or competencies. Key disempowering factors would also need to be addressed.

Finally, RBM priorities would be needed. Often the attention is directed toward this issue because shortfalls in "doing things right" are obvious. However, it is important that attention be directed toward "doing the right things." Therefore, it would be useful to ensure the above steps of assessing vision–reality gaps as well as finding the right path and formulating strategies. One can then pay attention to implementation. This is not to say that implementation is less important. Many well-designed paths and crafted strategies have delivered poor results or even failed because of flaws in their execution.

In summary, a leader needs to carefully diagnose where the problems lie and then seek to correct them. Often a commonly perceived problem may not actually be a problem. For instance, a team of government officials in a predominantly Muslim area in the Philippines felt that family planning performance was poor and had wished to popularize a fatwa in favor of family planning which had already been issued. However, systematic application of visionary leadership framework revealed that while religious concerns were important, even more important were the clients' concerns with the quality of care and addressing side effects of contraceptive use. Thus, actions are needed to improve the quality of care.

Sometimes, for a variety of reasons, it may not be possible to work with the most critical element in the leadership framework. Therefore, a leader can begin wherever it is feasible in the circle—creating a shared vision, assessing vision–reality gap, finding a path, and inspiring/empowering stakeholders to follow the chosen path. However, as we will see in the following paragraphs, to realize the vision of Universal Health Coverage (UHC) in India, it is necessary to carry out all these iteratively.

Applying Visionary Leadership Framework for Universal Health Coverage in India

United Nations Task Force, on the Post-2015 U.N. Development Agenda,[3] says that ensuring people's rights, health, and education is vital for inclusive social development; one of the four core dimensions along with environment sustainability, inclusive economic development, and peace and security.

In India, the Planning Commission of India constituted the High Level Expert Group (HLEG) in 2010 on UHC. Several of its recommendations are a part of the 12th Five-Year Plan (2012–2017). During the last decade, the Government of India has also taken many steps to universalize elementary education. Therefore, we will present the HLEG recommendations in the visionary leadership framework, review government steps to universalize elementary education, and discuss leadership challenges through comparison of these experiences in promoting UHC. We believe that these learnings and challenges will help in getting insights to ensure UHC. We also believe that application of visionary leadership framework discussed in this book will help

[3] UN Systems Task Team on the Post-2015 UN Development Agenda. (2012). Realizing the future we want for all: Report to the secretary general. New York.

in many core competencies and skills required for leadership to translate the vision of UHC into reality.

Universal Health Coverage

The HLEG[4] defined UHC as

> Ensuring equitable access for all Indian citizens resident in any part of the country, regardless of income level, social status, gender, caste or religion to affordable, accountable, appropriate health services of assured quality (promotive, preventive, curative, rehabilitative) as well as public health services addressing the wider determinants of health delivered to individuals and populations, with the government being the guarantor and enable, although not necessarily the only provider, of health and related services.

The given definition incorporates three dimensions of universal health assurance: health care, health coverage, and health protection. The Foundation for UHC is a universal entitlement to comprehensive health security and intrinsic to the notion of universality which is a fundamental commitment to health as a human right.

Vision

The vision of UHC by 2022 comprised the following:

- Entitlement: Universal health entitlement to every citizen
- National health package: Guaranteed access to an essential health package (including cashless inpatient and outpatient care provided free of cost) at primary, secondary, and tertiary care by the central government

---

[4] High Level Expert Group. (2011). Report on universal health coverage of India. Instituted by the Planning Commission of India. October 2011. Retrieved from www.planningcommission.nic.in/reports/genrep/rep_uhc2111.pdf/.

- Choice of facilities: Public sector facilities and contracted-in private providers

Vision–reality gap

There is a large gap between the above vision and reality.[5] Despite significant economic growth, health outcomes have not correspondingly improved. Total health-care expenditure is variously estimated to be between 4.8 and 6 percent, and around 70 percent of this expenditure is out-of-pocket, much of it is on outpatient consultation and medicines. It is estimated that 3.4 million households fall below the poverty line every year due to catastrophic health expenditures. The government only spends about 1.2 percent of gross domestic product (GDP), one of the lowest in the world, and this is expected to increase to 1.5 percent by the end of the 12th Plan. The HLEG has estimated that 3 percent of GDP would be required for UHC.

Path for UHC

The HLEG review of global experience with UHC concluded that there does not appear to be a single universal method of financing UHC and that HLEG-proposed approach of UHC is unique, building upon lessons learned in India.

Paths toward UHC used by countries can be broadly differentiated by financing mechanisms and service delivery organization. Sri Lanka realized universal coverage by largely relying on public health facilities. Thailand's Universal Coverage Scheme is financed through government taxes and pays largely public providers on capitation basis. Canada has a publicly financed and privately run health-care system that provides free universal coverage to all its citizens. Sweden has a universal delivery system with decentralized decision-making and implementation with minimal use fees. Since its launch in 1948, the National Health Service in the UK has grown to become the world's largest

---

[5] Planning Commission of India. (2012). Health Chapter 12th Plan. New Delhi.

publicly funded health service. On the other hand, Japan relies on insurance mechanisms which are well-regulated.

The proposed architecture of UHC by HLEG has specific recommendations in six critical areas:

1. Health financing and health protection
2. Health service norms
3. Human resources for health
4. Community participation and citizen engagement
5. Access to medicines, vaccines, and technology
6. Management and institutional reforms

Inspire and empower stakeholders

Although management and institutional reforms have been recommended by HLEG, most of the reliance is on incentive structures through introducing competition or capitation type payments to and empower service providers and community. HLEG comments, "It is crucial for any UHC scheme to incorporate economic incentives and provider payment mechanisms that encourage principles of quality, efficiency, cost-effectiveness and safety." Unfortunately, there is not much discussion in the HLEG report on ways to create a shared vision among providers and community to inspire them and reinforce underpinning values of UHC that will empower them.

Results-based management

UHC outcomes are expected to have (1) achieved greater health equity, (2) improved health outcomes with gradual but significant reduction in disease burden, (3) improved health promotion, and (4) improved health surveillance.

HLEG recommends developing a national health information technology network and the need to ensure accountability to patients and communities as well as several regulatory, development, and education authorities. However, most of the focus seems to be on outputs and inputs and less on outcomes such as improvement in health status, reduction in out-of-pocket expenses, or increased efficiency of health care.

HLEG document recommendations are appreciable and it is envisaged that it will help charter a path toward providing UHC. The HLEG document further emphasizes the learning from Indian experiences in making UHC a reality. In this context, a similar program on universalization of elementary education (*Sarva Shiksha Abhiyan*) by Government of India may help in learning the lessons and understanding the challenges in providing UHC.

Universalization of Elementary Education

The constitutional, legal, and national policies and statements have upheld the cause of universal elementary education (UEE).[6] The Constitution in 1950 mandated,

> The State shall endeavour to provide, within a period of ten years from the commencement of this Constitution for free and compulsory education to all children until they complete the age of 14 years. Although progress was made over six decades towards this goal, The Free and Compulsory Education for Children Bill (RTE) was introduced and passed by parliament in 2008, and became effective in April 2010.

Vision

The Right to Education (RTE) Act symbolizes the vision of UEE. It defines various aspects of the rights and entitlements of children and obligations of governments with respect to quality of education.[7] It mandates that no child shall be prevented from pursuing and completing elementary education for lack of money for fees or charges. The appropriate government and local authorities should provide and ensure compulsory admission, attendance,

---

[6] The World Bank Group. (2012). India economic update. Economic policy and poverty team, South Asia region.

[7] *The Gazette of India*. (2009). The Right of Children to Free and Compulsory Education Act, 2009. Ministry of Law and Justice, New Delhi, Government of India.

and completion of elementary education by all children in the 6 to 14 age group. The Act specifies standards for schools, prescribes norms for teachers, and deals with curriculum and evaluations.

Vision–reality gap

By the year 2000, out of the 200 million children in the age group of 6 to 14 years, 59 million children were not attending school.[8] There were problems related to dropout rate, low levels of learning achievement, and low participation of girls, and tribal and disadvantaged groups. That year the government launched the *Sarva Shiksha Abhiyan* (SSA, Movement of education for all), which is discussed in the following paragraphs.

By 2009, the number of out-of-school children in the age group of 6 to 14 years reduced to 8 million and enrolments climbed from around 160 million in 2002 to 193 million in 2011.[9] The average annual dropout rate fell to 6.8 percent in 2010–2011. Around 150,000 new primary schools and 93,000 upper primary schools were opened. However, this success in improving access was not supported by retention, satisfactory curricular interventions, and classroom practices.

Path

The main path for UEE is SSA, launched in 2001.[10] SSA was conceived as a centrally sponsored scheme to improve the educational status in the country through interventions designed to improve accessibility, reduce gender and social gaps, and improve the quality of learning. It is being implemented in partnership with state governments to cover the entire country and address the needs of 192 million children in 1.1 million habitations. The SSA seeks to open new schools in those habitations which do not have

[8] Ministry of Human Resource Development (MHRD). (2000). *Sarva Shiksha Abhiyan*: Programme for universal elementary education in india. Retrieved from www.educationforallinindia.com/.

[9] The World Bank (2012); Ibid.

[10] Planning Commission, Government of India. (2007). *Eleventh Five Year Plan (2007–2012)*. Oxford University Press.

schooling facilities and strengthen existing school infrastructure through provision of additional classrooms, toilets, drinking water, maintenance grant, and school improvement grants. Existing schools with inadequate teacher strength are provided with additional teachers, while the capacity of existing teachers is being strengthened by extensive training, grants for developing teaching-learning materials, and strengthening of the academic support structure at the cluster, block, and district level. SSA seeks to provide quality elementary education including life skills.

The objectives of SSA are

- All children in school, Education Guarantee Centre, Alternate School, "Back-to-School" camp by 2003; extended to 2005
- Bridge all gender and social category gaps at primary stage by 2007 and at elementary education level by 2010
- Universal retention by 2010
- Focus on elementary education of satisfactory quality with emphasis on education for life

The RTE Act further provided boost to operations of SSA.

Inspiring and empowering stakeholders

Despite significant achievements, its efforts to inspire and empower stakeholders were inadequate. Banerjee et al. argue that public participation in improving education is negligible.[11] Participation of community is believed to provide "voice" to the people and also facilitate "demand-driven" initiatives that make a difference. In SSA, local action is an essential element in the process of ensuring UEE. Primary vehicles for participation are Village Education Committees (VECs). An evaluation by Planning

---

[11] Banerjee, A., Banerji, R., Duflo, E., Glennerster, R., Kenniston, D., Khemani, S., & Shotland, M. (2007). Can information campaigns raise awareness and local participation in primary education? *Economic and Political Weekly*, 42(15), 1365–1372.

Commission[12] had this to say, "Community ownership of schools which was to be the backbone for the successful implementation of the program at the grassroots level has met with partial success as most VECs took a ringside view of school activities." This evaluation also found that motivation levels of teachers were low and the quality of learning varied considerably among the states. Ministry of Human Resources Development (MHRD) in its report of second year of RTE implementation mentions,[13] "Community involvement would be key to improving attendance and therefore deserves to become significant part of the agenda in the year to come."

Results management

The reporting system of SSA includes data on enrolment, retention, completion, and school facilities. The outcomes in terms of learning are measured through student's learning assessment and state-level achievement surveys.

However, the Annual Status of Education Report (ASER, 2011) by Pratham, a leading NGO, found that not only are India's learning levels poor on an international scale, but also the levels in government schools in the North have generally declined.[14] Despite RTE, enrolment in private schools is increasing. It argues that the learning level of a child in government school results from many factors where school is an important but only one of the factors. Nevertheless, an energized school system for learning focus can enhance learning effectiveness. Therefore, ASER makes a case that there is perhaps a need to rethink from a "right to school" to "right to learning." It recommends that there is, therefore, a need to rethink educational finance.

[12] Programme Evaluation Organization, Planning Commission, Government of India (2010). *Evaluation Report on Sarva Shiksha Abhiyan.* PEO Report No. 203.

[13] Department of School Education and Literacy, MHRD, Government of India. (2012). *The Right of Children to Free and Compulsory Education Act, 2009: The 2nd year.*

[14] Pratham Organization. (2012). *Annual Status of Education Report (Rural) 2011.*

Implications from UEE experience to UHC

As can be seen from the above description, there is considerable similarity in the vision for UEE and UHC. Both visualize universal access. However, the vision of UEE is enshrined in a legal act with rights framework. This is not yet so for right to health.

Also, the situation with regard to vision–reality gap is similar except for the time difference. There was considerable gap in access and enrolment in primary education in the year 2000. This gap has been largely bridged by SSA. The National Rural Health Mission (NRHM) launched in 2005, like SSA, sought to strengthen infrastructure including facilities and human resources, enhance community participation, and improve management. By 2011, access had been improved, although much remained to be done. The 12th Plan seeks to continue such investments both in rural and urban areas. Thus, the paths chosen for UEE and UHC are also comparable. They both focus on access and emphasize inputs and activities. Although emphasis on quality is sought, to date SSA has experienced difficulty in achieving it and this has implications for UHC.

Therefore, several issues that have arisen in the quest for UEE are also likely to arise in the progress for UHC. These include resource requirements, the role of private sector, inspiring and empowering stakeholders (Chapter Six), and RBM (Chapter Seven).

RTE Act includes a provision that private unaided schools must assure that 25 percent of the first-year students are children from economically weaker sections of the society. It is a measure to push universal enrolment, enhance education quality, and promote social integration. This provision was, however, challenged in the courts and it gained particular prominence in the media.

Jain and Dholakia[15] estimate that resource requirements for UEE, that completely rely on government schools, would be much higher even if 6 percent of GDP is allocated for the education sector. This is so because average salaries of teachers in government

---

[15] Jain, P. S., & Dholakia, R. H. (2009). Feasibility of Implementation of Right to Education Act, *Economic and Political Weekly, 44.*

schools are much higher than for private schools without a demonstrated difference in quality of education. They argue for a mix of private and public schools or, as an extreme measure, reliance on voucher system. Most of the state governments have shunned the recruitment of full-time qualified and trained teachers, and appointed para, contractual, and part-time teachers.[16] Some have opposed this on the ground that one cannot rely on private sector to ensure UEE and government needs to provide the necessary resources for UEE. Venu Narayan[17] says that it is difficult to generalize in terms of quality of education delivered at public and private schools. He argues that the case for public provision and control of education (and its close cousin, health care) is well known because of its large external social effects. However, he prefers facilitative regulation of private schools and quality-driven reforms in public schools which is a better alternative to public–private partnership. Thus, there is a whole range of options: from fully public to a substantial public with private sector responsibilities to a separate but well-regulated private and public sector.

Similar situation is likely to arise for UHC also. Currently, nearly two-thirds of health-care expenditure is private out-of-pocket. UHC envisages reversal of this situation and anticipates that the out-of-pocket expenditure will reduce to about one-third of the total with growth in public expenditure. Almost all the countries are struggling with cost escalation in health sector. Therefore, it is not clear what the total expenditure in the health sector would be and, of that, what proportion of expenditure will be in private sector. The HLEG also recommends contracting-in of private sector to utilize its available capacity. It is not clear how well that would work out. In addition, there is ideological opposition by some to the role of private sector, which they see as exploitative.

---

[16] Rustagi, P. (2009). *Concerns, conflicts, and cohesions: Universalization of elementary education in India*. New Delhi: Oxford University Press.

[17] Narayan, V. (2010). The private and the public school education. *Economic and Political Weekly*, 45(6), 23–26.

SSA faced implementation challenges in inspiring and empowering stakeholders.[18] There were challenges on both the number and quality of teachers. Of the roughly 1.2 million candidates taking the tests for primary or upper primary grades, less than 10 percent passed. Universal enrolment by no means ensures universal attendance and completion. On an average, only two-thirds of the students enrolled in primary classes are present in government schools. Financial constraint was one of the reasons. Poor households did not give adequate emphasis on attendance and completion as they often did not see the value of education and perceived its quality to be low.

It is not easy to inspire parents and communities. Banerjee et al. tested three interventions:[19] (1) information campaign in the village, (2) direct experience of parents and community members in terms of children's learning ability, and (3) in addition, training a group of volunteers to conduct an educational camp. The results showed that none of the interventions increased community participation in a significant way in education except that children's learning was better for those who attended the education camp in the third intervention. Very little difference was made in the functioning of VECs.

RBM is another challenge. As mentioned earlier, one of the criticisms against RTE has been that it focuses too much on the (physical) input side and does not pay adequate attention to quality issues despite plentiful evidence that the overall level of student learning outcomes is very low. The RTE Act offers a holistic vision of quality, but does not set benchmarks and indicators to turn the vision into reality. It is difficult to measure outcomes. Therefore, attention shifts to measuring inputs and activities. Mechanisms need to be found to ensure that the focus shifts to measuring and rewarding providers and communities for outputs and outcomes, particularly in terms of quality.

[18] World Bank (2012); Narayan, V. (2010). The private and the public school education.

[19] Banerjee, A., et al. (2008). *Pitfalls of participatory programs: Evidence from a randomized evaluation of education in India.* Working paper 14311. Retrieved from www.uber.org/papers/w14311/.

The World Bank[20] review of UEE concludes that what is important now is to build consensus among all stakeholders—governments, teachers, communities, parents, as well as the private providers—and ensure better implementation with a focus on quality improvements, the benefits of which need to be distributed in an equitable manner. These indeed would also be the challenges for UHC and the leaders of both UEE and UHC should be prepared to meet them if the goals are to be realized.

Constraints in Applying Visionary Leadership Framework

There are several patterns of working which may inhibit application of visionary leadership framework.

1. *Tendency to do things the same way*: Many leaders fall into a habit of doing things the same way even after the context or needs have changed. While at one time this pattern of working may have yielded results, there is no assurance that this will be the case in the future. So, a visionary leader should periodically review and apply the framework for the issue at hand. Often the signal to rethink comes after the performance has deteriorated substantially. This reactive response results in considerable delay to reverse the performance trend and precious time is lost in the process.

2. *Tendency to jump to the solution*: Often leaders have the tendency to jump to a quick answer as they may feel that their past success and current position warrants this. Unfortunately, this may result in incorrect diagnosis and possibly a prognosis which may be suboptimal. It is better to apply the framework even though a similar situation may have arisen earlier or elsewhere. Of course, it should not come as a surprise if a similar plan of action results.

---

[20] The World Bank (2012); Ibid.

3. *Limiting participation to follower group*: Often a leader begins to lose touch with wider constituency or people who think differently. He/she needs to be on guard against like-minded thinking and seek diverse perspectives, particularly from the individuals/households and communities. Sometimes leaders create an informal group which can provide such feedback directly or as a distillate.

4. *Looking only at zone of control*: A leader's role is to influence others, particularly those not in his/her direct control. However, many leaders are reluctant to influence other sectors, perhaps concerned that those influenced may also wish to influence them. However, many problems can only be effectively addressed when several agencies work in partnership to address them, building on their distinctive competencies.

Conclusion

There are a large number of leadership theories, as we have seen. Nevertheless, the field remains open and many vexatious questions remain. Before concluding, we discuss some of these questions here.

What is the primary significance of leadership? Attempts to link leadership to organizational performance in corporate sector have varying findings.[21] Some say that it is not significant compared to external forces such as industry structure and company history. Others argue that even after taking these factors into account, the influence of leadership on absolute performance is substantial. Another school of researchers put more importance on leaders' ability to influence purpose of and meaning into lives of people over their impact on economic performance. Perhaps leaders have indirect influence on performance through influenc-

[21] Noharia, N., & Khurana, R. (2010). Advancing leadership theory and practice. In N. Noharia, & R. Khurana (eds), *Handbook of leadership theory and practice*. Boston, New York: Harvard Business Press.

ing social nature and structure of organizations such as goals, incentives, culture, member composition, etc.

Leadership development has to also address two issues: (1) Can leadership be developed? If the leader is seen as a special person with unique personality and character traits, then short-term leadership development programs may have a limited role. On the other hand, some things could be done to develop competencies for leadership as a social role where it is seen as an influence relationship with the followers. (2) Should the leadership development emphasize leader's capacity for "thinking and doing" (emphasizing on various competencies) compared to "becoming and being" which puts an emphasis on evolving identity? The latter argues that what makes someone a leader is not because they have special attributes such as charisma but that they are able to fulfill vital functions that meet their followers' needs for meaning, social order, group identity, and goal accomplishment. Generally scholars agree that leadership development should do both.

Most models of leadership posit that universal attributes, functions, or relationships are core to any leadership. However, many equally realize that there is no best way to lead and an effective approach is contingent upon the situation and the characteristics of a leader. However, the variations in situations and characteristics may be so large that it is not possible to prescribe actions for all such combinations. It is hard to imagine that leadership does not have core set of leadership functions. On the other hand, leaders need to tailor their actions to situations and their own personality.

The answer to the above dualities does not seem to lie in "either–or" but rather "and."

However, as we have presented in the preceding chapters, there is much agreement on what leaders need to do—create a shared vision, assess vision–reality gap, develop paths to bridge this gap, and inspire and empower stakeholders to traverse that path. They also need to create strategies, structures, and systems for achieving the desired results. This is the leadership journey that this book seeks to spark and assist prospective and current leaders of public health.

Examples of Applying the Framework

In the following, we discuss two examples of ways of applying the visionary leadership framework. These include:

- Enhancing gender equity: Addressing violence against women
- Improving adolescent health

Visionary Leadership for Enhancing Gender Equity: Addressing Violence against Women

There is a strong link among gender equality and equity, domestic violence (DV) and women's health. The International Conference on Population and Development (ICPD), 1994, laid out the following Principle 4: Advancing gender equality and equity and the empowerment of women, and the elimination of all kinds of violence against women.

Violence against Women (VAW), also referred to as gender-based violence (GBV), arises from unequal power relationships between men and women. It has received increasing attention as a human rights issue since the late 1980s, and the international community has now made great strides in setting standards and elaborating a legal framework through the enactment of various treaties and covenants.

The Declaration on the Elimination of Violence against Women[22] adopted by the United Nations General Assembly in 1993 defines GBV and VAW as:

> Physical, sexual and psychological violence occurring in the family and in the general community, including battering, sexual abuse of children, dowry-related violence, rape, FGM, non-spousal violence,

[22] United Nations. (1993). Declaration on the elimination of violence against women. Retrieved from www.un.org/documents/ga/res/48/a48r104. htm/.

sexual harassment, trafficking in women, forced prostitution, and violence perpetrated or condoned by the state. (Article 2)

Despite such efforts, women continue to be subjected to various forms of violence throughout their life cycle (see Box 8.1). Most of this is DV perpetrated by an intimate partner and includes by definition "violence that occurs within the private sphere, generally between individuals who are related through intimacy, blood, or law." DV remains a widespread phenomenon in many countries. A review of studies from 35 countries[23] indicated that:

- Ten to 52 percent of women and girls reported physical abuse
- Up to 30 percent experienced sexual violence by an intimate partner

Box 8.1: *VAW Globally*

One out of three women in the world has been beaten, coerced into sex or abused in some other way, and most often by a man she knows, including her husband or other male relatives. Worldwide violence against women and girls causes more deaths and disability for women and girls between 15 and 44 years than cancer, malaria, traffic accidents, and war.

Source: UNFPA, 2005, *State of World Population Report.*

The health implications of DV are equally alarming and range from fatal to non-fatal outcomes affecting a woman's physical, mental, and RH. Studies suggest that DV is a frequent cause of suicides among women, and women who are beaten by their husbands or boyfriends are 48 percent more likely to become infected by HIV.[24]

---

[23] WHO. (2005). WHO *multi-country study on women's health and domestic violence: Summary report of initial results on prevalence, health outcomes and women's responses.* Geneva: WHO.

[24] UNFPA. (2005). *Beijing at ten: UNFPA's commitment to the platform for action.* New York: UNFPA.

The causes of violence are extremely complex and has its roots in the interaction of many factors—biological, social, cultural, economic, and political.[25] These include harmful traditional or religious practices, unequal access to resources, education, and employment opportunities which perpetuate women's subordinated status in society and VAW.

The focus in this case example is on DV as it is the most predominant form of VAW in the region. To effectively tackle DV, country leaders must now move beyond legislation on VAW to coordinated action on multiple levels and in multiple sectors. This vision must then be translated into action plans backed by enforced laws that protect women's and their sexual and reproductive health (SRH) rights. Sufficient resource allocation for a coordinating body is necessary for implementing DV policies across different sectors and stakeholders.

Creating a shared vision for addressing domestic violence

The magnitude of domestic/intimate partner violence is strongly tied to the cultural context and existing gender biases. There needs to be strong political commitment to address these multifaceted issues including a shared vision by a wide range of actors—from local health authorities and community leaders to NGOs and national governments.

Where awareness on VAW is low or political commitment is weak, it may be necessary to first carry out IEC and advocacy at different levels. For example:

- The annual worldwide campaign on the "16 Days of Activism against Gender Violence" brings together a diverse range of organizations and actors including survivors of violence to educate the public, press for changes in the law, and development of national plans of action.
- At the regional level, the Mekong Sub-Regional Network (Cambodia, Lao PDR, Myanmar, Thailand, Vietnam)

---

[25] WHO. (2002). *World report on violence and health*. Geneva: WHO.

jointly advocates for changes in policies, laws, and attitudes on sexual harassment, DV, and rape.

* After much lobbying and advocacy on marital rape by women's groups in Malaysia, a Domestic Violence Act was passed in 1994 and One Stop Crisis Centers (OSCCs) were established in hospitals to manage rape cases.

Campaigns to end violence require long-term efforts and funding. Besides advocacy, a shared vision can also be created through consultation and by engaging stakeholders in policy dialogues for improved DV legislation, programs, and financial/human resources (see Box 8.2).

Box 8.2: *Leadership to Address Domestic Violence*

Leadership Checklist

1. Does a policy framework to address DV exist in the country?
2. Is necessary legislation on DV in place?
3. Have IEC advocacy campaigns on VAW been carried out?
4. Is information on the magnitude of DV in the country available and widely shared?
5. Are there consultative processes to address DV involving all stakeholders?
6. Do you and your colleagues have a personal vision on eliminating DV? Can you jointly create a shared vision?

Source: Authors.

Experience of the Philippines: The President issued a Call to Action against DV in July 1997 and convened government officials for consultation on implementation strategies. Through this collective process, a multi-sectoral Plan of Action was adopted for the (1) formation of an interagency task force on generating statistics, (2) adoption of a fast-lane and one-interview system of investigation, (3) center and hospital-based assistance to victims, and (4) counseling services for both victims and offenders.[26]

---

[26] Special rapporteur on VAW. (1999). *Violence against women in the family*. Commission on Human Rights 55th Session.

Experience of Thailand: A Task Force of Women was formed under the 1997 Constitution to address DV and sexual harassment in the workplace, bringing together key players from NGOs, professionals, and universities. A Policy and Action Plan to end VAW and children was approved by the Thai Cabinet in 2000. The national plan integrated components in different areas—prevention, legal reform, protection and welfare, education and research, cooperation mechanisms, monitoring and evaluation systems, and the need for national budget allocations for implementation by government agencies and NGOs.[27]

Although these countries experience illustrate consultative processes for developing action plans, they tend to be top down and lack active participation of all stakeholders, particularly communities. There exists a leadership opportunity here to motivate and mobilize stakeholders, including building their capacity, for cocreating a shared vision beyond advocacy efforts.

Assess vision–reality gap of DV prevalence

In addition to understanding the root causes of DV, the challenge for leaders is to generate evidence to ensure that policies are informed by accurate data on the incidence and severity of violence. Unfortunately, this is seriously lacking in many countries due to the culture of silence surrounding GBV and no specific statistics is available since DV is often categorized as general assault.

National data collection needs to be strengthened for continually monitoring the prevalence of DV and existing "vision–reality" gaps (see Box 8.3). Research and evaluation studies should be further supported for evidence-based advocacy and identifying successful interventions to scale up.

---

[27] Jacobs, G. (ed.). (2003). Not a minute more: Ending violence against women. New York: UNIFEM.

Box 8.3: *Recommendations from UN Agencies*

WHO (2005)

- Data collection systems to monitor VAW under the responsibility of an institution, agency, or government unit.
- Support research and collaboration for a stronger basis for advocacy and scaling up.

UNFPA (2004)

- Accurate, timely, and cross-country comparable data to provide benchmarks and monitor ICPD implementation.

United Nations Development Fund for Women (UNIFEM) (2003)

- Strengthen national and international capacities to provide evidence to inform public policies.
- Research initiatives on the causes, consequences, costs, and remedies of VAW; evaluate effectiveness of programs.

Special Rapporteur on VAW (2003, 1999)

- Compliance to international standards by focusing on a set of indicators and gender-disaggregated data on VAW.
- Up-to-date statistical data collected and recorded in a public forum to evaluate the impact of law and policies.

Source: UNFPA. 2004. *Investing in People: National Progress in Implementing ICPD Programme of Action 1994–2004.* New York: UNFPA; Special Rapporteur on VAW. 2003. *International, Regional and National Development in the Area of VAW 1994–2003.* Commission on Human Rights 59th Session.

Seeing the Big Picture

Before the next step of designing appropriate interventions (i.e., finding a path), visionary leaders must "see the big picture." It is crucial that programs are based on the right kind of information on the magnitude, causes, and impacts of DV (see Box 8.4).

Box 8.4: *Assessing Vision–Reality Gap on Domestic Violence*

Leadership Checklist

1. Can you generate evidence on vision–reality gap on DV?
2. Are there country research and evaluation studies on DV?
3. Do you know who the key stakeholders for addressing DV are?
4. Are there benchmarks and indicators to monitor DV?

Source: Authors.

Trends over time. Changes in the incidence of DV against women and the related reasons need to be identified. These serve as important indicators of the current situation, emerging trends, and the effectiveness of VAW program interventions.

Increasing incidence of violence, Bangladesh. Data collected between 1996 and 2002 by the Ministry of Women and Children's Affairs shows an alarming rise in the number of reported cases of VAW. Beatings and murders of women within households have been linked to the escalation of dowry demands and more general harassment. Despite a number of existing laws to protect the rights of women, such an increase points to urgent action required in adequately enforcing laws and addressing the root causes.

Geographical variations. DV also varies over space especially in regions or areas where traditional sociocultural values and practices reinforce the lower status of women. Prioritizing efforts and resources for the communities most in need will create the highest impact and ensure cost-effectiveness.

Different levels of administration. In involving a range of stakeholders, the reality must be understood at all levels—village, town, district, province, and state. This will enable different perspectives to be incorporated in planning and strategies.

Multiple objectives. Reducing DV/VAW not only promotes women's rights and health but meets wider objectives such as gender equality, improved family relationships, and women's empowerment.

Finding a Path: Learning from Best Practices in VAW

Once the vision and shared values are established, the next step for leaders is finding the path to address DV. They should develop strategies to strengthen institutional capacity development and coordination across sectors.

Lessons can be learned from best practices that have enabled operational systems and built organizational capacity. Successful interventions may be identified from VAW programs, contact with and reports by international/national NGOs and peers, and the relevant websites.

Leaders must first know of best or promising practices, then they should be able to adapt such experiences to the local context, particularly sociocultural norms, and learn from any failures. Where best practices are limited, operations research helps in testing improvements and innovative activities in the community.

Implementing policies: Effective DV interventions

Several case studies from Asia and East Africa demonstrate what cross-sectoral interventions have worked in one or more of the following areas:

- Gender-sensitive and DV protocols in RH services and hospitals
- Gender sensitization and training for service providers and related sectors (e.g., criminal justice system)
- IEC and advocacy on gender equality and VAW
- Community awareness and mobilization

CASE STUDY 1: *Integrated Model for RH and DV*

Thousands of Tanzanian women are living in abusive relationships and women in the Mwanza region are among the most affected by violence. They are denied a voice by the traditional community practices that place them at a lower social status than men and restrict them from leaving their homes and receiving health care from male providers. The Jijenge Project in Mwanza, Tanzania,[28] aims to improve the reproductive and health rights of women. The project has been implemented by the African Medical and Research Foundation (AMREF) and consists of several components.

- Clinical component in district health facilities to improve knowledge and skills among health workers in the provision of women-friendly services. This includes training on gender-sensitive services, capacity building for management teams on gender-sensitive council health plans and budgets, and encouraging men's participation in services.
- Community component in wards to raise awareness on women's SRH rights and strengthen community structures. Activities included training community resource persons, building capacity of Ward Development Committees on gender-sensitive planning and budgets, and sensitizing and mobilizing communities (training community leaders on VAW, DV watch group, and community-based counselors trained in GBV).
- Combined community mobilization and clinical interventions.
- Advocacy at the community and district levels for policies supportive of women's RH rights (e.g., community by-laws against GBV, resource allocation for RH). Multi-sectoral partnerships, networking, and coalition building to promote health and rights of women.

---

[28] Matasha, E., Swalehe, Z., Kamanya, V., Mohammed F., Gavyole A., & Waibale P. (2002). *Gender focus in primary health care: A case study of improving women's sexual & reproductive health & rights in the context of gender relations, the Jijenge Experience.* Retrieved from www.aeci.es/vita/docs/ftp/ponencia-edna-matasha.pdf/.

CASE STUDY 2: Working *with the Criminal Justice System*

In the South-Asian context, VAW is a serious problem with high incidence of domestic abuse, dowry-related violence, and honor killings. Gender-sensitizing and training law enforcers (judges and police) have been critical, particularly in upholding VAW legislation. Collaboration with NGOs has proven to bring about change in the gender biases of the judiciary and practices discriminatory to women.

Bangladesh: The Centre for Women and Children's Studies (CWCS) brought together police officers and NGOs to design a training manual for law-enforcement personnel on GBV. More than 400 officers were trained in 12 regions.

India: A women's NGO, Sakshi, trained judges on women's rights in the judicial system. Activities included visits to women's shelters and meetings with NGOs to better understand women's needs. Some of the trained judges later became peer-educators and training has expanded to Bangladesh, Nepal, Pakistan, and Sri Lanka.

Pakistan: Local NGO Rozan conducted 21 behavioral change workshops for the police force (mostly policemen) on several issues—self-growth, gender and the implications of stereotyping men and women, and sensitization to VAW/children and the role of the police. Rozan also advocated for capacity building in the police system and institutionalization of community–police collaboration.

CASE STUDY 3: *One Stop Crisis Center (OSCC)*

A range of services need to be improved, integrated, and scaled up for both DV prevention and rehabilitative care for victims. At tertiary levels of care, health ministries and hospitals should develop standard protocols for documenting reports of partner violence, rape, and sexual abuse.[29]

[29] Watts, C., & Mayhew, S. (2004). Reproductive health services and intimate partner violence: Shaping a pragmatic response in sub-Saharan Africa. *International Family Planning Perspectives*, *30*(4), 207–213.

Linkages and joint efforts with NGOs are essential for offering support services such as counseling, shelter homes, and legal aid centers. The role of RH providers is also being increasingly recognized in helping to identify, support, and refer victims of partner violence.

Bangladesh: A few police headquarters have special cells for women and all divisional headquarters have an OSCC.

Malaysia: The Ministry of Health (MOH) established OSCCs in hospitals since 1986 based on the concept of "Integrated and Coordinated Teamwork of Multi-sectoral and Inter-agency Network for the Management of Survivors of VAW and Children."[30] By 1997, 90 percent of the hospitals had OSCCs providing a number of VAW services (medical attention and referral, counseling from NGOs, legal aid, special police desks, and provision of shelter). A standard operating procedure known as "Crisis Intervention Levels" or "Critical Pathways" was drawn up as a guide on the roles and responsibilities of the various agencies and departments involved. The NGOs working with the OSCCs are mostly women's organizations and federal departments which include health, police, social welfare, legal aid bureau, religious department, universities, judiciary, and law.

Inspiring and empowering stakeholder

Leaders must pay attention to inspiring and empowering key stakeholders involved in implementing policies. Gaining their support and increasing their capacities is instrumental in the fight against DV.

Stakeholders include public and private service providers, the criminal justice system, and communities (community and religious leaders, men and women, adolescents). Possible strategies and actions to inspire/empower them are to

---

[30] Satia, J., & Hii, M. (2001). *Innovative approaches to population programme management: VAW (Vol. 9)*. Kuala Lumpur: ICOMP.

1. Involve them in the whole process from vision sharing to management
2. Advocate and influence them at an emotional level taking into consideration political and sociocultural factors
3. Provide support for them to effectively perform their roles such as through resource mobilization, budgets, sensitization and training for VAW

Health-care practitioners, law enforcers, and social workers are at the forefront in dealing with abused women. Therefore, they must be sensitized and equipped with the skills to provide gender-sensitive and quality services for the care of victims as well as prevent DV. Training for these stakeholders to effectively address DV includes:

1. Gender awareness and analysis
2. Crisis management strategies: Identify symptoms of violence, document injuries, provide individual and family counseling, make referrals, and take legal actions

Empowering Communities

Mobilizing local communities to change gender-biased attitudes/practices and empowering them is key to reducing DV through

1. Awareness-raising campaigns including media coverage
2. IEC materials on available help (e.g., legal aid, shelter home, crisis centers)
3. Community watch groups, support networks, peer groups
4. Training community leaders and organizations, women, and men
5. Outreach activities: Counseling, hotline, and education activities
6. Encouraging men's and boy's involvement as partners

Planned Parenthood Association of Thailand (PPAT): Men's perceived superiority in Thai society results in DV as a common practice. PPAT (an NGO) created a support network at the grassroots level by forming a VAW Watch Group and setting up

Box 8.5: *Applying Visionary Leadership Framework to Address Domestic Violence*

Leadership Checklist

1. As a visionary leader of health, what should you do to address DV using the visionary leadership framework?
2. Have key stakeholders received the necessary support and training to implement policies?
3. How have communities been mobilized?

Source: Authors.

referral systems. It raised awareness and collaborated with the mass media, health professionals, police force, community leaders, government, and NGOs (see Box 8.5).

> *I have never thought of the importance of DV but with an incident of a husband killing his wife due to jealousy in the community, I became more aware of the impact of DV and have since taken action.* (A VAW Watch Group Leader)

Management lessons for DV programs

With committed leaders and appropriate strategies, eliminating DV can be an achievable goal. Sound program management is needed in planning and design, implementation, and monitoring and evaluation.

In tackling a multidimensional issue such as DV, strengthening cross-sectoral partnerships and their roles is essential. Joint forces among the civil society, private sector, and government agencies enable each to play effectively individual roles in undertaking preventive, treatment, or rehabilitative measures to counter the pandemic. Collaboration amongst stakeholders is also important for pooling the existing resources.

Research findings show that when assessing the vision–reality gap and diagnosis of the root causes, DV needs to be integrated into planning. This will help in highlighting the seriousness of the problem and in identifying effective program strategies.

A management strategy and coordination mechanism is then needed to organize and streamline the roles of different partners.

This would draw on each partner agency's strengths and avoid unnecessary duplication or confusion of roles. Monitoring mechanisms, such as regular meetings for a working committee represented by all sectors, help ensure exchange of information and experiences to improve DV programs.

Visionary Leadership for Youth Reproductive Health Programs that Empower Young People

The world's population of young people in the age group of 15 to 24 years stands at 1.16 billion. The threat of HIV infection has brought the issue of youth RH into focus. Worldwide, half of new HIV infections are among youth, and the majority of those infected are female. Rising HIV/AIDS rates and young people's special vulnerability due to migration, unemployment, and rising age of marriage signaled the need for accelerated action.

Investing in adolescents' health and rights will yield large benefits for generations to come.
(UNFPA State of World Population Report 2003)

The issue of SRH is culturally sensitive in many countries and there is no consensus on how best to address this. For instance, some have favored advocating "abstinence only" programs whereas others favor a broader approach of "abstinence, be faithful, or use condoms" or popularly known as "ABC" approach.

Youth's access to RH care

The data on access to RH by young people using three indicators for universal RH care access,[31] agreed by UNFPA/WHO,

---

[31] Ashford, L., Clifton, D., & Kaneda, T. (2006). World's youth data sheet 2006. Washington, D.C.: Population Reference Bureau; Demographic and Health Surveys (DHS 2003); Ross, J., Stover, J., & Adelaja, D. (2005). *Profiles for family planning and reproductive health programs, 116 countries* (2nd edition). Glastonbury: The Futures Group International.

reveals large differentials in deliveries assisted by skilled birth attendants for young women. Low rates of deliveries attended by skilled birth attendants and lack of emergency obstetric care make maternal mortality and morbidity a significant risk for young women. Pregnancy is the leading cause of death worldwide for young women aged 15–19.[32] Married adolescent girls aged 15–19 are less likely to use modern contraceptives than married young women aged 20–24 in Asia. Young women's unmet need exceeds that of women of all ages considerably— 23 percent versus 16 percent. Only a small percentage of youth have comprehensive knowledge of HIV/AIDS prevention.[33] Data indicates that among women in the age group of 15–24 years, only 1 percent in Indonesia, 3 percent in the Philippines, 25 percent in Vietnam, and 37 percent in Cambodia have comprehensive knowledge. Although they are more vulnerable, young women in general have lesser knowledge than young men.

Neglecting the SRH of young people can lead to high social and economic costs, both immediate and in the years ahead. For example, it has been estimated that Thailand lost an estimated 400,000 lives and over one million person-years from the labor force due to premature deaths from HIV/AIDS alone.

The benefits of SRH interventions, on the other hand, are far reaching.[34] For instance, improving SRH of young people reduces the likelihood of teenage pregnancy and its associated social and economic costs. It also encourages couples and individuals to decide freely and responsibly the number, spacing and timing of their children, which enables higher household savings and investment, and facilitates higher productivity. Delayed marriage and well-timed parenthood allow for greater educational achievements and thus greater career and employment opportunities.

---

[32] International Center for Research on Women (ICRW). (2006). *Child marriage and education*. Washington, D.C.: ICRW.

[33] Comprehensive knowledge of HIV/AIDS prevention is defined as "correctly identify[ing] at least two ways of preventing the sexual transmission of HIV, who reject the two most common local misconceptions about HIV transmission, and who know that a healthy-looking person can have HIV."

[34] UNFPA. (2003). *State of world population report*.

The prevention and treatment of STIs including HIV/AIDS also reduces stigma and help young people to stay healthy. Healthy families can earn more and save more, spurning economic growth.

Visionary leadership challenge

However, improving the SRH of youth is a complex, multifaceted task. This poses many leadership challenges including:

Making a Difference: Kirby et al.[35] reviewed 83 studies that documented impact of sex and HIV education programs on sexual behaviors of young people in developed and developing countries. Half of these studies focused only on preventing HIV or STIs; and about one-third covered STIs, HIV, and pregnancy. The review showed that 40 to 60 percent of the studies reported impact on one or more of the following aspects of sexual behavior: initiation of sex, frequency of sex, number of sexual partners, condom use, contraceptive use in general, and composite measure of sexual risk-taking.

Involving Multiple Sectors of Government: Most youth RH programs are implemented by NGOs. Many governments have shied away because of the sensitive nature of programs as many politicians even view them as impinging on cultural and religious sensibilities. There is also a need for different sectors to get involved—education, health, social welfare, sports, and others. The World Bank (2006)[36] estimated that although 82 percent of all countries have national youth policies, 70 percent of them are focused on narrow youth issues, with few links to other sectors. Where multi-sectoral youth policies exist, they fail to establish clear lines of accountability among the different sectors.

---

[35] Kirby, D., Laris, B. A., & Rolleri, L. (2005). *Impact on sex and HIV education programs on sexual behaviours of youth in developing and developed countries*. Youth Research Working Paper No. 2. California: Family Health International.

[36] World Bank. (2006). *World development report 2007: Development and the next generation*. Washington, D.C.: The World Bank.

Addressing Gender Issues: Throughout much of the world, families and societies treat girls and boys unequally with girls facing deprivation, lack of opportunity, and lower levels of investment in their health, nutrition, and education. Societal gender norms confront girls with special challenges including restrictions on their independence and mobility, inequality in educational and employment opportunities, pressure to marry and start bearing children at an early age, and unequal power relations that limit their control over their sexual and reproductive lives. Therefore, youth programs need to make special efforts for girls.

Youth Participation: For successful youth programs, young people themselves need to be involved in all phases of the program—advocacy, planning, implementation, monitoring and evaluation. Therefore, capacity of adults and youth needs to be strengthened for meaningful adult–youth partnership.

These and other challenges need to be addressed by applying visionary leadership competencies, as we will discuss now (see Box 8.6).

Box 8.6: *Creating Shared Vision on ASRH*

Leadership Checklist

1. Is there evidence of current reality on youth/ASRH?
2. Who are the key stakeholders for youth RH?
2. Can the evidence be used to create a shared vision among the stakeholders?
4. Can stakeholders with diverse perspectives have youth empowerment as the shared vision?

Source: Authors.

Creating a shared vision

Generally, most youth/adolescent RH programs address HIV/AIDS and, therefore, their vision is avoidance of risky behavior. This vision is widely accepted. However, it raises sensitive issues related to sexuality of youth. Some have argued for a broader vision: improving SRH as teenage pregnancy is also an issue in many countries.

Adolescent health had not received much attention in the past as adolescence was usually considered a healthy period of life. However, as substance abuse, road accidents, and other problems among the youth have increased, there is an argument that one should center the vision on adolescent health including SRH. However, the health-related vision has difficulties. One, programs that include activities on less controversial youth issues such as livelihood or literacy skills are more likely to be accepted. Two, different stakeholders (youth, parents, teachers, health workers, community leaders) have different priorities. A more holistic vision of overall youth development, although more attractive to many, is too complex for mobilizing support for programs.

Growing experience with SRH programs shows that youth programs that empower young people can make a difference. It means that youth are assisted to develop competencies (attitude, knowledge, skills, practice, and behavior) that lead to their empowerment, which they can utilize for their self-development as well as to influence family and community (see Figure 8.1). Thus, to empower youth is to give them power to successfully approach and face challenges that relate to their everyday life, specifically to their SRH and rights.

Evidence-based advocacy is needed to influence legislation, policies, programs, and strategies to promote health and development of young people. Thus, analysis of vision–reality gap can be used to create a shared vision among key stakeholders.

Vision–reality gap

It is difficult to assess and analyze the vision–reality gap because data is often lacking and fragmented. For instance:

- Demographic and Health Survey (DHS) provides information on teenage pregnancies, contraceptive use, and on knowledge of HIV.

Figure 8.1: *Empowerment of Young People*

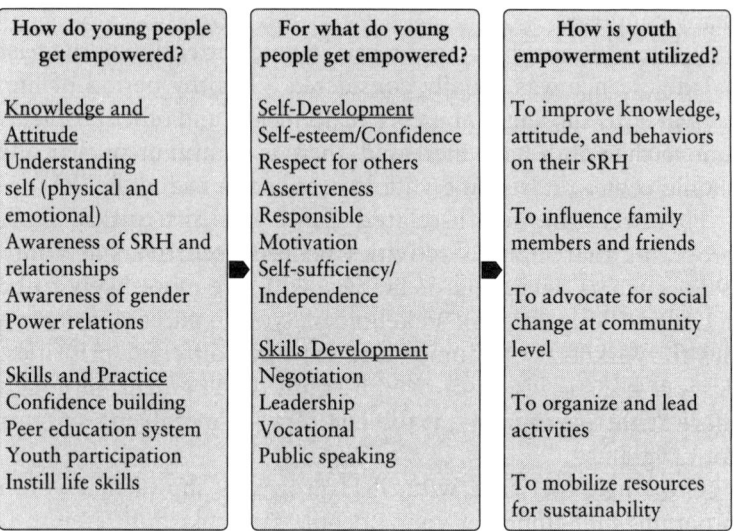

How do young people get empowered?	For what do young people get empowered?	How is youth empowerment utilized?
Knowledge and Attitude Understanding self (physical and emotional) Awareness of SRH and relationships Awareness of gender Power relations Skills and Practice Confidence building Peer education system Youth participation Instill life skills	Self-Development Self-esteem/Confidence Respect for others Assertiveness Responsible Motivation Self-sufficiency/ Independence Skills Development Negotiation Leadership Vocational Public speaking	To improve knowledge, attitude, and behaviors on their SRH To influence family members and friends To advocate for social change at community level To organize and lead activities To mobilize resources for sustainability

Source: Authors.

- HIV/AIDS surveillance provides information on risky behaviors as well as estimates of HIV prevalence.
- Hospital statistics provide an indication of admissions due to abortion complications among youth.
- Drug control department would estimate prevalence of substance abuse.
- Transport department would have statistics of road accidents involving young drivers.

The vision–reality gap also differs among different youth segments and special surveys may be needed. For instance, Young Adults Fertility Survey (YAFS) in the Philippines provides valuable information on vision–reality gap (see Box 8.7).

Analyzing vision–reality gap requires changes in mental models and systems thinking. *One*, visionary leaders need to see the *big picture* including a range of issues affecting youth: education, employment, income generation, migration, SRH as well as needs of vulnerable groups like orphans and street children. *Two*, they need to analyze changes in these variables over time and over

Box 8.7: *Vision–Reality Gap for Youth RH*

Leadership Checklist

1. How is the reality of youth RH changing overtime?
2. How does the reality of youth RH differ among different segments of youth by age, residence, education, sexual behavior, and so on?

Source: Authors.

different geographic areas. *Three*, they need to understand a variety of influences on youth: self-experiences, peer influence, family, teachers, communities, media, relevant laws and policies, and broader socioeconomic environment. *Four*, they need to develop capacity for working partnership with youth. This is a challenge for most program managers as they may believe that their greater experience makes them more suited to make decisions affecting young people. Youth partnership is a key to progress in improving youth SRH (see Box 8.8).

Box 8.8: *Youth Involvement in Improving SRH*

Leadership Checklist

1. Is there a clear national framework for youth RH? If not, can one be created?
2. Is there a supportive environment for youth empowerment?
3. What mix of interventions—behavior change, youth-friendly services, and youth leadership development—can be a path to bridge vision–reality gap on youth RH?

Source: Authors.

Finding path/strategy

Clear National Framework

The World Bank recommends a clear national youth framework to set priorities and guide coordination. The framework should be developed and backed by youth-related ministries and the finance ministry, and it should establish a plan of action specifying sector responsibilities for various youth goals. Sector ministries are best placed to implement youth policies within their own sectors and to complement, or at least not hinder, other sector efforts. The youth ministry or focal body can guide or coordinate and follow up on policy implementation by, for example, convening youth constituents to obtain their feedback on program quality.[37] Integrating youth policy in overall national development planning is one way to help ensure budget allocation for youth policy implementation. An example is that of Thailand's youth policy which coincides with that of the national development plan.[38]

Creating an Enabling Environment: Working with Gatekeepers

Many factors that impact adversely upon the SRH of young people stem from their immediate social environment, including poverty and unemployment; restrictive social and gender norms, especially those that reduce equitable access to information and services; and the impact of social and economic changes. While programs to improve the SRH of young people cannot focus directly on inequities and injustices in society, they must create an immediate social environment that fosters personal development and open communication to encourage young people to adopt healthy types of behavior. (See Box 8.9 for an example of getting approval from gatekeepers.)

Families, communities, media, and others can communicate positive norms and actions to promote healthy behavior among young people and adults alike. It must be remembered that program efforts need to take into account the fact that young people are not all alike, and that interventions and the ways in which they are delivered will vary according to the differing needs and circumstances surrounding young people's lives. For this reason, it is imperative that young people themselves should also play an active role in improving their immediate environment and the conditions that affect their SRH. For gatekeepers and other stakeholders, capacity-building for gatekeepers and other stakeholders to become supportive of young people's programs could include

[37] World Bank. 2006. *World development report 2007: development and the next generation*. Washington, D.C.: The World Bank.
[38] Retrieved from http://www.unescap.org/esid/hds/Youth/ypol.asp/.

Box 8.9: *Integrating Non-RH Interventions to Win Gatekeepers Over*

The Adolescent Girls' Literacy Initiative for RH in Nepal reaches rural and poor girls through literacy classes. Where the status of girls was particularly low, a "parent-friendly" strategy was employed because it would not have been possible to reach these girls and others with limited mobility due to social or financial constraints. To reach this marginalized group, the project presented the gatekeepers (in this case, parents) with an obvious, non-controversial benefit for their daughters—literacy skills. RH was integrated with literacy classes—literacy being important to promoting RH care access as well—and the girls benefited from both.

Source: Adhikari, Ramesh, Nepal, Binod, & Tamang, Anand. Undated. *Adolescent Girls Literacy Initiative for Reproductive Health (A GIFT for RH).* Nepal: CEDPA (Center for Development and Population Activities), AMK (Aaama Milan Kendra), and CREHPA (Center for Research on Environment Health and Population Activities).

opportunities for them to learn and understand as well as inject their own inputs into the project (see Box 8.10).

Box 8.10: *Developing Path to Address Youth RH*

1. Has a participative process been followed in developing path?
2. Are there coalitions of NGOs that advocate for youth RH?
3. Do youth fully participate in youth RH programs?

Source: Authors.

Programs to empower youth through youth-friendly and youth-empowering services. The Government of Thailand has established youth-friendly "corners" to provide primary prevention, link health, and social networks. Gender needs special attention as young girls suffer more. Globally, of the HIV-positive youth, about two-thirds are girls.

Behavioral change. Changing the risky behavior of young people is a key challenge for youth SRH programs. The behavioral change communication would provide an opportunity for youth to get insight into their personal situation. It will instill the motivation and skills needed to adopt and maintain a changed behavior. The change would be to improve the condition of one's own life and the society.

Youth leadership development. Youth leadership development programs would enable community young leaders to

- Expand their vision and technical knowledge to strengthen their leadership skills
- Create innovative solutions to SRH challenges faced by youth
- Take an active role in their communities for the development of youth RH programs
- Participate and contribute to program development, implementation, monitoring and evaluation
- Dialogue with authorities at higher levels for youth to have an effective voice in policy decisions related to youth SRH and be able to mobilize resources

Inspiring/empowering stakeholders

A broad range of stakeholders are involved in youth SRH: young people, parents, teachers, spiritual leaders, employers, various government ministries, NGOs, and communities. Many of them would need to be inspired/empowered for implementation of the path chosen.

Political commitment is a key to implementing any path for improving youth SRH. For instance, countries most successful in addressing HIV/AIDS are those where top political leaders took the epidemic seriously and expressed their commitment publicly.

The process of developing a path/strategy is crucial for inspiring/empowering stakeholders. The anticipatory learning and action approach has been used in many countries to design programs, which has mobilized various stakeholders including communities to examine their own situation including concerns, values, and priorities and devise their own solutions to the challenges they face.

Coalitions need to be created for advocating legal reforms, enforcement measures, and legislative reviews to safeguard adolescents' rights, especially in critical areas such as violence, marriage, education, and RH.

Youth–adult partnership is influenced by the adult's attitude toward youth. Young people can be perceived as objects, as recipients, or as partners. Both parties would need to develop capacity for partnership.

Implementing Youth Programs that Empower Young People

Research has shown that a number of key elements determine the level of youth SRH program successes, which include:

1. Youth participation at all levels of the program
2. Program components that address common roots and determinants of youth attitudinal and behavioral problems
3. Interventions that incorporate youth-friendly collaborative models for comprehensiveness (health, education, life skills, etc.)
4. An enabling environment for youth empowerment

UNFPA recommends the following building blocks for programs for adolescent girls programs:[39]

1. Creating an environment conducive to keeping girls in school through the secondary level, or at least ensure that they are literate.
2. Ensuring that the particular RH needs of adolescents are addressed and youth-friendly services provided.
3. Working with communities, including local political and religious leaders, to increase public awareness on SRH issues affecting adolescents.
4. Providing life skills and counseling so that adolescent girls are aware of their rights and know about the available services.

[39] UNFPA (2003). State of World Population 2003. p.45.

5. Developing vocational training and income-generating programs for adolescent girls to increase their status, independence, and opportunities.
6. Mobilizing support of decision-makers at all levels to support programs aimed at improving adolescent SRH
7. Contributing to equitable and sustainable development by reinforcing the capacity of national governments to engage girls in the social, economic and political life of the country.

Thus, planning and implementation of youth SRH programs should ensure that they are youth-focused, youth-empowering, gender-sensitive, and participative. They should be tailored to fit diversity of youth concerns, behaviors, and needs. Monitoring and evaluation should be an integral part of the program from the start. Resource mobilization is a key challenge for youth programs as many ministries and agencies are involved. Ideally, these should be mainstreamed in the relevant programs of the ministries and agencies concerned. Once again, following a participative process in all the phases of program development would help in mobilizing necessary resources (see Box 8.11).

Box 8.11: *Multi-sector Response to Youth RH*

Leadership Checklist

1. Can you advocate for holistic youth RH policies?
2. Can you catalyze multi-sector action?
3. Can you ensure full participation of youth in youth RH programs?

Source: Authors.

PART II

Leadership Competencies

Nine

Your Personal Leadership Journey: Focus on Self

Knowing others is intelligence; knowing yourself is true wisdom.
Mastering others is strength; mastering yourself is true power.
—Lao Tzu, Tao Te Ching

Introduction

Leaders who want to change an organization must be able to change people. To change others, you have to first change yourself. Therefore, there is only one starting point that makes sense: Learning to lead oneself better is the only way to lead others better.

You have to be the change you want to see in others.
(Mahatma Gandhi)

Leaders are often seen as having a separate or extra set of values or characteristics, things that make them different. When you see what is expected or demanded of people we call leaders, you will understand that they are not your average person, at least not during the times when he/she is assuming the role of a leader.

Leaders are generally perceived to have a heightened sense of self-awareness, of their own personal "dream," "mission," "capability," or may even feel to "...have greatness thrust upon them."[1] In this chapter, we discuss how you can create your own personal leadership journey. The framework in Chapter Two is designed for leading health programs, but with some modifications it can be used to chart out one's own personal leadership journey. First, we look at ways to create personal vision, followed by a discussion on finding a path to bridge the gap between vision and reality. Finally, some tips are provided on how you can keep yourself inspired. However, you will need to hone some critical skills in your personal leadership journey (see Chapter 10).

Becoming a More Effective Leader

Leadership is about the whole of you. Influences from early childhood, education, experiences and learning from failures all count toward molding a leader's vision, mind-set, and behavior. But also important are the conscious efforts that leaders take to continuously learn and improve themselves, and become more effective leaders.

Creating a Personal Vision

One of the most famous and inspiring vision statements is in a speech by Martin Luther King Jr, delivered at the height of the civil rights movement in the US, in Washington, D.C. in 1963.

Martin Luther King was a great orator and one of the most recognizable leaders in the world. As a leader of the civil rights movement in the US in the 1960s, he was the right leader for the right cause at the right time.

He was a visionary leader who also understood very well how to communicate effectively, and used his oratorical skills to full advantage. He knew how to move people simply with words, by

---

[1] This is a very popular quote from William Shakespeare's *Twelfth Night*. The full quote is "Be not afraid of greatness; some are born great, some achieve greatness and some have greatness thrust upon them" (Act II, Scene V).

communicating his vision and his values. To this day, there are still frequent references to his speech "I have a dream" message and this illustrates his power and enduring stature as a leader (see Box 9.1).

Box 9.1: *Excerpts from Martin Luther King's "I have a dream"*

I say to you today, my friends, that in spite of the difficulties and frustrations of the moment I still have a dream. It is a dream deeply rooted in the American dream.

I have a dream that one day the nation will rise up and live out the true meaning of its creed: We hold these truths to be self-evident; that all men are created equal.

I have a dream that one day on the red hills of Georgia the sons of former slaves and the sons of former slave owners will be able to sit down together at the table of brotherhood.

I have a dream that one day the state of Mississippi, a desert state sweltering in the heat of injustice and oppression, will be transformed into an oasis of freedom and justice.

I have a dream that my four children will one day live in a nation where they will not be judged by the color of their skin but by the content of their character.

I have a dream today ....

Source: www.archives.gov/press/exhibits/dream-speech.pdf accessed on March 29, 2014.

Pause for Reflection
Analyze the above vision statement in terms of what it embodies.

The leader finds the dream and then the people. The people find the leader and then the dream. (John Maxwell)

Thus, the personal leadership journey begins with a vision. A vision is truly an extraordinary thing that can go on to influence and change you.

It is more emotional than analytical. It is something that touches the heart, not just the mind. It should embody what you wish to be and would come to be identified with it.

Your vision may be derived from the vision you have for the community you wish to serve. You may wish to reflect upon your vision of the community you serve or wish to serve. How does health contribute to or is integral to this vision? (See Table 9.1)

Table 9.1: *Ask Yourself These Questions*

What Are You Passionate About?	What Personal Values Have an Impact on You? ⇩	Who Inspires You? ⇩	What Inspires You? ⇩	Who Would Have an Influence on Your Vision? ⇩
Example: Empowerment of women and girls	Example: • Persistence • Fair-mindedness	Example: Mother Teresa	Example: Indonesia's commitment to civil society	Example: • Midwives • Outreach workers

Source: Authors.

You can use the following exercise to develop your personal vision (see Figure 9.1). It takes two "P"s and three "I"s to get you to reflect on yourself as a person, and what drives you.

Figure 9.1: *Creating a Personal Vision: Some Useful Questions*

	Questions to ask
Evocative descriptor ➡	What will I see?
	What will I hear?
Core values ➡	What do I value?
	What achievements have meaning for me?
Priorities ➡	What do I want?
	How will I recognize when I see it?

Source: Ciampa and Watkins, 1999.[2]

[2] Ciampa D. and Watkins M. (1999). *Right from the start: Taking charge in a new leadership role.* Boston, USA: Harvard Business School Press.

The personal vision

- Evokes a clear and positive mental image of a future state
- Creates pride, energy, and a sense of accomplishment
- Is memorable
- Is inspiring
- Is idealistic
- Clarifies purpose and direction, inspires enthusiasm
- Focuses attention
- Moves people to action

> **Review your Vision**
> How many of the above attributes does it meet?

Draw Your Vision

Represent your vision in a drawing using elements such as rainbow, cartoons, bridges, trees, people, buildings, flowers, and so on. Be creative. Consider: (1) current situation, (2) personal attributes, and (3) future. What is your rationale?

In our program to develop visionary leaders, the personal vision among emerging leaders differed. A few of them expressed it as what they wanted "to be." For example,

- Be at the forefront of the HIV/AIDS initiatives in the state and region
- Be an advocate and raise awareness to control the scourge of obstetric fistula

Several others expressed their vision as what they wanted "to do." For example,

- To forge partnership with the private sector to respond to the needs and enhance service delivery

- To keep serving people with a clear focus now and an eye to the future
- To integrate food and health for the poor and marginalized
- To create a new model for integrating livelihood and SRH
- To build an effective new model for government programs in family planning and health
- To help disadvantaged young people
- To improve women's socioeconomic situation
- To influence change in society through appropriate religious tools and messages
- To establish our institute as a recognized national institution for leadership development
- To improve the status of women

A few other emerging leaders expressed their personal vision in terms of "see it happen." For example,

- To see Ethiopian women, children, and young people lead healthy and productive lives
- To see that malnutrition is no more a public health problem
- To see people with HIV/AIDS live a life without stigma
- To see that people at all levels participate in campaign against FGM
- To know that there is widespread consistent and correct use of condoms

Exercise What About You?

What do you want... **To be?**   ....

....

What do you want... **To do?**   ....

....

How do you... **See it happen?**   ....

....

Assess Vision–Reality Gap

Leaders have to be practical and realistic. In the context of your vision, you will have to understand the environment you are in and prioritize what needs to be done first. Therefore, an assessment of the vision–reality gap is necessary.

Assessing the reality means taking stock of your strengths and weaknesses, as well as the external environment in which you currently operate or are likely to operate in the future. You will need to know your talents and reflect upon your experiences. You also need to know what the systemic capabilities of the organization are, such as office infrastructure, equipment, technological facilities, supplies, and other resources. The dynamics of the external environment exert an equally important impact on the reality which you as a leader will have to deal with. You will have to be aware of the trends and patterns such as the changing needs of clients, government regulations and policies, competitors' behavior, or the social and political conditions in the community that affect demand or service delivery.

Once an audit is done of the internal and external realities, you will need to seek information and ways to deal with any prospective problems. Having and sharing a vision is an essential first step but knowing and narrowing the vision–reality gap is critical to progress in your leadership journey.

Choosing a Path to Realize One's Personal Vision

An analysis would be needed for identifying these competencies depending upon the vision–reality gap and ways to bridge this gap. Participants of a leadership development program chose a mix of the following to realize their personal visions:

1. Strengthening and utilizing their leadership competencies
2. Strengthening their organizations
3. Inter-organizational partnering

4. Development of community capacities
5. Participation in policy and program activities

Strengthening and utilizing their leadership competencies

A variety of skills depending upon the challenges in realizing a personal vision may need to be strengthened and/or utilized. Some of these are discussed in Chapter 10 including listening, negotiation, conflict management, communication, public speaking, and building and leading the top teams. Other skills may include ability to think and act strategically, willingness to use leadership potential, and enhanced persuasive ability.

Strengthening their organizations

Often emerging leaders are working in an organization. Depending upon their position, they can contribute to strengthening their organization through developing and sharing a vision, mobilizing support and resources from within, aligning organizational values and systems, strengthening program performance, and initiating new ideas and approaches to implementation for better organizational results.

Inter-organizational partnering

For synergy, nothing can beat networks and alliances promoting an idea or getting things done. Leaders recognize the value of people and organizations pooling their talents, experiences, and resources but the challenge is initiating and then sustaining it. Leaders can form networks to address a need or expand the range as well as reach of health services. Government–NGO–private sector alliances in health can not only advocate for causes but can partner to achieve results building upon their distinctive strengths. Finally, leaders can use their competencies to build such competencies in other organizations.

Development of community capacities

Community values, norms, and practices have significant bearing on health status. Leaders need to recognize them and use them creatively to realize their vision. Sometimes, there may be hostility to new ways of doing things and leaders need to demonstrate their utility and may need to persist despite the opposition. It helps to understand the reasons behind the current practices and address these reasons.

Most leaders desire to bring change through influencing policies and programs

However, the ability to do so effectively may not be easy. The skills and competencies are rather specific (such as negotiation, conflict resolution, communications, consensus building, and so on) and certain traits may take time to acquire (such as politics-smarts, knowledge base, and credibility). Sometimes, the opportunity may present itself such as being a member of the policy drafting committee or technical working group, or a professional association.

Establish goals and strategies

Every vision effort needs not just a broad vision and an assessment of vision–reality gap, but also specific path, strategies, and realizable goals. Goals represent what you will commit yourself to do, often within a well-defined and short period of time.

Inspire Self to Pursue the Personal Vision

Awareness of "self" is the beginning of being inspired. The elements of self-awareness include perceptions, focus, energy, and clarity, as can be seen from the following comments of some emerging leaders:

- I became aware of my perceptions and skills
- Became reenergized and focused

- Leader with a vision never gets tired
- I became aware of my negative traits

The source of inspiration varies for leaders and may emanate from some experiences, parents, family, world leaders, and high achievers such as athletes, mentors, and program leaders. Even poverty and ill health can be inspiring to some emerging leaders:

- I was touched and traumatized by exposure to the real problems of people in my area.
- It was the pain of seeing young people going through major challenges related to reproductive health and child care.
- Memory of seeing how hungry poor people rushed for food at a mosque spurred me into development work.

Some others saw how weak (or lack of) leadership had affected the lives of people and, thus, realized the importance of good leadership and chose to test their own mettle and become strong leaders.

Early influences, whether from family members or from others, often become a strong source of inspiration. These influences can be instrumental in shaping early perspectives in life and their choice of vocation:

- My mother could extend her love and affection beyond her family boundary, every villager in some way or other got her blessing...that is how I was prompted to think for the poor.
- My grandfather was pioneer in women's education, while my parents taught about sharing responsibilities and working with others.

Some derive their inspiration from world leaders such as Mahatma Gandhi and Nelson Mandela.

The people's capacity to achieve is determined by their leader's ability to empower. (John Maxwell)

When leaders talk about inspiring people, their prescription is remarkably consistent:

- Communicate continuously
- Listen carefully
- Tolerate failure as a learning experience
- Build on people's desire to make a positive difference
- Maintain a commitment to innovation, creativity, diversity, social responsibility, and continuous development

> **Pause for Reflection**
> How is a vision in your organization established? Should it move to the next higher stage? Why?

Followers May Determine Your Leadership Style

Traditionally, leaders were viewed by followers as leaders by virtue of their titles or positions. The study of leadership as a discipline has evolved rapidly in the past 50 to 60 years, moving from titles or positions to behavior or personality styles, to action-oriented approach (what followers expected leaders "to do"). Therefore, to be an exemplary or effective leader, the aspirations of your followers should be woven into your behavior and action.

Being a leader is about managing those who "follow" you, either because they are your subordinates (employees/staff), partners, or just people who look up to you, believe in you, or count on you to achieve something. In short, effective leaders need to develop good followership.[3] To foster this, as a leader you need to pay some attention to these four areas:

- *Authenticity*: You have to feel comfortable and real in your role as a leader. Followers need to feel they can trust

---

[3] O'Brien, P. (2011). Change your leadership style. *New Straits Times*, December 20.

you and that you have a certain pattern of behavior that is authentic and predictable.

- *Bridging*: Leaders create a better future but to get there, they must first lay a clear path that manages this transition that is a bridge between today and tomorrow. Followers look toward a better tomorrow through a leader's vision which is aligned or resonates with their own hopes and aspirations.

- *Communication*: Followers want their leaders to be able to convey their vision and messages clearly, honestly, and sincerely. Communication is a two-way process, so they want their leaders to listen to their views and concerns. Hence, communication can strengthen the leader–follower relationship, in direct and indirect ways.

- *Emotional Engagement*: Ever since Daniel Goleman put forward his "emotional intelligence (EI)" theory,[4] the emotional connection has been hugely influential in the leadership debate in recent years. High IQ does not always mean success or happiness while high EI may determine or generate emotional bonding, loyalty, trust, and admiration from followers. An example of an exceptional success-ful leader is the former US President Bill Clinton who is renowned for his ability to make an emotional connection with each and every person he speaks with.

> *Leadership and learning are indispensable to each other.*
> (President John Kennedy)

Leadership Development Is a Lifelong Process

One of the outstanding traits of effective leaders is that they are not only willing to learn from failures but they are constantly learning. It is a lifelong process and commitment. But what does learning mean?

[4] Goleman, D. (1995). *Emotional intelligence. Why it can matter more than IQ*. Bantam Books.

Learning has two meanings[5]—acquiring knowledge and acquiring skills. Or, respectively, know-how and know-why. While "know-how" is important, for a leader, the "know-why" is more critical to complement their visionary mission because skills are the building blocks to inspiring and empowering followers. Here are a variety of ways you can learn (see Table 9.2).

Table 9.2: *Akin's Model of Learning*

Emulation	⟹ In which one emulates either someone one knows or a historical or public figure
Role taking	⟹ In which one has a conception of what one should do and does it
Practical Accomplishment	⟹ In which one sees a problem as an opportunity and learns through the experience of dealing with it
Validation	⟹ In which one tests concepts by applying them and learns after the fact
Anticipation	⟹ In which one develops a concept and then applies it, learning before acting
Personal Growth	⟹ In which one is less concerned with specific skills than with self-understanding and the "transformation of values and attitudes"
Scientific Learning	⟹ In which one observes, conceptualizes on the basis of one's observations, then experiments to gather new data, with a primary focus on truth

Source: Bennis Warren, 2003.[6]

Pause for Reflection
How do you learn?

---

[5] Boyett, J., & Boyett, J. (1998). *The guru guide. The best ideas of the top management thinkers.* New York, USA: John Wiley & Sons, Inc.

[6] Bennis Warren (2003). On becoming a Leader. Philadelphia, USA: Perseus Books Group.

Exercise

What or Who Inspires You?	How do You Learn?
1.	1.
2.	2.
3.	3.
4.	4.
5.	5.

Taking a Journey to Leadership Development

Becoming an effective leader is a very personal journey (see Figure 9.2). It will lay bare your sense of self, tease your sense of direction, challenge your self-esteem, test your patience, question your decisions, and delve into your resolve and resilience. But mostly, it will be exhilarating and deeply rewarding because, as all travelers well know, it is not the destination that we look forward to but the journey itself.

Figure 9.2: *My Personal Journey to Leadership*

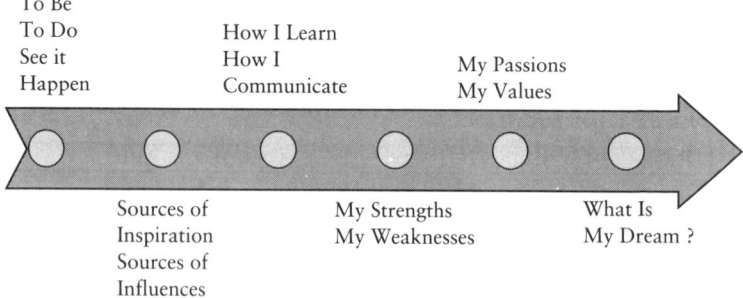

To Be
To Do
See it
Happen

How I Learn
How I
Communicate

My Passions
My Values

Sources of
Inspiration
Sources of
Influences

My Strengths
My Weaknesses

What Is
My Dream ?

Source: Authors.

Remember the famous Chinese proverb:

Every thousand-mile journey begins with a single step.

Ten

Public Health Leadership Attributes

...Success in a flatter, more distributed and collaborative world will require a new generation of leaders in public health with new mindsets, an appetite for innovation and interdisciplinary collaboration and a strong dose of political savvy.[1]
—J. R. Kimberly

Introduction

Public health is a constantly evolving field, with new challenges and new forces that necessitate agility and creativity to protect our communities. High performance and flexibility are not just useful attributes. They are daily survival requirements for public health. Public health has added to its capacity to evolve quickly and adapt in a changing environment.[2]

Recent developments in the field have highlighted that public health leaders should:[3]

---

[1] Kimberly, J. R. (2011). Preparing leaders in public health for success in a flatter, more distributed and collaborative world. Public Health Reviews, 33(1), 289–299.

[2] The Public Health Leadership Society, the National Public Health Leadership Development Network, and the National Public Health Leadership Institute. (2009). Now more than ever: The case for public health leadership programs. Presented to the leadership of the Centers for Disease Control and Prevention, p. 2. Retrieved from www.phls.org/CMSuploads/Now_More_Than_Ever-83499.pdf/.

[3] See, Association of Schools of Public Health (ASPH) Education Committee: Master's degree in public health core competency development

- Demonstrate transparency, integrity, and honesty in all actions
- Apply social justice and human rights principles when addressing community needs
- Engage in dialogue and learning from others to advance public health goals

These are discussed in the second, third, and fourth sections.

Integrity, Honesty, and Transparency

When asked, what was the most important characteristic people sought in their leaders, integrity was by far considered the most important.[4] Followers need to trust their leaders to do what is in their best interest. Therefore, leaders need to lead with integrity and honesty.

Integrity and honesty are guided by personal and organizational values. Each leader needs to define his/her values and organizations should define and commit to their values. There can be many potential values that one could choose. So, there is a need to prioritize them and find basic values that will determine most of the other values.

Values need to be emphasized again and again in terms of conversations, actions, and dialogues within the organization.

Webster's Dictionary defines integrity as firm adherence to a code of values or the quality or state of being complete or undivided. Integrity means consistent behavior that matches the values system a person or organization has. Trust is created when leaders "walk the talk" and model the values in difficult circumstances. Maintaining integrity and honesty guided by values by a leader will result in these qualities permeating within the organization.[5]

---

project, Version 2.3. Retrieved from http://srph.tamhsc.edu/health-policy-mgmt/master-of-public-health/mph-competencies.html/.

[4] Covey, S. (2005). *The 8th habit: From effectiveness to greatness*. Free Press.

[5] Retrieved from www.corneliusassoc.com/.

Human resources management has a critical role to play in creating a culture of integrity and honesty.[6]

1. Recruit new employees with a concern for integrity
2. Model integrity in selection, appraisal, promotion, and other rewards within the organization
3. Discipline the transgressors

Transparency is not an act, it is a process. A leader or an organization that strives for transparency not only does not hide anything, but also proclaims that "we are proud of what we do and how we function." This is only possible if the leaders and their organizations have integrity and honesty. Transparency, on the other hand, also supports integrity and honesty.

Stephen Covey[7] says that just as trust is the key to all relationships, so also is trust the glue to all organizations. It is the cement that holds the bricks together. Trust is the fruit of trustworthiness of people and their organizations. The trust comes from three sources: personal, institutional, and one person consistently choosing to give it to another—an act that leads one to feel another's belief that one can add value. Trust is a verb AND a noun. When it is both a verb and a noun, it is something shared and reciprocated between people. That is the essence of how a person becomes the leader or their boss. They merit trust by giving it. A trustworthy organization will keep its promises. People will do what they say and they will do it consistently.

Without integrity, trust is never achieved. The best leaders are transparent: they do what they say; they "walk the talk." Therefore, people believe them. Integrity comes from a strong sense of values. Behaving with integrity also means being consistent with one's choices and actions.

Integrity requires personal courage to uphold the values in benign as well as difficult circumstances.[8] Principle-centered leadership is often accompanied by a strong sense of humility

---

[6] Retrieved from www.johnbaldoni.com/.
[7] Covey, S. (2005). *The 8th Habit: From effectiveness to greatness.*
[8] Ibid.

and courage which has integrity at its heart. The power, wisdom, and guidance for a leader increase as these principles are applied.

Leaders in the public health sector need to adhere to the highest level of integrity and ethics in their behavior. Their honesty must apply to their dealings with public, colleagues in their organizations, collaborating partners, and the media.

The key to high performance is for integrity to be part of a leader's day-to-day actions and thinking, not just when big decisions are needed but even when small ordinary ones have implications for or impact on someone.

Social Justice, Health Equity, and Human Rights

The three fields of social justice, health equity, and human rights have different fundamental concepts, perspectives, languages, and tools of action; but have many points of intersection.[9]

Social Gradient

In arguing for closing the gap in health disparities and life opportunities within a generation (30 years), the Commission on Social Determinants of Health (CSDH) says that in countries at all levels of income, health follows a *social gradient*—that is, the lower the socioeconomic position, the worse the health. Putting these inequities right—the huge and remediable differences between and within the countries—is a matter of social justice (see Box 10.1).[10]

Health equity is determined not only by the social determinants of health—conditions of daily life and inequitable distribution

---

[9] Braveman, P. (2010). Social conditions, health equity and human rights. *Journal of Health and Human Rights*, 12, 31–48. Retrieved from www.hhrjournal.org/.

[10] Chapman, A. (2010). The social determinants of health, health equity, and human rights. *Journal of Health and Human Rights*, 12, 17–30. Retrieved from www.hhrjournal.org/.

Box 10.1: *Social Gradient in Health*

The poor health of the poor, the social gradient in health within countries, and the marked health inequities between countries are caused by the unequal distribution of power, income, goods, and services, globally and nationally, the consequent unfairness in the immediate, visible circumstances of people's lives—their access to health care, schools, and education, their conditions of work and leisure, their homes, communities, towns, or cities—and their chances of leading a flourishing life. This unequal distribution of health-damaging experiences is not in any sense a "natural" phenomenon but is the result of a toxic combination of poor social policies and programs, unfair economic arrangements, and bad politics. Together, the structural determinants and conditions of daily life constitute the social determinants of health and are responsible for a major part of health inequities between and within countries.

Source: CSDH, Closing the gap in a generation: Health equity through action on the social determinants of health: Final report of the Commission on Social Determinants of Health. (Geneva, Switzerland: World Health Organization, 2008). Retrieved from http://www.who.int/social/._determinants/final_report/en.

of power, money, and resources, gender, poverty, and social exclusion—but also by other determinants of health such as safe water, adequate sanitation, adequate nutritious food and housing, healthy occupational and environmental conditions, and access to health-related education and information. The public health leaders need to understand the relative role of various determinants of health in the context—place and time—where they are working.

While social gradient is said to lead to health gradient, the reverse relationship has not been investigated in as much depth as the former. The issue at hand is—how much the impact of social injustice can be mitigated by policies in fields such as water and sanitation, food security, targeted nutrition interventions, and primary health care. Often it is argued that even when such policies and programs are in place, better-off people tend to benefit more than those who are needier. Nevertheless, it could be argued that health equity indicators can be a measure of social inequities in a society.

Rights-Based Approach

On the human rights side, Article 12.2 (b) of the International Covenant on Economic, Social and Cultural Rights[11] enumerated the following four steps to be taken by the State parties to achieve the full realization of the "highest attainable standard of physical and mental health":

1. The provision for the reduction of the stillbirth rate and of infant mortality, and for the healthy development of the child
2. The improvement of all aspects of environmental and industrial hygiene
3. The prevention, treatment, and control of epidemic, endemic, occupational, and other diseases
4. The creation of conditions which would assure to all medical service and medical attention in the event of sickness

A rights-based approach including treatment of underlying determinants of health in the approach tends to identify the state's obligations and assesses the extent to which they are fulfilled. In this approach, people are not beneficiaries but "claim holders" and the service providers are "duty bearers."

The approach to the underlying determinants by members of the human rights community tends to be narrower both in concept and emphasis from the role that social determinants play in the CSDH report. While health system is an important factor in human rights considerations, the CSDH report treats it as one of the social determinants.

There is a difference in health inequalities versus health inequities. Inequality in health cannot differentiate health outcomes independent of any assessment of cause or fairness. On the other

    [11] U.N. General Assembly, International Covenant on Economic, Social and Cultural Rights. (1966). United Nations, Treaty Series, Vol. 993, p. 3, December 16. Retrieved from http://www.unhcr.org/refworld/docid/3ae6b36c0.html/.

hand, CSDH says,[12] "Where systematic differences in health are judged to be avoidable by reasonable action globally and within society they are, quite simply, unjust. It is this that we label health inequity."

Generally, health equity can be considered from four dimensions:[13]

- *Universal access to health care*
  Many countries do not have financial resources to pay for effective health systems delivering comprehensive health services, including preventive services to all its citizens. In addition, other barriers—informational, social, and physical—also operate to detract from universal access.
- *NCDs*
  While universal access to health care and preventive public health services, including water and sanitation, can address many communicable diseases and there is some success on that front, NCDs have emerged as a major threat. It is estimated that by 2020, NCDs will be responsible for 60 percent of sickness worldwide and seven deaths in every 10. Most will be in the developing world. Generally, the risk factors are the results of rich diets, lack of physical activity, alcohol, and tobacco use although poor may also suffer as a result of infection, inadequate food, pollution, and lack of basic health care.
- *Role of community*
  Strong advocacy is needed within the communities if health is to be prioritized. Among populations most vulnerable to illness, capacity for effective grassroots action rests on approaches that build local capacity not only to access

[12] CSDH. (2008). *Closing the gap in a generation: Health equity through action on the social determinants of health: Final report of the Commission on Social Determinants of Health*. Geneva, Switzerland: World Health Organization. Retrieved from http://www.who.int/social_determinants/final_report/en/.

[13] Summarized from editorials of Volume 13 of *Journal of Health and Human Rights*. Retrieved from www.hhr.org/.

health care and other services but also to address other determinants of health.

- *Settings of natural disasters and emergencies*
  Rights-based frameworks can offer considerable advantage to ensure health services in such situations.

The emphasis in human rights is on equality of dignity, legal standing, and legal status, and not equality in social or economic position. The former may not necessarily lead to the later and possibly even vice versa. Nondiscrimination as human rights can be an important measure for health equity.

The areas of convergence and complimentarity between social justice, health equity, and human rights are substantial although their nature of concerns, approaches, and emphasis vary.

The public health leaders concerned with health equity need to pay closer attention to social determinants of health and underlying social injustices and be prepared to use legal human rights enshrined in human rights framework to influence them (see Figure 10.1).

Figure 10.1: *Social Justice, Human Rights, and Health Equity*

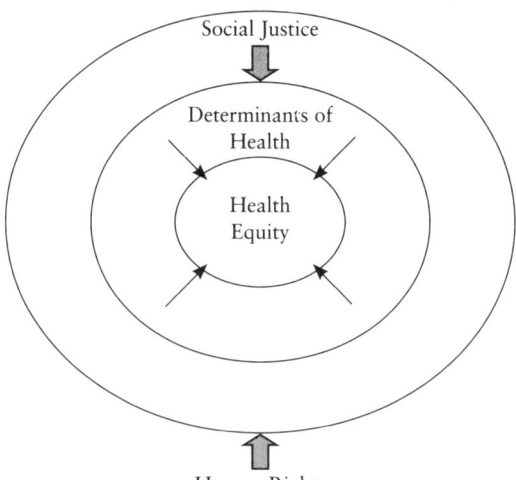

Source: Authors.

Dialogue and Learning

Public health leaders need to keep up with the rapidly changing and increasing complexity of the public health field. Therefore, they need to continue to learn. They would need to receive feedback and solicit new ideas from a diversity of stakeholders. The vital sources of information would include people and community leaders, leaders of other health institutions, professionals working in other related sectors, researchers, and politicians. They can seek the feedback in a variety of ways—through direct and indirect contacts, social networking, surveys, and interpersonal dialogues.

> *The leader of the past was a person who knew what to tell. The leader of the future will be a person who knows how to ask.*
> (Peter Drucker)[14]

The public health agencies need to become learning organizations.[15] The learning organization will need leaders who will continuously learn. Peter Drucker said that individuals have different styles of learning—through listening, reading, and through observation, experience, and reflection.[16] They need to identify a mix of their styles and organize their learning.

However, there is a possibility of information overload. Therefore, leaders need to prioritize. On their personal leadership journey, they can identify a few (one to three) key areas that they seek to improve, prepare an action plan, implement, and follow-up with coworkers to see if improvements have taken place.

In conclusion, public health leaders of the future will have to learn, change, and grow on the job. They will need to reach out to multiple stakeholders, ask for inputs, respond in a positive manner, and implement action plans. Through this iterative process, they will become more effective.

[14] Retrieved from www.marshallgoldsmithlibrary.com/cim/.

[15] Senge, P. (1990). *The fifth discipline: The art and practice of the learning organization.* New York, USA: Doubleday.

[16] Drucker, P. (2005). Managing oneself. *Harvard Business Review*, *83*(1), 100–109.

Effective Dialogue as a Means of Learning

Dialogue is a spoken conversation or written exchange between two or more people. For effective dialogue, there has to be mutual respect and willingness to actively listen to other participants. It requires the following:

- *Participation from both sides.* Dialogue recognizes that people have different perspectives, viewpoints, knowledge, and skill sets. These need to be respected.
- *Freedom.* Dialogues are not to be conducted under coercion or threat.
- *Valued contribution.* Each participant should value the benefit they will derive through the dialogue.

A public health leader would need to have the ability to dialogue with community, stakeholders in health sector and other sectors that have substantial bearing on their work and mission.

When effective dialogue takes place, both parties experience change and can participate in adaptive work of change through collaboration discussed in Chapter 12. Dialogue creates trust, understanding, and empathy for others' positions.

Stephen Covey says that "you should understand first and then seek to be understood." He recommends that you should articulate positions and views of other parties and seek confirmation that you have understood them correctly. The other participant could repeat the same process. Thus, increased understanding will not only remove sources of misunderstanding and conflict, but also result in better ways to address issues.

Thus, dialogue will

- be useful to increase trust, reduce conflicts, and enhance mutual understanding
- lead to creating shared interests and willingness to address common problems
- generate creative ways to address problems through collective action

Effective Listening

For a leader, it is important to listen well to (and posing appropriate questions to) his/her followers, subordinates, and peers, not only to get information but also to establish or strengthen interpersonal relationships. For the speaker, it is a positive feeling when he/she gets a sense of not only being heard but also understood. The power of effective listening is in the hands of the leader.

What is effective listening? Effective listening comes from a combination of active listening and good questioning. Active listening and good questioning act to encourage open communication of ideas and feelings between two parties—the listener and the speaker.

Here are some useful tips given in Tables 10.1 and 10.2.

Table 10.1: *Tips for Active Listening*

	Your Tools	*Action*	*Reasoning*
Active Listening	Your eyes	Look at the person who is speaking	This shows you are interested in what he/she is saying and also that you understand.
	Your body	Be aware of what your body is telling the other person	The body has a nonverbal language of its own and it can convey messages from openness and friendliness to hostility and aloofness. How does your body behave when you are listening to someone? As a leader, you want your body language to show that you are open and welcoming of the speaker's message.
	Emotional vibes	Nonverbal communication	It is not difficult to get a sense of the emotional vibes the speaker is sending you. Is what he/she is saying being said in a calm, smooth manner or in an excited, agitated manner? And what does that tell you about the speaker?
	Reflection	Summarizing what you have heard	It is useful to pause at appropriate moments to summarize the main points of what you have heard. This tells the speaker that you have been paying attention and have understood what was said.

Source: Adapted from several sources.

Table 10.2: *Tips for Good Questioning*

	Types	Example
Good Questioning	Open-ended questions	An example is: "What was the meeting like?" not "Did you go to the meeting?"
	Probing questions	"What do you mean by women not being able to use the clinic?"
	Clarifying questions	"Do you mean that services are underused due to location of clinic or the hours of operations?"
	Ask for personal views and feelings	"What do you think of the way the new counseling service for adolescents was introduced into the area?"
	Ask for (and give) feedback	Ask for feedback after group work or discussion to assess whether the work or discussion has been productive or completed satisfactorily.

Source: Adapted from several sources.

Exercise

Identify a person who you think is a good listener. Observe how he/she listens to other people and list down five characteristics.

1. _____

2. _____

3. _____

4. _____

5. _____

The principle of silence is important for improving listening skills. Some actions include:

✓ Pause a few seconds before answering someone.
✓ Accept silence as a normal part of conversation.
✓ Work to balance speaking and listening time during conversation.
✓ Break eye contact for a moment to allow the other party to feel comfortable with silence.

Exercise

→ Practice the above actions with five people you speak in the office for a week.
  • How do you see their reaction and response to you?
  • Has it improved the quality of the conversation and information you received?

How to Listen Effectively[17]

An unwillingness to listen is too common among the host of poor leaders we have to put up with. And nearly 60 percent of all management problems stem from faulty communications.

Leaders have to learn to touch the hearts of people before they can ask for their hand. In the workplace, the manager has to first know what's in the heart of his/her people, and listening to them enables this. When the manager listens, he/she connects with those people, and learns of their joys and concerns.

  • *Listen to your followers.* Follow this piece of advice from a British Earl, Philip Stanhope: "Many a man would rather you heard his story than granted his request." Good leaders do more than conduct business when they interact with their people—they take time to get to know their people, a feel for each as a person. As managers, you want to be the kind that people want to follow. If you are in the habit of listening only to the facts and not the person who expresses them, you are strongly advised to change your focus—take time to listen to your people.
  • *Listen to your customers.* Whether you are running a business, a service, or an administration, you have customers to deal with. These people represent your greatest opportunity

[17] Appleby, D. (2003). Article in *New Straits Times* (Malaysian newspaper), Appointments Section, January 25, 2003.

and they should be your priority at all times. Unhappy customers should always be a concern. If you are caught up in your own ideas and fail to listen to their concerns, complaints, and suggestions, you will be in trouble. The American Red Indian Tribe Cherokee have a wonderful saying, "Listen to the whispers and you won't have to listen to the screams."

- *Listen to your competitors.* This might seem odd at first. As a leader, you don't want to base your actions on what the other guy is doing, but you should still listen and learn what you can improve upon. Larry King, the American television talk show icon, puts his thoughts across plaintively when he remarks, "I remind myself every morning: nothing I say this day will teach me anything. So if I am going to learn, I must do it by listening." King does not make the mistake of others, who see other organizations as competition and focus their attention on building and championing their own cause, to the extent they forget to learn what the other group is doing.

- *Listen to your mentors.* No leader is so advanced or experienced that he/she can dispense with a mentor. You are always learning from observing and listening to leaders who have more experience than yourself. If you do not have a mentor, you should go out and identify one to be there for you. While you get the process going, begin by reading the success stories of others—sports and media personalities, bureaucrats and businessmen, politicians and statesmen, scientists and philosophers.

Improving on Your Listening

Are you a good listener or are you too busy doing your own thing? When was the last time you really paid attention to people and listened to what they have to say? Do more than just grab the main points, start listening to not only their words but also their feeling, meanings, and undercurrents, if any.

- *Change your schedule.* As mentioned, spend more time listening to your followers, customers, competitors, and mentors. Give them more attention and on a regular basis—daily, weekly, or monthly.
- *Meet people on their own turf.* A key to being a good listener is to find a common ground with people, whether they are your employees or customers. It is a good practice to discipline yourself to ask at least four to five questions about the individual as a person whenever you meet up—this way you get to know the person better. And seek common ground to cement your connection with him/her.
- *Read between the lines.* As you interact with people, pay attention and listen closely to both the factual and emotional content of their conversation. Sometimes by listening and reading between the lines, you begin to know what is really going on. Try listening with your heart.

Eleven

Team Building, Negotiation, Communication, and Conflict Management Skills for Leaders

There are many ways to describe and sort the competencies and skills that it takes to lead, and there are many frameworks for thinking about leadership. Some of these are specific to public health.
—Association of Schools of Public Health[1]

Critical Leadership Skills

To be effective, leaders require vital attributes and competencies, comprising attitude, knowledge, skills practice, and on-the-job behavior. Leaders need a set of competencies that will help them to translate a vision or mission into action, and these competences can be grouped as (see Figure 11.1):

1. Self-related individual competencies

   • Commitment to public health concerns
   • Innovative ways of addressing problems
   • Sensitivity toward gender and equity issues
   • Articulating a shared vision
   • Deriving individual and organizational vision

[1] Retrieved from www.asph.org/userfiles/competencies-reources, accessed on June 2, 2012.

- Effective communication and public-speaking skills
- Creative problem-solving, decision-making, and inter-personal relations

2. Organization-related capabilities

   - Updated knowledge on developments and policy/program interventions in public health
   - Strategic management skills
   - Capacity to inspire and empower people in the organization
   - Create a learning environment
   - Ensure accountability

3. Inter-organizational skills

   - Create a shared vision
   - Advocacy, negotiation, and consensus
   - Build strategic alliances
   - Sustain policy dialogues

4. Community-related skills

   - Create empowered communities to meet their own aspirations
   - Strengthen positive community values, norms, and institutions

5. Policy and program-related capacity

   - Articulate, advocate, and manage public health concerns in national and regional contexts
   - Generate and consolidate actions on public health at all levels
   - Engage in dialogue with leaders and potential leaders on policy and program options
   - Keep future leaders fully updated on latest developments

Figure 11.1: *Critical Leadership Skills Categories*

Source: Authors.

Peter Drucker, the grand old man of management, says that the whole discussion of characteristics and traits is a waste of time.[2] While social skills are vital for one person, another may be an equally effective leader by being a loner. He believes leaders are successful in their own ways.

> *It is a terrible thing to look over your shoulder when you are trying to lead and find no one there.* (Franklin D. Roosevelt)

While there is considerable debate about what constitutes essential leadership competencies, almost all agree that leaders need followers. Motivating or inspiring others to follow you is an integral part of leadership but to be successful in this and be able to sustain this allegiance from followers, whether within an organization, from partner organizations or the larger environment of public health, involves the following critical competencies for public health leaders:

[2] Boyett, J., & Boyett, J. (1998). *The guru guide: The best ideas of the top management thinkers.* New York: Wiley & Sons, Inc.

- Building and leading top teams
- Successful negotiations
- Conflict management
- Effective communications
- Public speaking

In this chapter, we discuss these competencies.

Pause for Reflection
If you are a leader or aspiring to be one, ask yourself why should anyone be led by you?

Building and Leading a Top Team

Leaders often make a difference in health practices in their country or region. They do this by making their organization or institution more effective, making it a leader in the field, a center of excellence for others to turn to for advice and authority. Bringing about change in your organization and, subsequently, the environment within which you work is a major challenge but one that can be highly motivating for both you and your staff.

A mission of such magnitude can only be achieved with a strong and dedicated team of senior professionals working alongside you. The leader may provide the vision, the motivation, the confidence, the direction but bringing about fundamental change in behaviors of people and health practitioners requires a strong team of operational managers who are committed to the cause.

In this section, we focus on building, maintaining, and strengthening the top team in order to enhance performance, achieve excellence, or deliver superior results. Teamwork has to be developed, maintained, invested in, and continually worked at. Good teams do not just happen by bringing together the right mix of well-intentioned and competent individuals. This is only half the work; providing the impetus for these individuals to go beyond 100 percent is the work of an effective leader.

As we have seen in the last chapter, the most effective teams are made up of a mix of personalities that may not, by nature, automatically enjoy working together. This dynamic must be cultivated through inspired, caring, and sensitive leadership.

First and foremost, the leader must make the purpose of the top team clear and ensure that all team members internalize, own, and commit to this purpose. Given the time constraints on all staff, particularly senior managers, it is important to define exactly what the purpose of the top team is and to identify some medium- and long-term clear measurable performance goals because the team composition should include members with all the necessary skills and the team needs to develop mutual accountability.[3]

In short, a team can be defined[4] as:

> A small number of people with complementary skills who are committed to a common purpose and approach with agreed performance goals for which they hold themselves accountable.

Top teams cannot and should not micromanage the organization. Top teams must ensure that they both collectively and individually provide consistency and focus for all stakeholders on the primary purpose of the organization and its strategic directions. The success of a team depends upon several key factors including the chair as well as diversity and balance in the team composition (see Box 11.1).

Box 11.1: *Success of a Team: Six Key Factors*

1. The person in the chair
2. One strong "Plant" in the team
3. A good spread of mental abilities
4. A spread of personal characteristics
5. A good match between team members' attributes and their responsibilities
6. Recognition of imbalance in the team and the ability to adjust to it

Source: Adapted from several sources.

---

[3] Retrieved from www.coach4growth.com.
[4] Retrieved from www.enbconsulting.com/downloads/Topteams.doc, accessed on November 27, 2011.

The top team ensures that the organization is moving in a clear and consistent direction, one that they are all totally committed to. If the top team starts to take on more than they can efficiently and effectively handle, frustration and dysfunctional behavior will develop.

Each individual's role within the team needs to be recognized by the whole team, and mutual trust and respect between all members of the team has to be established. Team members require continual support from each other and especially from the leader. Team members need coaching, motivation, feedback, and encouragement. When negative conflict erupts between members, the leader should be quick to respond and help to resolve such dynamics that can undermine the performance of the whole team.

Top teams continually face challenges and potential difficulties. Top teams should include people who can collaborate, can ask for help, are willing to take small steps and ask for feedback, are adaptable, and are willing to work outside their expertise.[5] (See Box 11.2)

Box 11.2: *Key Behaviors of Successful Teams*

Behaviors of successful teams include:

1. Planning before action: Agree on a strategy before starting the task
2. Selecting a competent leader for the task
3. Mutual support and trust in each other
4. Willingness of team members to be led by the person selected
5. Ability to identify and learn from mistakes
6. Importance of good communication
7. Ability of team members to influence their leader

Source: Adapted from www.stanford.edu/class/e140/e140a/effective.html (accessed on April 7, 2014).

Top teams are made up of strong personalities, people who may be or are leaders in their own field. They are used to being recognized authorities in their fields and this expectation needs to be recognized by top team leaders as they mold a strong team of highly accomplished individuals.

[5] Retrieved from www.jrothman.com/.

Each time a person leaves or joins the top team, the team dynamics will be affected. Each new challenge the top team faces will initiate a new set of tensions within the team. Team leaders need to understand and be sensitive to the reality that as top teams take on new challenges each team member has their own professional perspective, their divisional responsibility, and their commitment to the top team and the whole organization.

The Role of the Leader in Building the Top Team

The leader must invest in team building. This happens collectively in regular meetings, in special team-building sessions, and through counseling and mentoring individual members. Team building involves some group dynamics activities and working on team definition, strategic thinking, and engagement in organizational tasks.

Effective and efficient meetings reflect that the leader is valuing the time of the top team and its members. Leaders need to ensure that the team keeps within its functional areas, that they care for each individual member of the team, recognize their contributions, and take quality time with each member.

- Be clear about what you are looking for
- Define membership
- Define purpose: Role and function
- Support and empower the team
- Manage effective meetings
- Ensure quality interaction and communication: Consulting and informing
- Build mutual understanding, trust, and respect: Give credit and praise for contributions of members
- Recognize and build on experience
- Provide feedback, individual coaching, caring, and respect to each member of the team
- Review progress and evaluate team strength

While the twin roles of empowering and coaching have been recognized as good leadership practices in the West for half a century, it should be remembered that acceptable styles of leadership do vary between cultures and that while this is good leadership practice, it is rarely followed.

> (Sven-Goran) Eriksson's one-to-one style can be boiled down to two elements—empowering and coaching.
>
> Empowering is about delegating responsibility to the people who work for you, sharing decision-making with them and appreciating their initiative.
>
> Coaching is about making everyone feel a part of the team, encouraging players to cooperate, keeping them informed and taking an interest in their individual performance.
>
> (Julian Burkinshaw and Stuart Crainer)[6]

Part of the reason is the tension between empowering people to perform and investing in building people's capacity through coaching. Empowering can be seen as letting people "sink or swim," while coaching can easily become micromanaging! The art is getting the right balance with both teams and individuals.

While the role of a visionary leader carries many important demands both inside and outside the organization, none is more important than making quality time for the members of your senior team. Good leaders genuinely care for their team colleagues and their staff. This attribute is felt by everyone it is bestowed upon. It is a fundamental ingredient in building excellence within your top team (see Box 11.3).

Motivation is about creating an environment and context within which each member of your team can satisfy their needs. Everyone is different, as are their situations; however, the common needs are: security, money, status, recognition, responsibility, and job satisfaction. Beyond individual motivation, once you have established a strong team with spirit and focus, team success will also become an important need and motivational factor for each member.

---

[6] Burkinshaw, J., & Crainer, S. (2002). *Leadership the Sven-Goran Eriksson Way*. Capstone Publishing Ltd.

Box 11.3: *Empowering and Coaching People*

Key Elements of Coaching

- Caring for each individual
- Motivation
- Counseling
- Mentoring
- Tutoring
- Confronting and challenging

Source: Adapted from several sources.

Counseling is about talking to people about individual problems as they arise and arrive at a solution, or to enable them to arrive at their own solution. There are three critical aspects to counseling: (1) setting the scene, (2) discussing the problem, and (3) finding the solution (see Box 11.4).

1. "Setting the scene" involves arranging a special time, adequate to enable a full discussion. It should be private with absolutely no interruptions! Create a comfortable and relaxed environment, with appropriate refreshments.

Box 11.4: *Managing Counseling Session: Important Guidelines*

- Meet privately, with plenty of time and in a conducive atmosphere
- Plan carefully: Identify specific examples of the points you wish to make
- Do not exaggerate, generalize, or be judgmental
- When you speak to the person talk about "how I feel when," rather than "you make me feel"
- Explain why you feel this way
- Listen to what the person has to say
- Focus on how they behave, not what you think they are
- Relate their behavior to the team's effectiveness
- Give credit and be positive where appropriate
- Suggest a solution (prepared)
- Listen and discuss

Source: Adapted from http://www.washington.edu/admin/hr/roles/mgr/ ee-performance/corrective-action/initial-counsel.html (accessed on April 7, 2014).

2. "Discussing the problem" involves outlining the problem or symptom of the problem you have observed and then indicating that you acknowledge there may be something else deeper that is the real problem. Try to open up your colleague to analyze their own problems. Don't be afraid of silence, it tells both of you something important. There is time and more time can be made available at a later date. In summary, acknowledge the person's feelings, encourage them to talk, and examine the options together.

3. "Finding the solution" is a matter of enabling the person to find his/her own solution.

Team Composition: Nine Team Roles

Dr Meredith Belbin of Belbin Associates Ltd[7] has identified the following nine roles that team members need to perform:

1. *Plant*: They are highly intelligent and original thinkers. They generate new ideas and provide ways of solving difficult problems.

2. *Resource investigator*: They are also creative people but they generate their ideas from building on other people's experience. They are relaxed, extrovert, and inquisitive, usually extremely popular and are good at networking.

3. *Coordinator*: Highly disciplined and controlled, has a natural inclination to focus on objectives. This helps the team to work toward a shared goal and to keep on track.

4. *Shaper*: Dynamic and full of nervous energy, outgoing, impulsive, and impatient, often edgy—sometimes on the verge of paranoia. They love to set challenges and be challenged, very achievement-oriented.

5. *Monitor evaluator*: Intelligent, stable, and introvert. Can be dry and unexciting personalities, even cold. Their strength

---

[7] Retrieved from www.belbin.com/.

lies not in generating ideas but in clear, dispassionate analysis of other people's ideas.

6. *Team worker*: Supportive, sensitive, and social; recognizes the emotional undercurrents in the team most clearly. Team workers make good listeners and diplomats, loyal to the team, popular, and mild-natured.

7. *Implementer*: Do the core work of the team. Have organizational skills, common sense, and self-discipline to turn ideas and decisions into defined and manageable tasks.

8. *Completer*: Anxious and introvert by nature, although may appear calm. Worry about what might go wrong, not happy until they have checked every detail.

9. *Specialist*: Dedicated to acquiring highly specialized skills or knowledge. Real interest in their own subject area which they are enthusiastic and highly professional about.

Follow-up: The challenge for the visionary leader is in finding the right mix of people and in developing the right balance of individual team skills. Most people have one or two strong role preferences and others they are comfortable with.

Common Problems with Top Teams

The effectiveness of the top team is largely a reflection of the team leader, although it also takes supportive team members who work with the leader. It is the team leader who defines the role of the top team, its culture and norms. While the leader will normally use participatory methodology and ensure ownership of the parameters that define the top team, it is the leader who largely defines the top team, provides it with credibility, and enables it to define the organization and how it operates.

Problems may be viewed as either problems relating to the team as a whole or those that are largely individual problems. All teams and groups have problems and they can be sorted by investments on team building and individual counseling and motivation.

Team-building exercises can assist team members to identify how they contribute to team dynamics. Remedial action can then be taken.

Team problems

- Whole team is not up to the new role you have envisaged for them
- Lack of clear purpose and roles
- Attempting to micromanage the whole organization, rather than provide a direction
- Too many meetings
- Meetings badly managed: Lack of preparation by leader and members and poor decision-making
- "Groupthink": Too easy agreement on everything

Sometimes, it becomes clear that one or two members of the team may not be suited for the task, no matter how much support and coaching they are provided; in these cases, the team members have to be changed, in a manner that further strengthens the team and the organization as a whole. This involves two separate tasks of great importance to the credibility and success of leaders: the removal of unsuitable team members and the recruitment and induction of new members.

Problems with individual team members

- Inadequate capabilities of individual operational leader
- Lack of mutual respect and trust between members
- Lack of engagement and participation by some members—fragmentation
- Frequent conflict between members—harmful rivalries
- Poor communication between members
- Lack of commitment to decisions made
- Lack of transparency
- Undermining the team and other personality problems

Problem people

Problem people should be seen as a challenge for the leader to build a more productive relationship and a more productive team player. Difficult people exist everywhere and, indeed, they can play important and constructive roles in an organization and as a member of a team. By "difficult," we are looking at people with difficult personality traits, not people who are incompetent or lack knowledge, skills, and attitudes necessary to do their job. The leader has to engage the problem or difficult person with constructive feedback; positive where warranted and negative to clarify the unacceptable behavior and the impact it is having upon the team. Constructive negative feedback is an important and, sometimes, challenging skill for the leader (see Box 11.5).

Remember that you cannot change people's personalities. Be satisfied with reasonable improvements. You can change people's behavior and their contribution to the team and the organization.

Box 11.5: *Some "Problem" Personalities*

• The person who never listens	• The manipulator
• The daydreamer	• The buck-passer
• The loner	• The over-competitive person
• The secretive person	• The sulker
• The moaner	• The oversensitive person
• The control freak	• The martyr
• The prima donna	• The prejudiced person
• The pessimist	• The "jobsworth" type
• The know-all	• The aggressive type
• The rowdy person	• The rule bender
• The domineering person	

Source: Adapted from several sources.

Removing Team Members

Good leaders give people a chance and environment within which they may prove themselves. When new leaders are introduced into an organization, it is important to give members of your team time to adjust and demonstrate their commitment and contribution.

Likewise, when new members join a strong team they require time and support to find their natural place within the team. Never write off a new team member too quickly. Remember that you are taking on the whole person: the excellent traits that underpin why the person was hired and the negative or dysfunctional aspects that everyone has stored away.

Having said this, there are people who just don't fit into the team, are continually dysfunctional, negative, and undermining of all you are trying to achieve. They are underperformers, sometimes even incapable of achieving what they are supposed to. Their continued inadequacy actually fuels their dysfunctionality. Some people have been promoted to their level of incompetency; others have used connections to move beyond their competency levels. Other people have never been managed, never held accountable, have never been part of a team, and just do not wish their peaceful and comfortable life to be interfered with. In such cases, it is important to root them out of the team, if not the organization.

There are several options available when you have consistently unproductive team members, destructive team members, incompetent and unsatisfactory performance. Reshuffles consist of moving people around in top jobs. Reassignments involve promoting upwardly mobile middle-level managers, reassigning senior people to important staff positions from leadership roles they have demonstrated they cannot handle. Staff secondments and exchanges between offices and organizations also provide a refreshing break for some people, new challenges for others.

Finally, there is the option of dismissal or early retirement. While never a pleasant option, it is critical that team members who do not contribute are removed from the team and replaced by high caliber top team members.

Appointing New Team Members

Probably the most important decision you ever make. Make sure you search the market and cast the recruitment net wide, there is nothing worse than having no candidates to be appointed at the final selection phase. For the top team, invest in recruitment and selection agents with a track record of successful placements. Avoid selecting clones of yourself and choose people of real ability and stature.

Mistakes in appointments reflect directly on your own performance in the eyes of your board. Follow due process. The opinion of the whole team matters!

Successful Negotiations

Negotiation is an integral part of everybody's life. Today's leaders have to constantly negotiate with actors in external and internal environments. It plays an important role for public health leaders for the following reasons:[8]

- Public health leaders not only have to negotiate with staff within their own departments but also with other sectors on which they do not have authority and need to influence them. For instance, public health laws need to be negotiated with law ministry and lawmakers.
- Public health leaders need to negotiate with other segments of health sector, such as curative care institutions, to increase emphasis on prevention. Thus, they need to infuse these segments with public health values, methodologies, and approaches.
- Many issues arise at different levels. For instance, at community levels, change of behavior norms may have to be negotiated. At the time of emergency, coordinated response would need to be negotiated. At the global level, public health leaders have been involved in intellectual property protection issues or counterfeit drugs issues.

Thus, there are many occasions where public health leaders would seek to influence colleagues or partners to adopt a specific

[8] Retrieved from www.ghd-net.org/training/.

course of action, persuade peers or stakeholders to take part in joint projects or collaborate to secure common objectives.[9] Therefore, competencies for effective negotiations are critical for public health leaders to succeed.

Negotiation involves two or more parties, who have something the other wants. The process has four components:

1. Common interests of the parties
2. Conflicting interest that forms an important component
3. Criterion or bottom line
4. Willingness to compromise (everything is negotiable)

Thus, negotiation is the interaction between people who are interdependent but whose needs are different. Although each side may have a position, the challenge during negotiation is to figure out alternatives, create values where none was there before, trade desires that are valued differently, achieve agreement, and maintain relationships for the future.[10]

It is often said that successful negotiations are win-win negotiations in which both parties get a fair compromise. Both parties need to have defensible positions and options. It is not useful to negotiate when one party is in competition with the other party. Both sides want win-win options. If there is no way a win-win can be achieved, it is best not to enter into a negotiation.

We first explain the principles of negotiation. You can strengthen your skills and confidence to plan and conduct the negotiation by providing tips for planning, conducting, and closing the negotiation process.

There are five basic principles for successful negotiations:[11]

1. Be hard on the problem and soft on the person
2. Focus on needs/interests, not on positions

---

[9] Retrieved from www.healthknowledge.org.uk/.

[10] Wilcox, L. Effective negotiation skills. Harvard University. Retrieved from www.chidlrenhospital.org/.

[11] Retrieved from http://www.healthknowledge.org.uk/public-health-textbook/organisation-management/5a-understanding-itd/negotiating-influencing (accessed on April 7, 2014).

3. Emphasize common ground
4. Be inventive about options
5. Make clear agreements

Develop and Strengthen Your Negotiation Skills

To become a good negotiator, you should learn to read the other party's needs. It is useful to practice negotiating to improve your skills. You could sit in as an observer in other people's negotiations. Also, many excellent books are available and you can learn tactics from the reading of famous negotiations.

Planning for negotiations

Strategy

Negotiations should be for win-win, not win-lose. The true meaning of a win-win settlement is a negotiated agreement where the agreement reached cannot be improved further by any discussions. So, the outcome cannot be improved for your benefit, and similarly, the agreement for the other party cannot be improved for their further benefit also.[12] By definition, there is no value left on the table and creative options have been thoroughly explored and exploited.

Therefore, negotiating strategy needs to vary according to the type of negotiation. You should examine all your options—strengths, weaknesses, limits, and the range of options. Therefore, you should be clear about your Best Alternative to Negotiated Agreement (BATNA).[13] It is important to write down all your objectives and then prioritize them. You should also identify issues that are open to compromise and those that are not. Each objective should be specified in a single sentence. In this process, unrealistic objectives should be abandoned even before the start

---

[12] Retrieved from www.negotiations.com/.

[13] Fisher, R., & Ury, W. (1981). *Getting to yes. Negotiating without giving in*. Boston, USA: Houghton Mifflin.

of the negotiation, recognizing differentiation between wants and needs. Negotiating strategy should be simple and flexible.

You should know your interests and not positions as different positions could still serve your interests. In this process, some conflicts would most likely arise but most of them can be resolved if both parties are interested in a win-win outcome.

If you think you are in a less powerful position then you should explore whether you can improve upon your BATNA or weaken the other party's BATNA.

When you do not expect to deal with people ever again, then it may be appropriate to "play hardball," seeking to win a negotiation while the other person loses out.[14] Similarly, when there is a great deal at stake in a negotiation, it may be appropriate to prepare in detail and legitimate "one-upmanship" to gain advantage. However, neither of these approaches is usually much good for resolving disputes with which you have an ongoing relationship. Such approaches may lead to reprisals later or can undermine trust and damage teamwork. In such situations, honesty and openness are almost always the best strategies.

Preparation

Psychologically, you should think about gains not losses and should be prepared to compromise when you negotiate. Clarify your priorities; be ready to concede less important points. It is important to be aware that the opposition may have a hidden agenda.

Successful negotiators need to prepare very well; there is nothing like too much preparation. They would gather all the key information relevant to negotiation and talk to people who know the other party in negotiations. They should research in advance about who will be representing the opposition.

Roles and responsibilities of the negotiating team should be defined clearly, who will be a leader, a good person who understands, a bad person who makes opposition feel "small;" hard liner, sweeper, bringing together views, and putting them forward in a single case.

---

[14] Retrieved from www.mindtools.com/.

Conducting negotiations

Negotiating Style and Behavior

It is important to dress according to the need of negotiations. Be flexible—it is a sign of weaknesses not strengths. Begin any negotiation with uncontroversial points. You should put forward your proposal in an unemotional way and pay close attention to the proposal of the other party. You should wait for the other party to finish before responding and look for any similarities. If you agree in haste, you may repent later. You need to hide your short temper and frustration when negotiating. There are cultural differences in negotiations; you need to understand them and use them to your advantage. Leave enough room for maneuvers in your negotiation. Feel free to reject the first offer. Make conditional offers such as "If you do this, we will do this." Indicate that every concession you make is a loss to you. You should not make an offer that you cannot keep. Retracting an offer will often destroy the spirit of negotiations. Lying or misrepresentation may be grounds to invalidate the arguments. Respond to ploys.

Keep testing your assessment of the opposition against how they behave during negotiations. Whenever possible consult with people who know the opponent. Arrive a bit early to look professional. Be careful with the sitting arrangements and place: home, neutral, or "away" grounds. Observe nonverbal communication. Probe the attitudes of the opposition. Always use stalling practices subtly and sparingly. You could ask smart questions—close-ended, direct, and open-ended—to elicit information, to ascertain that you have understood the position of the other party; you may wish to repeat back your own understanding of that position and seek affirmation. This avoids many misunderstandings and often helps in appreciating each other's position as well as interest underlying that position.

Being able to negotiate well is a highly developed skill. Experienced and effective negotiators are a successful combination of psychologist, diplomat, and language expert!

The following are some guidelines on how to negotiate:

- What we say first is most important

- The use of personal pronouns is revealing of the position of the speaker on the topic at hand ("I and we" means more commitment)
- Expressions such as "People think," "We," "Experts in the field," "In my humble opinion" are screens that often hide arrogance and false modesty
- A "Yes" followed by a "But" generally announces an attack or a killing
- Skillful negotiators use expressions such as "I think that you will like what I am about to say" (*some good news is coming up*), "It goes without saying" (*you must agree on this one*), "Off the top of my head" (*I share with you what I think right now, without any preparation*), "Would you be kind enough to" (*I need your help*), "I am sure that someone as intelligent as you" (*a big stroke on the other party's ego*) as softeners
- Skillful negotiators can also use effectively foreboders such as "Nothing is wrong" (*there is something wrong for sure*), "It really does not matter" (*it matters a lot*)
- Statements such as "And do you know what we did," "Guess what he decided," "You are not going to believe this" can be used to arouse interest
- Keywords such as "Go on," "Excellent," "I like it," "And then" are incentives to keep the other party talking
- Negotiators who want to put the other party down use expressions such as "Are you happy now," "Don't make me laugh," "Don't be ridiculous," "Needless to say"
- What is important in a negotiation process is not so much what the speaker is saying or what he/she thinks, but what the other party thinks the speaker is saying

Often tactics are used in negotiations to take the other party to yield to demands. Some of these are making threats, offering insults, bluffing, using intimidation, divide and rule, using leading questions, making emotional appeals, and testing the boundaries. Some of these can be countered by helpful behaviors including emphasizing results, encouraging and applauding, avoiding a win-lose situation, and giving openings for saving face.

Negotiation Schedule

Agenda should be set so as to be able to influence the meeting. A written schedule of times for briefings and rehearsal tactics should be prepared. Negotiations should not run longer than two hours; keep the clock where everyone can see. You should ask for a break to consider any new proposals.

Closing negotiations

You will know that negotiations have finished when there is success on both sides, as each party achieved its own critical objectives and is satisfied. If there are irreconcilable differences or one party has had to capitulate then the negotiations can be considered a failure. Reasons for such an outcome include poor preparation, wrong intentions, greed, indecisions, and emotional responses.

When negotiations are successfully concluded then the agreements should be summarized and reviewed, parties thank each other and leave the room open for further negotiations maintaining their relationship.

To further improve your own negotiating competence, you should reflect on your experience in terms of what went well, what went wrong, and what you would do differently in the future.[15]

Conflict Management

One of the core abilities of today's leader is conflict avoidance and management. Problems and conflicts arise daily in a leader's work. How effectively these conflicts are managed, will to a great extent influence the overall performance of the organization.

Conflicts are destructive when they consume so much of people's energy that work is affected. They can be so vicious and violent that they may lead to the destruction or neutralization

---

[15] Wilcox, L. Effective negotiation skills. Harvard University. Retrieved from www.chidlrenhospital.org/.

of one party or the other. Conflicts within an organization can have a destructive effect as they can lead to conservatism and conformity, high turnover of staff and absenteeism, distortion of information, and duplication of efforts.

Some conflicts may be good if they lead to constructive end, energize and motivate people, and get us the best idea. Resolution of such conflicts can lead to better relationship, increased problem-solving capacity, improved creativity, and increased productivity.

As a public health leader you would want to identify a conflict early and determine its causes. Causes of conflicts could be categorized as:[16]

1. *Instrumental conflicts* that concern goals, means, procedures, and structures.
2. *Conflicts of interest* that concern the distribution of means such as money, time, staff, and space, or concern factors that are important for distribution of these means such as importance, ownership, competence, and expertise; aspects of relationships including loyalty.
3. *Personal conflicts* are about question of identity and self-image, and important aspects in relationships including loyalty, breach of confidence, and lack of respect or betrayal of friendship. It is important to identify the source and cause of the conflict to identify ways to resolve it.

It is important that conflicts are managed, otherwise they may escalate and lead to destructive outcomes. There are several ways in which conflicts are resolved.[17]

1. In order to avoid conflicts, people may agree to superficial consensus. However, underlying causes of conflict may persist and lead to more serious conflict later on.

[16] International Federation of University Women. (2001). Workshop on conflict resolution. Prepared by Judy Kent and Ann Towen. Retrieved from www.ifwu.org/.
[17] Adams, B. (2001). *Everything leadership book*. Retrieved from www. everything.com/.

2. The two parties may fight to finish; one would emerge as victor and another as vanquished. This may lead to hidden resentments among those defeated and can give rise to another conflict later.

3. The two parties may negotiate and agree to a compromise in the spirit of give and take.

4. They may collaborate in seeking to find a win-win solution following the six steps process (see Box 11.6).

Box 11.6: *Six Steps to Managing Conflicts in a Collaborative Process*

1. *Clarify*: What is the conflict? Team members gather information and views of other team members on the nature of the conflict. A dialogue should continue until all point of views are understood.

2. Agree on the *common objectives*: Team members should try to find common objectives and preferred outcomes. It is important to find the common ground that is acceptable to all.

3. *Options*: Team members discuss their ideas with the other team members. They collect suggestions and explore options.

4. *Remove barriers*: What are the barriers? What would happen if barriers were removed? Team members discuss things that can be changed and agree on things that cannot be changed. They should systematically try to remove barriers, one at a time.

5. Agree on what best *meet the needs* of both parties, the solution that is most acceptable.

6. *Acknowledge*: The win-win solution should be recognized, credit should be given where possible.

Source: Adams Bob, 2001.[17]

The six steps require careful problem-solving approach. The win-win approach means that the leader and team members use positive and not negative action. In groups, the participants identify positive action at every step in problem solving.

Stephen R. Covey takes this approach to a much higher level in his book *The 3rd Alternative: Solving Life's Most Difficult Problems*.[18] We had briefly discussed it in Chapter Five. He argues that the attitude of "my team" or "my idea" versus "your

---

[18] Covey, S. R. (2011). *The 3rd alternative. Solving life's most difficult problems*. UK: Simon & Schuster.

team" or "your idea" is a self-defeating and destructive attitude. Instead of compromise, we should be open to another, third alternative which, is a whole new approach leading to a superior outcome that both parties to a conflict have not yet seen. The third alternative transcends beyond "your way" or "my way" to a higher and better way—one that allows both parties to emerge from conflict to a far better place than either had envisioned. With the third alternative, nobody has to give up anything and everyone wins.

Such an approach to seeking the third alternative begins with a question: May be we can come up with a better solution than either of us had in mind. Would you be willing to look for third alternative we have not even thought of yet? If both parties agree to this approach, then Covey offers a four-step paradigm:

1. I see myself: I have to see myself as a creative, self-aware human being. I should be willing to challenge my own assumptions and be willing for creative engagement with other people.
2. I see you: I accept the other, care for him, and have authentic respect.
3. I seek you out: I need to understand you, have a broad inclusive view of the problem and see conflict not as a problem but as an opportunity. This requires empathetic listening. He recommends "talking stick" approach where the other person must express in his/her own words what the first person has said and seek agreement on that understanding before speaking himself. The talking stick then passes to the first person who should then repeat the same process.
4. I synergize you: The process of synergy requires the following: (1) Define criteria of success: Together both parties need to define what would look better, (2) Create the third alternative: Start experimenting with ideas that will meet the criteria for success including brainstorming new frameworks, turning thinking upside down and, in short, engaging in adventurous open-ended thinking, (3) Arrive at synergy: A creative answer has been found that everyone can embrace.

Unless specifically sought, the third alternative does not automatically emerge. For instance, by the early 1960s, malaria had been contained with the use of extensive Dichloro Diphenyl Trichloroethane (DDT) spray. However, DDT leached out into fields and water streams.[19] Worldwide action followed. This led to resurgence of malaria. Only by the late 1990s, comprehensive solution to the problem was sought in terms of a mix of approaches combining vaccines, insecticide impregnated bed-nets, early detection and treatment, careful use of DDT sprays, and mosquito control. These had begun to yield results as discussed in Chapter One.

Communications

Effective communication is another leadership skill that can be learned in order to overcome the many barriers that exist. As we discussed earlier, listening is a skill usually taken for granted. Many leaders believe that they get what they want through talking. Many successful leaders, however, spend more time listening than talking. When they talk, they ask questions in order to learn more.

Leaders have the responsibility to communicate effectively with the people whom they lead. To be effective in this, they must transmit their messages in a way that ensures the listeners understand the intent of the message. Similarly, the listeners need to interpret the messages from the leader as intended.

Developing good communication skills is challenging. Leaders will be more effective if they strive to transmit messages clearly and listen carefully to what others have to say. Communication involves a sender of the message and a receiver. The communication model shows how communication between a sender and a receiver can be distorted by different factors. The model also presents some strategies for overcoming the distortions.

[19] As highlighted by environmentalist Rachel Carson in her famous book Silent Spring, which facilitated the ban of the pesticide DDT in 1972 in the US.

The following mistakes are often made during communication. The mistakes are usually through many elements that one as communicators assume or take for granted.

A Few Basics of Communicating Effectively

Often, the message that the sender wants to communicate is NOT the message that is understood by the receiver. This is because of distorting factors pertaining to the sender and those pertaining to the receiver. Any time a person begins speaking (the sender), the message is influenced by the speaker's beliefs, attitudes, and knowledge. The same factors influence the way the receiver interprets the message.

In addition, the message can be distorted by

- The speaker's tone of voice
- Choice of words
- Physical condition
- Personal feelings toward the receiver
- The environment and time of day when the communication is taking place

At the other end of the transmission is a set of distorting factors that affect how the message is received:

- The level of interest
- Personal feelings toward the sender
- Position/status of sender
- Physical conditions
- Demands on time

Communication can be improved by adopting strategies for reducing or eliminating distortions such as:

- Using both open and close-ended questions and following up with probing questions to help clarify the meaning

- Using multiple communication channels to verify the message and its meaning
- Using simple language when speaking
- Paraphrasing what has been said to ensure understanding

Effective Public Speaking

Good public speaking is a mark of effective leaders especially those hoping to inspire others. It accomplishes two of the main functions of leaders: speak comfortably and effectively to groups and, with this, attract people to their ideas.

Public speaking is a common source of stress for everyone. But if we want to be leaders or achieve anything meaningful in our lives, we need to speak to groups, large and small, to be successful.

The truth about public speaking, however, is *it does not have to be stressful*! If you correctly understand the hidden causes of public-speaking stress, and if you keep just a few key principles in mind, speaking in public will soon become an invigorating and satisfying experience for you. The primary reason is that speakers are afraid of looking foolish in front of other people. The way to overcome this fear is through preparation, a safety net, and a positive attitude toward the audience.

The basics of public speaking[20]

Winston Churchill famously said: "For every minute of speaking I spend at least one hour of preparation."

> *Public speaking requires preparation and practice, the same as in other areas of life. If you don't prepare and practice it, you can't expect to deliver a speech as well as you might.*[21]

---

[20] Youthspeak. The Australian Speak Easy Association. Retrieved fromwww.639120.toastmastersclubs.org/BetterSpeaker.html (accessed on April 7, 2014).
[21] Ibid.

1. Preparations

   - Prepare early and not at the last minute.
   - Public speaking requires preparation in the same way an athlete requires preparation for a sporting contest. You have to practice just like most things in life.
   - A speech is the developing of an idea, opinion, and belief.
   - Select a topic you are familiar with or have strong thoughts on.
   - Always carry a pencil and paper with you and jot thoughts down when they come to you, i.e., brainstorming. You can jot down the main points of a good speech in moments.
   - Write the speech out fully to get a feel and timing.
   - Fine-tune and sort out what is necessary and unnecessary.
   - Practice the speech on a tape. Listen back, correct, and time it.
   - Have the speech prepared at least a few days prior to presenting it. Listen to your speech a couple of times a day leading up to the day of delivering it.
   - Condense notes into keywords. It is a speech, not a reading, spaced out on small cards. If using cards, remember to number them according to the sequence the points appear in your speech.
   - Practice your speech often. Put A4 faces on a wall to simulate an audience.
   - Your last rehearsal should be as close as possible to speech delivery time.

2. Speech Structures

   - There are three types of speeches: to inform; to persuade, inspire, or motivate; and to entertain.
   - A speech should always have an opening, a body, and a closing. You tell them what you are going to tell them (opening), you tell them (body), and you tell them what you told them (closing).

o Opening: Right from the outset it must be clear what the purpose of the speech is. It may include attention grabbers in the form of some statistics or an anecdote or personal experience, etc.

o Body: You can break the body into points. It is better to limit the main points to three or four with sub-points for each main point.

o Closing: The closing should include a brief summary and a memorable statement.

3. Make "Butterflies" Fly in Formation (Or take steps to feel confident and settle nerves) Before your presentation, acclimatize yourself to the room and where you will be speaking.

- Dress well and appropriate to the audience and occasion.
- Get to know your audience. Greet them as they arrive. It is easier to speak to friends than strangers.
- Have your speech thoroughly prepared. Know it backwards.
- Make sure that the preparation includes that it will be obvious to the audience what your one main message is. They have to be able to walk away knowing what it was.
- Memorize your opening.
- Don't apologize for your speech or for your nerves. The audience is hoping you succeed. Just have the intention of doing your best.
- Take yourself seriously if you want your audience to. Speak with conviction, enthusiasm, and sincerity.

4. What Audiences Like

- If the speaker is prepared, committed, comfortable (confident and not fidgety), and interesting
- Voice: Be yourself and include vocal variety, i.e., volume, pace, tone, and pausing

- Eye contact: Engage the members of your audience with eye contact
- Hands: Hand gestures should match the spoken words
- Uhms and ahs: It's almost impossible to eliminate them altogether but too many are distracting

The basics of impromptu public speaking[22]

Impromptu speaking is a speech without any planning or preparation. It is a speech with little or no notice, for example, when you are called upon, unexpectedly, to offer your opinion or provide instructions (see Box 11.7).

Box 11.7: Impromptu *Public Speaking*

Leaders are expected to be called upon to speak with no notice especially if they are known to be good speakers or an expert in a subject.

The advantage of speaking from the cuff is that the action is instant and should be done with no hesitation. It is important, at this stage, to be in control of any panic that may arise and get on to think of what to say immediately.

It is important, too, to remember to introduce yourself first and give your credentials so as to win the confidence of your audience: in what capacity are you saying what you want to say. The same rules apply to when you are standing up to present a speech that was prepared in advance.

Source: Authors.

Have the attitude that it's a wonderful opportunity rather than "why me!" The best way to be able to respond effectively to an unexpected request such as this is to practice like most things in life. You can always practice by yourself, for example, look around you and speak to yourself for 60 seconds on the first noun you see written.

[22] Adapted from several sources: http://nustm.wordpress.com/ 2006/12/09/thinking-on-your-feet-a-guide-to-impromptu-speaking/; http://sixminutes.dlugan.com/how-to-impromptu-speech/; http://webuser. bus.umich.edu/Organizations/umbstoastmasters/file/members/prepare/ ImpromtuSpeakingHints.pdf (accessed on April 7, 2014).

What to do when you are asked to give an Impromptu Speech?
Make sure you understand the question and you answer it. For
clarity, you can ask for the question to be repeated.

- Appear confident. Don't be rushed, be calm, and try to
  emulate a confident person
- Rise with confidence
- Organize your thoughts. Take a moment to determine your
  answer, i.e., the main point(s) of your answer, then support
  this view with two or three reasons
- Structure the mini-speech, i.e., by having an opening, body,
  and closing
- Have a strong closing

You may use any of the following methods:

1. P.R.E.P. Method

   a. State your *Point* of view.
   b. Give *Reason* for the point of view.
   c. *Explain* how the point of view came about. Give your
      experience or other real-life experience if possible.
   d. Summarize what you said and repeat the *Point* of view.

2. PPF (Past, Present, Future) Method

   a. Start with "There was a time when…"
   b. Develop with "But now we find that…"
   c. Close with "In the future I expect…"

3. The Three Important Things Method

   a. Start with "There are three important things that come
      to my mind about this subject…" This hopefully gives
      you a good start and you can start to think of some
      things while you are saying it. If you think of one thing,
      you have something to go on with and hopefully other
      thoughts will happen along the way. If they don't, just
      say you forgot what they were very confidently.

4. The Pros/Cons Method

    a. Start with "There are two sides to this argument..." and continue on or start with "I firmly believe that... but on the other hand."

5. The Six-Question Method

    a. Ask yourself: "Who, What, When, Why, Where, and How," as you are speaking to jog your memory.

Visual aids

Visual aids help to divert attention from the speaker. In a long presentation, this is a good thing for both the speaker and audience.

- *They increase understanding.* Learning occurs more through watching than listening.
- *Saves time.* One picture is worth 1,000 words. People process information faster when provided visually rather than verbally.
- *Information is retained.* Surveys show that people can digest and retain information from what they read, hear, and see in the following proportions:

    1. *Promotes attentiveness.* People think faster than they speak, so minds can wander when you are speaking. Visuals help the audience to maintain focus on your message.

    2. *Interesting/memorable.* Visuals add variety to a presentation and this makes it more interesting and memorable.

    3. *Helps the presenter control nerves.* Nervous energy is spent without distracting the audience with fidgety actions such as pacing, rocking, swaying, and playing with notes.

Gestures

Gestures are the use of hands and arms to illustrate your words. There are four main groups of gestures as given below in Table 11.1:

Table 11.1: *Gestures for Effective Public Speaking*

1	Descriptive	Used to clarify or enhance. They help visualize size, weight, shape, location, function, direction, etc.
2	Emphatic	Moving forward a clenched fist suggests strong feelings, such as anger or determination
		• Hit your fist into your open palm to show importance or urgency • A folding of arms illustrates strength and determination • Clasping your hands together in front of your chest conveys unity • A forefinger pointed towards the ceiling means listen to me • Show your clenched fist to urge action
3	Suggestive	These are symbols of ideas or emotions
		• An open palm suggests giving or receiving • A shrug of the shoulders indicates ignorance, perplexity, or irony • Comparison and contrast can be illustrated by either moving hands in unison or in opposite directions
4	Prompting	These prompt or evoke a desired response from the audience. If you want your listeners to raise their hand, applaud, or perform some action, you'll enhance the response by doing it yourself as an example.

Source: HYPERLINK "http://www.toastmasters.org/201-gestures"www.toastmasters.org/201-gestures. Accessed on June 16, 2014

Facial Expression

Your face communicates your attitude, feelings, and emotions. Don't be scared to look angry, disappointed, to smile, etc. In particular, smile. Smiling conveys warmth and sincerity and makes the audience more receptive to what you are saying.

Mind maps: A tool for speech preparation

Mind mapping is a fairly recent phenomenon for recording, storing, and retrieving ideas in the most efficient and memorable manner. Tony Buzan has written many books on this subject. In the book on mind mapping,[23] Joyce Wycoff devotes a chapter to the use of mind maps for preparing speeches. Mind mapping is a way of note-taking and note-making. In regard to preparing a speech it is a way of note-making, i.e., a way of putting together the notes to be used for a speech. The entire map will be on one piece of paper. It is regarded as extremely useful when having to quickly prepare a speech.

How a mind map is drawn?

- Only a keyword or keywords are used. Only nouns or verbs should be used.
- Purpose of the speech is at the center: This should stand out and be a constant reminder to the speaker.
- Branches indicating main points flow out from the center.
- Sub-branches indicating sub-points fork out from the end of the branches.
- The keyword(s) of the points are written along the branch.
- Branches should be in one color and sub-branches should be in another. This enables the speaker to quickly differentiate between them.
- Opening and Closing "branches" can be neighbors to further remind the speaker of the purpose of the speech because the keywords for each should match up.
- Symbols familiar to the speaker can be used on the map to indicate such things as a handout to be given out now, or an overhead to explain further information which should be shown now, etc.
- Main branches should be numbered to show an order.
- Writing should be extremely legible.

Advantages

- The speech notes are contained on one piece of paper/card.

[23] Wycoff, J. (1991). *Mind mapping: Your personal guide to exploring creativity and problem solving*. New York: Berkley Books.

- The purpose of the speech stands out and is a constant reminder to the speaker.
- Only keywords are used; this assists in the preparation as the speech is not required to be remembered in "parrot-fashion." This makes the preparation more effective.
- Useful technique for a quickly prepared speech, e.g., to thank a speaker at a function. The map can be drawn in no particular sequence and "on the run."
- The speaker can maintain eye contact with the audience rather than having to look at lengthy notes (assumes notes of other methods are not in point form).

Disadvantages

- Opening and closing cannot be written word for word. So, perhaps the opening can be written word for word above the map and the closing written word for word below the map, i.e., still on the same piece of paper.

Twelve

Collaboration and Partnership

*We must be led by those who have mastery of the skills to
mobilize, coordinate, and direct broad collaborative actions
within the complex public health system...these skills
need constant refinement and honing.*

—Institute of Medicine[1]

What Is Collaboration?

Improving public health requires collaborative approach among
many actors and sectors. Therefore, public health leaders need to
cultivate leadership competencies to foster effective collaboration
with appropriate actions to build successful partnerships. In this
chapter we will:

- Describe alternative strategies for collaboration and partnership among organizations focused on public health goals
- Discuss ways to use collaborative methods for achieving
  organizational and community health goals
- Present strategies to motivate others for collaborative
  problem-solving, decision-making, and evaluation

Collaboration is defined as "exchanging information and sharing or pooling resources for mutual benefit to achieve a common

---

[1] Institute of Medicine (IOM). (2002). Future of the public's health in
the 21st century. Washington, D.C., USA: National Academies Press.

purpose."[2] Thus, collaboration goes beyond communication, cooperation, or coordination.[3] It means to "work together." It is a mutually beneficial relationship between two or more parties to achieve common purpose or goals by sharing responsibility, authority, and accountability for achieving results. It goes beyond sharing information or cooperating or coordinating to achieve each party's own goals. Thus, a common purpose or goals derived from a shared vision is fundamental to any collaboration.

Why Collaboration?

Traditionally, society has looked to the health sector to deal with its concerns about health and disease. Certainly, suboptimal distribution of health care—not delivering care to those who most need it—is one of the social determinants of health, or ill-health, in this case. But the high burden of illness responsible for appalling premature loss of life arises in large part because of the conditions in which people are born, grow, live, work, and age.[4]

Therefore, most public health problems are complex. These types of problems require many sectors to "own" the solution for it to be successfully implemented, utilizing a systems approach with diverse inputs and multiple perspectives. Many of the factors which determine health outcomes rest outside the health system. Primary prevention, a central goal of public health, requires productive relationship outside the health sector. For instance, tobacco use is responsible for one in 10 global deaths. It affects population health, the economy, the environment, and society. Efforts to prevent and control the global tobacco epidemic include

---

[2] Turning Point Leadership Development Collaborative Leadership. Retrieved from www.collaborativeleadership.org/.

[3] Chrislip, D. D. (2002). *The collaborative leadership field book*. San Francisco: Jossey-Baas.

[4] CSDH. (2008). *Closing the gap in a generation: Health equity through action on the social determinants of health. Final Report of the Commission on Social Determinants of Health*. Geneva: WHO.

population level education, legal and policy changes on use of tobacco, the ethical dimensions of tobacco control policies, and the activities of the tobacco industry and its allies.

> Who is responsible for health? Almost all sectors have more or less influence on health.

Action on the social determinants of health must involve the whole of government, civil society and local communities, business, global forums, and international agencies. Policies and programs must embrace all the key sectors of the society, not just the health sector. However, health sector can champion a "social determinants of health" approach at the highest level of society, it can demonstrate effectiveness through good practice, and it can support other ministries in creating policies that promote health equity. All this requires collaboration with other sectors and actors.

Thus, public health has many issues which cannot be resolved by technical expertise or routine behavior. Instead, it requires innovation and fostering change which, in turn, requires new learning about such adaptive behaviors.[5] To bring about such adaptive behavior, many agencies need to come together.

Building Collaborative Relationship with Other Sectors

As mentioned earlier, all sectors affect health albeit to a varying degree. To illustrate:

• A comprehensive approach to early child development would be critical for health later on.

---

[5] Heifetz, R., & Linsky, M. (2002). *Leadership on the Line. Staying alive through the dangers of leading.* Boston, USA: Harvard Business School Publishing.

- The daily conditions in which people live have a strong influence on health equity. Access to quality housing, shelter, clean water, and sanitation are human rights and basic needs for healthy living.
- Urban planning can promote healthy and safe behaviors equitably, through investment in active transport, retail planning to manage access to unhealthy foods, and through good environmental design and regulatory controls, including control of the number of alcohol outlets.

Strategies for such collaboration between sectors or among multiple sectors could be

- Coordinating activities and services
- Sectors other than health to include appropriate health education and services
- Public health sector to include education and services for other sectors such as water and sanitation
- Sharing information to improve population health
- Collaborating to improve health promotion and protection
- Collaborating to plan for future health system development

The implementation of these strategies can be illustrated through collaboration between medicine and public health synergies, as discussed in the following paragraphs.

The structural foundations that can be used in the collaborations include:

- Forming coalitions
- Entering into contractual agreements
- Designing appropriate administration/management systems
- Constituting advisory bodies
- Establishing intra-organizational platforms

In these collaborations, professionals continue to work within their own organization while, at the same time, transcending the boundaries of that organization to link up with professionals and organizations in other sectors.

Collaboration between Medicine and Public Health

To begin with, public health leaders need to build synergistic collaboration with medicine.[6] Because of health transition from communicable diseases to NCDs and from mortality reduction focus to morbidity reduction and enhancing wellness, the medical and public health sectors are becoming increasingly dependent on one another in achieving their missions. Although a specific collaboration may be designed to address a particular health problem, a set of common and generally applicable strategies have emerged from analysis of several experiences. One aspect of such a framework focuses on ways that professionals and organizations in medicine and public health—and often other partners in the community as well—combine their resources and skills, and the benefits that can be achieved by doing so. These reinforcing combinations provide "synergies" between the two sectors in health. Experience shows that these synergies could involve virtually every type of professional and organization in the two health sectors. They encompass all domains of medicine and public health—practice, policy, education, and research—and they occur at local, state, and national levels.

There are many assets that these two sectors bring to collaborative endeavors:

- Technical, scientific, and pedagogic expertise
- Methodological tools
- Individual-level services and population-based strategies
- Administration and management skills
- Legal and regulatory authority
- Convening power
- Influence with peers, policymakers, and the public
- Data and information systems
- Buildings and space
- Financial support

[6] Lasker, R. D., & The Committee on Medicine and Public Health. (1997). *Medicine and public health: The power of collaboration.* New York: New York Academy of Medicine.

These assets are valuable in and of themselves. But, by combining them in certain ways, the individual partners in the collaboration are able to transcend their own limitations and achieve additional benefits that are important to their patients, their populations, and themselves.

The synergistic relationship between the two can be operationalized in a mix of the following ways:

1. **Improve health care by coordinating services for individuals** through providing medical care and addressing determinants of health that go beyond medical care. These objectives can be achieved by combining clinical services with one or more of the following:

   a. *Wraparound services* that overcome logistical, cultural, and social barriers to care

   b. *Counseling and educational services* directed at personal risk behaviors

   c. The *management of particular health problems* and the use of health services

   d. *Outreach services,* such as home visits, that assure the delivery of needed care and that promote compliance with complex treatment programs

   e. *Case management services* that identify health-related needs of individuals, link individuals with health professionals and programs in the community, and coordinate care

   f. *Social services* that address socioeconomic determinants of health

2. **Improve access to care by establishing frameworks** to provide universal care by overcoming the logistical, financial, and legal barriers that medical practitioners face in delivering such care through collaborative activities that bring them together with one or more of the following:

   a. *Administrative services* to plan and coordinate the effort

   b. *Convenient sites* to provide clinical care

c. *Ancillary staff,* supplies, and services (such as lab, X-ray, pharmacy, etc.)
d. *Screening programs* to identify patients eligible for care
e. *Referral mechanisms* to link patients with appropriate practitioners
f. Offering *immunity from liability* for medical malpractice

3. **Apply a population perspective** to medical practice to improve the quality and cost-effectiveness of clinical care, as well as to ensure the economic viability of medical professionals and institutions. These collaborations may combine medical care for individuals with one or more of the following:

a. *Population-based information,* such as data about the prevalent health problems and health risks for a particular population; the underlying causes of health problems; the risks, benefits, and costs of various approaches to diagnosis and treatment; and health resources available in a geographic area
b. *Population-based strategies,* such as community-wide screening, outreach, and case finding
c. *Population-based analytic tools,* such as practice-based risk assessment, cost-effectiveness analysis, and the measurement and evaluation of performance

4. **Use clinical practice to identify and address community-wide goals** of public health through interactions that combine clinicians' access to and influence with individuals with one or more of the following:

a. *Community-wide frameworks* for collecting health-related information
b. *Population-based strategies* to facilitate the delivery of clinical services in mainstream medical practices
c. *Community programs* to address health risks in the social and physical environment

5. **Strengthen health promotion and health protection** through mobilizing community campaigns by working together on population-based strategies, professionals and institutions in medicine and public health to address underlying causes of some of the most pressing health problems, such as tobacco use, poor diet, inactivity, injuries, and violence, and strengthen essential functions of public health. They do so by bringing together two or more of the following non-clinical resources' influence with peers, policymakers, and the public:

   a. Legal authority
   b. Convening power
   c. Information
   d. Scientific and technical expertise
   e. Advocacy, lobbying, and public relations skills

6. **Shape the future direction of the health system by collaborating around policy, training, and research** by influencing health system policy, by educating the future generation of health professionals, or by expanding the knowledge base that supports health professionals' work. These are based on combinations of two or more of the following skills and resources:

   a. Influence with peers, policymakers, and the public
   b. Practical experience
   c. Scientific expertise
   d. Pedagogical skills

Collaborative Leadership

Collaborative leadership needs to be used to foster collaboration for achieving policies, programs, and systems change to improve public health.

A collaborative leader safeguards and promotes the collaborative process that includes activities and relationships in which a group and its members engage in collaboration. It is the type of leadership shown by a group that is "working together" to achieve common purpose by strategically addressing agreed-upon issues.[7] Collaborative leadership requires all the attributes and competencies of public health leadership. These include creating shared vision and values, assessing the vision–reality gap by analyzing environment, developing people and self-reflection. However, as collaboration will involve people and organizations with diverse perspectives and cultures, building trust and sharing power and influence become critical. Building trust comes from creating safe places for developing shared vision, purpose, goals and action. It requires higher level of negotiation, conflict management, and communication capability.

Collaborative leadership requires new notions of power. Often it is thought that when power is shared, the person sharing it will have less power. However, once common vision, purpose, and values are firmly established, the more power is shared, the more there is to use. It utilizes supportive and inclusive methods to ensure that all people affected by a decision are part of the change process. Therefore, sharing power and influence develops the synergy of people, organizations, and communities to accomplish a shared vision.

Sometimes, collaborative leadership is considered akin to "servant leader" as one who values the common cause much higher than self through an attitude of service. Such a leader is an "active listener," promotes a sense of community and keeps focus on what is best for the community or group versus individual self-interest.

Thus, collaborative leadership is the skillful and vision-oriented leadership of people and relationships by building structures and processes to support and sustain productive relationships over time.[8]

---

[7] Turning Point Leadership Development Collaborative Leadership. Retrieved from www.collaborativeleadership.org/.

[8] Hank, R. (2009). *Collaborative leadership: Developing effective partnerships for communities and schools*. California, USA: Corwin Press.

Focuses for Collaboration

Ad hoc collaborations may be organized around a specific issue or event. But for more durable collaborations with some sustainability, two focuses can be used: (1) community or regionally-based multi-stakeholder collaboration or (2) local health or government-based in which inter-organizational or inter-institutional collaboration takes place.

Community-Based Multi-Stakeholder Collaboration

Arising out of concern to create healthy communities, collaborative partnerships involving many sectors and organizations can be an important strategy for improving public health. Therefore, community collaboration is a cornerstone of public health practice. Successful community collaboration not only builds skills and capacity within the community but involves them in making decisions and taking actions, which are fundamental to improving health.

There are various levels of community collaboration moving beyond information dissemination, cooperation, or coordination. It involves joint planning and actions, financial contributions from the community, and ultimately community guiding the collective action, with the local health system as a partner. Such collaboration should stem from the needs, expectations, and desires of the community.[9] However, community can be defined in many ways such as:

- People: Socioeconomic, demography, health status, risk profile, cultural, and ethnic characteristics
- Location: Geography
- Connectors: Shared values, interest, or communication patterns

[9] Minnesota Department of Health. Community engagement. Retrieved from www.health.state.mn.us/communityeng/.

- Power relationships: Formal and informal lines of authority, influence, and resource flows

Typically three stages in engendering community collaboration can be seen:

1. Coming together: Sharing the dialogue, building trust and safe spaces for people to think, debating, reflecting upon and making decisions
2. Moving forward: Converting dialogue into activity, reaching out beyond the original planning group, and creating partnerships to implement programs and providing services
3. Sustaining momentum: Building structures, developing and sustaining leadership, assessing and improving programs, measuring change, and communicating results

Government public health agencies must find ways to improve communication and openness with the public to maintain and increase their trustworthiness. (Institute of Medicine, USA Healthy Communities, 1996)

For active collective action by the community, there is a need for professionals with public health institutions to understand that communities can deal with complex issues, and that people interrelate various community concerns. And that they can be mobilized to address their concerns with appropriate technical support. For a public health leader to build community collaboration, the following steps will be important for the above three stages:

- *Coming together*: Identify the community in which collaboration is to be built and clarifying its purpose; become knowledgeable about its socioeconomic conditions, politics, norms and values, health practices; establish relationships, build trust, and work with formal and informal community leaders
- *Moving forward*: Partnering with the community to create changes and improve health; identifying and mobilizing the community assets; developing capacities and resources for community health decisions and action

- *Sustaining momentum*: Release control to the community; commit to the activities for the long term

A community balanced scorecard has been developed[10] for generating community-focused collaboration (see Table 12.1).

Table 12.1: *Community Balanced Scorecard*

Balanced Scorecard Perspectives		Community Balanced Scorecard
Financial performance	→	Improve community health/quality of life outcome
Customer	→	Community implementation including investigations, enforcements, health promotion, and health services
Internal business processes	→	Community capabilities, processes and learning-policies and plans, evaluation, health status monitoring, and research
Learning and growth	→	Community assets including engaged community members, public health partners, and competent health workforce

Source: Paul, 2009. [11]

A "Healthy Living" theme, for instance, may focus on healthy eating, better exercise, reduced smoking and substance abuse, water and sanitation, and chronic disease prevention, early detection, and management. For this purpose partners, including health department, schools, parks, environment, nutrition, and so on, would need to collaborate. The collaborative process involves: creating a shared vision for desired outcome.

- Developing performance measures
- Developing strategies for each outcome
- Forming teams for each outcome
- Creating a "community results compact"
- Implementing strategies

[10] Paul, E. (2009). *Community balanced score cards for strategic performance management.* Presentation at ASPA Annual Conference, Florida, March 2005. Retrieved from www.RTMteam.net/.
[11] Ibid.

A feedback cycle from the gap between desired and current realities as well as the monitoring and evaluation system would help steer this process.

Local Public Health System Partnerships

National public health strategies operate within the broader health system, interacting and interdependent with all aspects of health care and health service delivery systems. Within the health system these involve a complex interplay of the range of activities which span from specialist clinical services to universal public health prevention and protection programs; their focus may range from the individual through to the entire population and their interventions may target the settings in which health services are provided or where people live. They may seek to modify health behavior and/or health care seeking behavior.

Thus, partnerships to improve public health may be initiated by the local public health agency. In this case, the partnerships are generally formed with other government agencies, hospitals, medical practices, or clinics. Sometimes, community-based organizations or direct citizen participation could be elicited.

The motive for forming partnerships could arise from the need to address a specific health problem or availability of finances, or government mandates.[12] The types of health problems that may be successfully addressed include maternal and child health, NCD prevention, and control of epidemics or emergencies. Sometimes such partnerships may be limited to specific collaboration for conducting community health events or disseminating information to the community. However, more complex form of partnerships would include joint-action planning and goal setting which are more difficult to engender.

The partnership success is predicated on many factors depending upon context, purpose, and content of partnerships and is,

---

[12] Zahner, S. J. (2005). Local public health system partnerships. *Public Health Reports, 120,* 76–83.

therefore, difficult to generalize. A mix of factors has been linked to successful local health system partnerships. These include having a budget, partners making financial contributions, and having a broad array of partners involved for a longer duration and more capacity to implement. Some other studies have identified as having a clear vision, conducting action planning, developing and supporting leadership, having systems for evaluation, and availability of necessary human and financial resources for successful local health partnerships.

Strategies for Successful Partnerships

For sustained collaborations, partnerships need to be established. However, partnerships are not always successful, and those that are, usually have difficult weather and stormy periods.[13] While collaborations fail for a variety of reasons, it is fair to say that most problems revolve around the relationships of the partners involved. Cross-sectoral collaborations bring together a broad range of individuals and organizations, not only in medicine and public health, but often from other sectors in the community as well. Many of these partners are separated by deep cultural differences; some are competitors; few have any history of working together. Viewed in this context, there would seem to be daunting barriers to getting potential partners to acknowledge their mutual interests in collaboration, let alone to establishing working relationships that allow them to put their ideas into action.

Research shows that for partnerships to succeed, partners must perceive a compelling *need* to work with professionals or organizations in other sectors and be *willing* to do so. To some extent, the willingness to participate in a collaborative enterprise depends on whether potential partners give it a high priority. That decision, in turn, relates to whether the expected benefits

---

[13] Lasker, R. D. (1997). *Medicine and public health: The power of collaboration.*

appear to be worth the investment and commitment, and whether the project is likely to be feasible and well-run. Willingness to participate also hinges on relationship issues. Unless potential partners have confidence and trust in the leaders of the enterprise and the other participants, they are unlikely to get involved in a meaningful way. If confidence and trust dissipate after the project gets started, it is difficult, if not impossible, to sustain a collaborative partnership.

Therefore, generally it is believed that for successful partnerships, partners should have a shared vision and interest in addressing common goals.[14] The relationship needs to be built around individual leaders and what partners know of each other. Finally, partnership benefits should exceed costs.

However, an alternative view has also emerged which holds that such stringent conditions may not be necessary for successful partnerships. Such partnerships involve the right combinations of partners to achieve partnership objectives that are shaped around common or shared objectives but also contribute toward each partner's aims. As partnership progresses, individual relationships need to be supplemented by structured methodologies defining roles and structures of functioning. A partnership's success often depends on its evolution in terms of memberships, wider relationships, or its purpose.

For determinants of successful cross-sectoral partnerships, the following eight strategies gleaned from literature may be helpful to leaders who are considering engaging with or leading medicine and public health collaborations:

- Build on self-interests as well as health interests
- Involve a "boundary spanner," somebody outside the partnership, in the project
- Seek out influential backing and endorsements
- Don't expect other partners to be like you
- Be realistic

[14] Business Partners for Development. (2001). Putting partnering to work. Retrieved from www.oecd.org/dataoecd/14/58/2082379.pdf/.

- Pay attention to the process
- Ensure adequate infrastructure support
- Be "upfront" about competition and control issues

Leading Beyond the Walls: How High-Performance Organizations Build Alliances for Shared Success[15]

We know that effective partnerships can be achieved. In fact, there are many success stories. What is needed is for leaders of all sectors to take leadership responsibility beyond their own sectors or institutions, leading beyond the walls, so to say. They have to lead not only entire institutions and lead them to performance but at the same time, take community responsibility beyond the walls of their institutions (see Box 12.1).

Box 12.1: *Leadership without Walls: Challenges*

- Build strategic alliances with partners to upscale success
- Change the mind-set of leaders
- Get commitment of leaders to address the health problem as a whole
- Leaders should be willing to learn from different values of partners, accept, and respect them

Source: Hesselbein, Goldsmith, & Somerville, 1999.[16]

This is not easy. There is a need not only to address performance and personal dimensions but also a different mind-set. Each institution is like an instrument in an orchestra that plays its own part. But it is the score that dictates how each instrument plays its part to achieve the end result for the pleasure of the listeners. The community is the score. And only if each individual instrument contributes to the score is there music. Otherwise, there is only noise.

[15] Hesselbein, F., Goldsmith, M., & Somerville, I. (1999). *Leading beyond the walls.* New York: The Drucker Foundation.
[16] Ibid.

Leadership Roles

First, leaders must define the inside and outside of the organization by reference to core values and purpose, not by traditional boundaries. *Second*, they must build mechanisms for connection and commitment rooted in freedom of choice rather than relying on systems of coercion and control. *Third*, they must accept the fact that the exercise of true leadership is inversely proportional to the exercise of power. *Finally*, they must accept the fact that the trend toward partnerships will accelerate.

It is often easier to build and sustain partnerships at the frontline who deal with people. As we move away from the grassroots, partnerships become more difficult. Therefore, partnership champions and managers need to be created in each institution/sector.

Partnerships are built on the mind-set of mutual benefits. It is a deep inner commitment toward achieving win-win. To build a strong relationship between organizations, both sides must win. By attacking a problem from several angles, a mutually beneficial solution will, more often than not, become apparent from both sides. However, having the right mind-set is only the first stage. Leaders will also need special skills set especially the skills of communication and synergy.

Communicating effectively requires that you first understand the other party's view before you try to explain your own. Once you understand other people's point of view, you must then get them to understand yours. If you fail to do this, the richness of your ideas will remain untapped. It is only through sharing of ideas that the next piece of puzzle can be put in place: Synergy!

Synergy is finding the third way that is better than the way either of us could come up with independently. The steps in creating synergy are

- Identifying what both parties really want
- Creating alternatives that lead to betterment of all organizations
- Determining acceptable solutions for all parties

- Fostering a spirit of mutual benefit
- Building relationships

Leadership Skills

The following four abilities are vital skills for leaders beyond walls:

- The ability to design powerful relationships: Many contributing factors—religious beliefs, differing views, diverse participants, and cultures—affect a leader's probability of success in developing powerful relationships. Diversity can make it difficult to create or sustain cross-domain relationships. Successful, powerful relationships require the creation of new culture and sustainable structures unique to the needs of the relationship.
- The ability to create a systemic change: Leaders in future must be able to envision and lead systemic change. Leaders will have to establish shared expectations and set clear priorities for performance and results.
- The ability to develop comfort with risk while building trust: There is no better way to reduce risk than to build trust. Leading beyond the walls will require learning new rules of trust and going beyond the old earned trust. Earned trust is built over time and is entirely based on performance. It is important but insufficient to build partnerships. Leaders must learn to generate granted trust, the trust individuals need to create with others and to obtain early action and results while establishing earned trust over time.
- The ability to value diversity and source of contribution: While leaders would need to establish common ground, the commitment to address health problems, they also need to establish uncommon ground, the ground of diversity of different sectors. They would have to learn to employ diversity on behalf of the common commitments.

CASE STUDY 1: Partnering with Civil Society Organizations, Communities, People Living with HIV (PLWHIVs), and Private Sector in HIV/AIDS Programs

One of the characteristics of successful national HIV/AIDS prevention programs is active involvement of multiple sectors of the society including civil society, religious leaders, and NGOs in the response to AIDS. Therefore, partnership has emerged as a message that we should embrace, share, adapt, and build upon.

The primary role of the government is to pave the way so that all sectors of society can contribute to the response. No one organization can do things on its own and attain success in AIDS prevention, treatment, and care. For instance, health education alone cannot even breach the surface for public education on HIV/AIDS, and, similarly, the national education system on its own cannot have the desired impact. Providing care and treatment is also multifaceted requiring not only involvement of the public health facilities but also professional associations, social and behavioral scientists, private sector, and communities. Another aspect requiring partnerships is programs to eliminate the stigma and discrimination against PLHIVs. Such programs cannot attain success without collaboration with human rights institutions.

As mentioned earlier, it is well recognized that success will require working in partnership with communities, civil society, PLHIVs and vulnerable groups, and private sector. Each has complementary strengths. Governments have decision-making power, political will, and infrastructure while NGOs have access to people and grassroots-oriented approaches. PLHIVs and vulnerable groups have both the understanding of needs and how best to meet them. They are not only the recipients of services but are a significant resource themselves. The private sector can assist in making the drugs available at low cost, in ensuring that appropriate drug regimens are followed, and in workplace programs. Experience on these issues is growing. Distilling lessons from these experiences and sharing them may enhance the capacity of the programs for effective partnerships.

In this regard, strategic competencies include building strategic alliances with partners to upscale success. However, this will require a different mind-set. Leaders are not only responsible and accountable for the performance of their organizations, but more importantly, the commitment to address the HIV/AIDS epidemic as a whole. This will involve acceptance of the different partners' values, respect for these values, and willingness to learn what these values are. All of these require commitment, conviction, and dedication to the common cause. The basic issues that leaders need to address are how to

- create a common vision for sustained partnerships?
- delineate synergistic roles for each partner?
- build alliance competence among partners?
- create effective institutional structures for results-oriented partnerships?

CASE STUDY 2: Leadership Development to Strengthen Partnerships in Ethiopia[17]

In early 2002, Ethiopia mobilized more than 250 leaders at all levels of government and civil society to step up efforts to reduce the number of people contracting HIV/AIDS and improve treatment and care for those infected with the disease.

UNDP and the Ethiopian International Institute for Peace and Development conducted a seminar for top government

---

[17] UNDP Communications Office. (2002). Retrieved from www.undp.org/content/undp/en/home/ourwork/hiv-aids/Projects-initiatives/hiv-epidemic-ethiopia-case-study-transformational-change/.

executives, in early 2002, to launch the Leadership Development Program to slow the epidemic.

Ethiopia was hit hard by the deadly disease, with 2.1 million adults and children living with HIV, according to the Joint U.N. Programme on HIV/AIDS (UNAIDS). Over 6 percent of Ethiopians aged 15 to 49 were infected with HIV, and an estimated 120,000 Ethiopians died of AIDS in 2001. Despite its devastating impact, many Ethiopians remained unaware of the risks HIV/AIDS poses. A survey in 2000, for example, found that more than 60 percent of women aged 15 to 24 did not know that a person who looked healthy could be infected with HIV.

President Girma Woldegiorgis, who chaired the National AIDS Council Secretariat, said while the community should be mobilized to fight the epidemic, there was a pressing need for leadership. "The Government should be in the forefront to coordinate efforts by all stakeholders for the control and prevention of the epidemic and alleviate its impact," he emphasized.

Experience from other countries showed that leadership was critical in combating HIV/AIDS and in achieving progress toward the objectives set by 2001 U.N. General Assembly Special Session on HIV/AIDS, the U.N. Millennium Development Goals, and the government's HIV/AIDS action plan.

The leadership program was a new approach that aimed to build on individual and organizational responsibilities to address the causes that fuel the epidemic. The process would take nine months, involving leaders from all sectors of the society including government officials and civil society organizations, such as youth groups, religious organizations, women's groups, and the private sector.

The seminar for government executives focused on the experiences of countries such as Thailand and Uganda in reversing the epidemic and how they could be applied in Ethiopia. They also discussed practical steps and strategies at the federal, regional, and local levels to combat the epidemic.

Support for the program was part of the overall UNDP strategy on HIV/AIDS, which helped countries to

- Promote advocacy and policy dialogue
- Build capacity to control the epidemic
- Mainstream HIV/AIDS programs across government agencies
- Protect the human rights of those affected by HIV/AIDS
- Carry out information and awareness campaigns

CASE STUDY 3: Regional Collaboration: Controlling Chagas Disease in the Southern Cone of South America[18]

Brazil's early success with the program demonstrated the technical feasibility of vector control efforts. However, the program also exposed two challenges facing the fight against Chagas disease: border-crossing insects and wavering political commitment. Despite the diligent mapping and control efforts within its borders, Brazil's campaign faced disease transmission from neighboring countries. The insect vector could easily cross borders and was thought to have originated in Bolivia and spread across a large swath of the continent, hidden in people's belongings as they moved from one place to another. As such, Brazil's experience demonstrated that unilateral control efforts would be unable to defeat the disease.

In 1991, a new control program known as the Southern Cone Initiative to Control/Eliminate Chagas (INCOSUR) addressed these challenges and marshaled the commitment of the countries of the southern cone region where Chagas was an endemic threat. The initiative was a joint agreement among the governments of Argentina, Bolivia, Brazil, Chile, Paraguay, Uruguay, and later Peru, which set out to control Chagas

[18] Center for Global Development. (2004). Millions saved: Proven successes in global health. Retrieved from www.cgdev.org, accessed in 2010.

disease through the elimination of the main insect vector. Led by the PAHO, the initiative was designed to bolster national resolve and prevent cross-border reinfestations.

Within the INCOSUR, each country financed and managed its own national program. However, regional cooperation has proved essential to the program's success and has been coordinated by PAHO. Each year, representatives from the collaborating nations shared operational aims, methods, and achievements at a PAHO-sponsored annual meeting of the Intergovernmental Commission of the Southern Cone. A series of inter-country technical cooperation agreements has fostered the sharing of information among scientists throughout the region and their respective government organizations.

Incidence in the seven countries covered by the initiative fell by an average of 94 percent by 2000. By 2001, disease transmission was halted in Uruguay, Chile, and large parts of Brazil and Paraguay.

CASE STUDY 4: **Collaboration with Private and/or NGO Sector: Cataract in India**[19]

Although the Blindness Control Program's quantitative achievements in India were remarkable in its early years, the impact on health was disappointing as outcomes were relatively poor. According to at least one study of 24 villages, less than half of those operated had good visual outcomes. The reasons for this underperformance were many. First, the intracapsular cataract extraction, known as ICCE surgery, itself had a significant failure rate, even under the best circumstances. And the camps where this was done were in no way the best circumstances. Surgeons were serving a rural population that did not always understand instructions for post-surgical care

[19] Center for Global Development. (2004). Millions saved: Proven successes in global health.

at home. It was difficult (and often impossible) to maintain a sterile field during the operation. Local doctors were either not present or not able to provide follow-up monitoring and care.

So, while the program was increasingly successful at stimulating a demand for surgeries, it was unable to keep up with that demand. A backlog of people asking for treatment led to long lines and increased pressure to work quickly and move on.

In part, in response to the shortcomings of the public sector program, the private sector—and particularly NGOs—sought to fill the void.

The Aravind Eye Care System, an NGO with a 30-year history of providing very low-cost vision care, has been a leading partner to the Government of India in its blindness program and a leading example of social entrepreneurship in the health sector. Among the NGOs providing cataract treatment in India, Aravind is by far the largest, conducting more than 1,000 screening camps and performing close to 1 million cataract surgeries each year. Within the context of the Cataract Blindness Control Program (CBCP), Aravind's role was particularly significant in Tamil Nadu, where some 95 percent of the surgeries were performed under the organization's auspices.

Aravind had its start in 1976 when its founder Dr Govindappa Venkataswamy, after mandatory retirement from government service at the age of 58, opened a 12-bed hospital in the South Indian city of Madurai. Starting with little money but a strong sense of mission toward saving the vision of those in need—and inspired, serendipitously, by the large-scale success of the McDonald's fast-food marketing strategy—over time Dr Venkataswamy established a network of specialty eye hospitals throughout India that uses a sustainable business model to provide high-quality patient care. He devoted himself to this effort until his death in 2006, his family continues his work. Three key elements define the Aravind business model:

1. Economies of scale: With excellent management and high patient volume, Aravind keeps productivity high,

with surgeons performing 25–40 procedures daily; unit costs are maintained at the very low level of about $10 per cataract operation.

2. Cross-subsidies: Aravind provides free or very low-priced care to two-thirds of its patients with the revenue derived from the one-third of patients who are able to pay moderate prices. The only difference in the treatment of those who do and don't pay is in the amenities, such as the air-conditioning in the recovery room.

3. Vertical integration: Recognizing that the imported intraocular lenses constituted a major component of the total surgical costs, Aravind obtained a transfer of technology through the US-based Seva Foundation, and additional support from the Combat Blindness Foundation, to permit it to manufacture these lenses at a fraction of the cost. The manufacturing activity scaled up quickly, from 35,000 in 1992–1993 to nearly 600,000 lenses today. Now, at the Aurolab subsidiary established for this purpose, a workforce of about 200 young women from rural backgrounds produces lenses to a global standard of quality that are used at Aravind, as well as at facilities throughout India. The affordably priced intraocular lenses are exported to some 85 countries around the world, providing another source of revenue for Aravind. The system of eye hospitals also is considered one of India's premier ophthalmic training institutions, providing a steady flow of well-prepared professionals and support staff.

Beyond the mechanics of the business model was the leadership of Dr Venkataswamy, a surprising combination of marketing savvy and spirituality. "If Coca-Cola can sell billions of sodas and McDonald's can sell billions of burgers," Dr Venkataswamy asked,

"why can't Aravind sell millions of sight-restoring operations, and, eventually, the belief in human perfection? With sight, people could be freed from hunger, fear, and poverty. You could perfect the body, then perfect the mind and the soul, and raise people's level of thinking and acting."

With this approach, he attracted both financial and technical support from many organizations outside of India, from Lion's Club to the WHO to the Seva Foundation, and inspired a generation of health professionals in South Asia and beyond.

Annexure 1

Major Strands of Thoughts on Leadership

When we think of leadership, many attributes of leaders come to mind: courage, charisma, vision, persistence, commitment to goals, and tenacity, to mention a few. While the interest in and study of leaders and leadership is not new, it is only in recent decades that "leadership" became a distinct and recognizable discipline for study, research, and training. For a long time, up until perhaps the 1900s, the so-called "Great-Man" theory—"leaders are born, not made"—was generally the accepted reference point. However, from 1950s onwards, different strands of thought on leadership began to appear, prompted by, and surely a reflection of, the great wave of socioeconomic changes and industrial development that followed the end of World War II. In response, theorists started to see other factors (besides nature—"being born") that exerted critical influences on behavior that could be befitting of leaders.

Generally, three factors influence leadership behavior: personality, situation, and the environment. They may go by other similar or related names but they formed the bases for new directions for thinking on leadership such as: Traits theory (what makes leaders different from other people?), Situational theory (situations determine who emerges as a leader), Transformational leadership (leaders are called upon to deal with a crisis), Results-based leadership, and so on. Over time, more hybrids inevitably came into being, as leadership thinking evolved from different environments and circumstances. Covey,[1] for example, goes so far as to say that five broad approaches in leadership theories

[1] Covey, S. R. (2004). *The 8th habit. From effectiveness to greatness.* New York: Free Press (Simon & Schuster), Appendix 2.

have emerged in the 20th century: (1) trait, (2) behavioral, (3) power-influence, (4) situational, and (5) integrative.

The study of leadership as an academic and professional discipline has its roots in the US where a successful and productive convergence of leadership in practice (the corporations) and leadership in theory (the academicians/theorists) has been happening for at least half a century. Today, given the proliferation of books, written materials and other resources on leadership, many names are as familiar to practitioners and students of leadership as mission statements and action plans.

This abundance shows up similarities and differences, many a matter of adaptation and refinement of theoretical parameters and frameworks. For example, Bennis as well as Kouzes and Posner both talk about vision but in different ways; for the former, vision is what guides leaders while for the latter, vision is about "igniting passions" in others. The following is a cursory look at some of the key leadership theorists or thinkers (see Table A.1).

Table A.1: *Leadership Is an Evolving Process: Some Examples from Research*

Type of theory	Basic concept
Great man →	Leaders are born, not made
Trait →	Leaders have certain traits, competencies, and behavior
Power and influence →	Leaders have power and influence
Results-based or → behaviorist	It is what leaders actually do that matters rather than what they are
Situational →	Different circumstances require different forms of leadership
Leader as servant →	Leaders are seen as serving others
Transactional leadership →	Leaders and followers have an exchange relationship
Followers' attribution →	What do the followers attribute to the leaders?
Transformational → leadership	The leader is a proactive and innovative visionary

Source: Covey (2004).[2]

[2] The 8th habit.

In tandem with the proliferation of literature on the subject, there are more and more "what experts say..." snippets about leadership than ever before. Are we any closer to an understanding of what leadership is? What is clear is that we can now generally understand what leadership entails or how it best functions.

Leadership is like a force that moves people and mobilizes resources to get things done. To accomplish this, it entails initiating and modeling values, respect, practices, learning, and often risk-taking. It involves creating an empowering and enabling environment to inspire and motivate people through effective communications and setting a personal example. Keywords often associated with leadership, such as "courage," "integrity," "passion," "conviction," "self-awareness," "charisma," and others, tell us that leaders possess certain common qualities. Warren Bennis, one of the foremost management gurus on the topic, thinks that the basic ingredients of leadership are as given in Table A.2.[3]

Table A.2: *Basic Ingredients of Leadership*

Basic ingredient	What it means
Guiding vision	You have a clear idea of what you want to do—professionally and personally—and the strength to persist in the face of setbacks, even failures.
Passion	You have an underlying passion for the promises of life, combined with a very particular passion for a vocation, a profession, a course of action. You love what you do.
Integrity	Your integrity is derived from self-knowledge, candor, and maturity. You know your strengths and weaknesses, are true to your principles, and have learned with experience how to learn from and work with others.
Trust	You have earned people's trust.
Curiosity	You wonder about everything and want to learn as much as you can.
Daring	You are willing to take risks, experiment, and try new things.

Source: Warren Bennis (1998). *On becoming a leader.* New York, USA: Addison-Wesley.

[3] Boyett, J., & Boyett, J. (1998). *The guru guide. The best ideas of the top management thinkers.* New York: Wiley & Sons, Inc.

Leaders are found at all levels of an organization and of the community. There are leaders at the front-line of service delivery, and they are crucial for effective implementation of services because they interface with the clients at a very personal level. Then, we have leaders within an internal network system in the organization who have influence in either an official or informal way. We also have the so-called "community builders"[4] to help extend an organization's influence to the outside. At the most obvious positions are the executive leaders such as the managing directors, chairman of the board of trustees, the operations managers, the supervisors, etc., that is, people who are paid to lead. Beyond the program organization, there are community leaders and political leaders who set the cultural and behavior norms, and lead their constituents toward espoused goals.

Certainly, alchemy of sorts needs to exist for leaders, especially the not-so-obvious ones, to emerge from unexpected places. Challenges or adversities appear to be an element conducive to leadership development as they draw out or motivate certain action-inducing behavior in people. People's leadership qualities are best tested in difficult times or environments. But first a path, guided by a vision needs to exist on how to confront these challenges or how to do things better, must be communicated to them. As Peter Senge puts in eloquently, "...[we can] see leadership as a systemic phenomenon inseparable from its context."[5]

Leadership is a force that needs a context and also competencies to do what needs to be done. Leaders need competencies to manage four things (see Table A.3).

Table A.3: *Four Competencies of Leadership*

Management of ATTENTION ⟹	Vision of leaders commands the attention of followers.
Management of MEANING ⟹	Leaders are able to skillfully communicate issues in simple images and language.
Management of TRUST ⟹	Leaders are admired for their consistency of purpose.

(Table Contd)

---

[4] Senge, P., et al., (1999). *The dance of change. The challenges to sustaining momentum in learning organizations.* New York: Doubleday.

[5] Ibid., p. 20.

(Table Contd)

Management of SELF	$\Longrightarrow$	Leaders are adept at identifying and fully utilizing their strengths and accepting and seeking to develop areas of weaknesses.

Source: Warren Bennis (1994). *The four competencies of leadership.* An Inverted Life Reflections on Leadership and Change (Chapter 5). Cambridge, Massachusetts, USA: Perseus Publishing.

Different thoughts of leading thinkers on leadership are articulated in Box A.1.

Box A.1: *Quotable Quotes on Leadership*

When the best leader's work is done, the people say, "We did it ourselves."

Lao-Tzu

A leader is a man who has the ability to get other people to do what they don't want to do and like it...

Harry Truman

My own definition of leadership is this: The capacity and the will to rally men and women in a common purpose, and the character which inspires confidence...

Field Marshall Bernard Montgomery

Leadership is influence. That's it. Nothing more; nothing less.

John Maxwell

Great leaders move us. They ignite our passion and inspire the best in us. When we try to explain why they are so effective, we speak of strategy, vision, or powerful ideas. But the reality is much more primal: Great leaders work through the emotions...

Goleman et al.

To lead is to live dangerously because when leadership counts, when you lead people through difficult change, you challenge what people hold dear—their daily habits, tools, loyalties, and ways of thinking—with nothing more to offer perhaps than a possibility.... By making the lives of people around you better, leadership provides meaning in life.

Heifetz

(Box A.1 Contd)

(Box A.1 Contd)

A leader is a dealer in hope.

Napolean Bonaparte

Leaders are pioneers.... They guide us to new and often unfamiliar destinations...

Kouzes and Posner

Leaders...are responsible for building organizations where people continually expand their capacity to understand complexity, clarify vision and improve shared mental models—that is they are responsible for learning.

Peter Senge

The greatest leader is seen as servant first because that is what he is deep down inside. Leadership is bestowed on the person, who is, by nature, a true servant...

Greenleaf

To link oneself with the masses, one must act in accordance with the needs and wishes of the masses.... We should help them to proceed from these things to an understanding of the higher tasks which we have put forward.... Such is the basic method of leadership.

Mao Tse-Tung

Leadership is defined as the capacity to effect changes from a forward-looking participatory perspective throughout society and not simply at the local level.

African Development Forum

Source: Adapted from several sources.

Level 5 Leadership: Going from Good to Great

Jim Collins, coauthor of the bestselling book *Built to Last*, believes that "Good is the enemy of great" because "being good" prevents someone or some organization from becoming extraordinary or great. A chance encounter with Bill Meehan,[6]

[6] Bill Meehan said to Jim Collins that while his previous book *Built to Last* was good, it was "useless." He said that the companies featured in the book stopped at being "Good" and mostly never made it to "Great."

managing director of the San Francisco office of McKinsey & Co., prompted him to undertake a five-year-long research project on what it takes for a company or organization to go from GOOD to GREAT, which is also the name of his book.

The basic premise of GOOD to GREAT is that it is about "timeless principles," of "how you take a good organization and turn it into one that produces sustained great results..."[7] Having analyzed the histories of 28 companies and sieving through thousands of pages of interviews and great amounts of data over five years of research, Collins and his team believe that top among the key determinants of "greatness" is leadership.

However, the leadership that is required for greatness to happen is not just any sort of leadership. It takes a very special leader to create an enduring organization that will not only sustain or improve its performance over time but will also outperform its peers. To differentiate between different types of leaders, Collins has devised a five-level hierarchy of capabilities, of which Level 5 (the highest) is the one necessary for "greatness" (see Table A.4).

Table A.4: *Level 5 Hierarchy*

5. Executive	Builds enduring greatness through a paradoxical blend of personal humility and professional will.
4. Effective Leader ⬆	Catalyzes commitment to and vigorous pursuit of a clear and compelling vision, stimulating higher performance standards.
3. Competent Manager ⬆	Organizes people and resources toward the effective and efficient pursuit of pre-determined objectives.
2. Contributing Team Member ⬆	Contributes individual capabilities to the achievement of group objectives and works effectively with others in a group setting.
1. Highly Capable Individual ⬆	Makes productive contributions through talent, knowledge, skills, and good work habits.

Source: Collins (2001), p. 20.

[7] Collins, J. (2001). *Good to great*. New York, USA: Harper Collins.

What are the traits and characteristics of Level 5 leaders? Collins says he was greatly surprised by the results of his research. Level 5 leaders go against conventional wisdom of behavioral patterns or characteristics expected of most traditional leaders such as inflated egos, high visibility, greater-than-life persona, tendency to be boastful, and so on. Collins considers the latter as Level 4 leaders, those likely to be colorful figures with a short-term vision and who might never be able to take the organization from "good" to great.

Collins' Level 5 leaders are quiet but resolute, ambitious but low-key. They think of the organization first and foremost, not themselves. They are results-oriented and concerned for the long-term sustainability of the company (not short-term gains). While they do not seek any glory for themselves, they nevertheless have resolute faith in their beliefs and vision for the organization, and the direction they want to take it. The key points of Level 5 leaders are as follows:

- "Level 5" refers to a five-level hierarchy of executive capabilities, with Level 5 at the top. Level 5 leaders embody a paradoxical mix of personal humility and professional will. They are ambitious, to be sure, but ambitious first and foremost for the company, not themselves.

- Level 5 leaders set up their successors for even greater success in the next generation, whereas egocentric Level 4 leaders often set up their successors for failure.

- Level 5 leaders display a compelling modesty, are self-effacing, and understated. In contrast, leaders with gargantuan personal egos often contribute to the demise or continued mediocrity of the company.

- Level 5 leaders are fanatically driven, infected with an incurable need to produce sustained *results*. They are resolved to do whatever it takes to make the company great, no matter how big or hard the decisions are.

- Level 5 leaders display a workmanlike diligence—more plow horse than show horse.

- Level 5 leaders look out the window to attribute success to factors other than themselves. When things go poorly, however, they look in the mirror and blame themselves, taking full responsibility. The comparison CEOs often did just the opposite—they looked in the mirror to take credit for success, but out the window to assign blame for disappointing results.
- One of the most damaging trends in recent history is the tendency (especially by boards of directors) to select dazzling, celebrity leaders and to deselect potential Level 5 leaders.
- Level 5 leaders exist all around us, if we just know what to look for, and that many people have the potential to evolve into Level 5 leaders.
- Ten out of 11 good-to-great CEOs came from *inside* the company.
- Level 5 leaders attribute much of their success to good luck rather than personal greatness.

Level 5 leaders have a winning combination of *Professional Will* and *Personal Humility*, see Box A.2.

Approaches to Leadership: Qualities, Situational, and Functional

Even as a schoolboy, John Adair was interested in the subject of leadership, something he later devoted much of his professional life to. He first made a public statement on leadership as the founder of the historical society at his school in London. Speaking on the topic of "Leadership of History" he first made the linkage between a leader and his personal qualities saying that "... although leadership may change in this aspect from age to age, the qualities of a leader are the same."

Later, having served in the British Army in the 1950s, he put his observations of how leadership was described and developed

Box A.2: *Level 5 Leadership*

Professional Will	Personal Humility
Creates superb results, a clear ⟷ catalyst in the transition from Good to GREAT.	Demonstrates a compelling modesty, shunning public adulation; never boastful.
Demonstrates an unwavering ⟷ resolve to do whatever that must be done to produce the best long-term results, no matter how difficult.	Acts with quiet calm determination; relies principally on inspired standards, not inspiring charisma, to motivate.
Sets the standard of building an ⟷ enduring great company; will settle for nothing less.	Channels ambition into the company, not the self; sets up successors for even greater success in the next generation.
Looks in the mirror, not out ⟷ the window, to apportion responsibility for poor results, never blaming other people, external factors, or bad luck.	Looks out the window, not in the mirror, to apportion credit for the success of the company—to other people, external factors, and good luck.

Source: Collins (2001).[8]

into what he believed were three distinct approaches to leadership—Qualities, Situational, and Functional.[8]

Qualities approach

In the early 1950s, the British Army prescribed the following 17 qualities as those necessary for "...influencing a body of people to follow a certain course of action; the art of controlling them, directing them and getting the best out of them":[9]

[8] Adair, J. (2010). *Effective strategic leadership*. London: Pan Books, Chapter 3.
[9] Adair, J. *Effective strategic leadership*. p. 64.

1. Ability to make decisions
2. Assurance (confidence)
3. Example
4. Calmness in crisis
5. Human element
6. Pride in command
7. Sense of duty
8. Ability to accept responsibility
9. Enthusiasm
10. Energy
11. Determination
12. Resolute courage
13. Sense of justice
14. Initiative
15. Loyalty
16. Humor
17. Physical fitness

However, trainee officers were encouraged to continue learning in order to be leaders and to profit by experience.

In institutions that have their own traditions of leadership such as renowned military institutions like West Point or exclusive gentlemen's clubs, the qualities approach continues to serve its purpose of distinguishing between the leaders and the followers. For practitioners of this approach, other personal qualities that are deemed to "qualify" for the leadership caliber are: temperance, justice, sagacity, amiability, presence of mind, tactfulness, humanity, prudence, fortitude, sympathy, courage, magnanimity, generosity, and so on.

Situational approach

The belief that leaders were leaders because they possessed a certain set of qualities soon came into disrepute when psychologists began to question its validity. They started to put forth the argument that leaders were leaders because they possessed certain attributes that responded well in particular situations, rather than having a set of prescribed qualities. This came to be known as the *situational* approach, thanks to a big expansion of research activities in the social or behavioral sciences after the World War II period.

The *situational* approach puts much emphasis on *knowledge* (especially technical or professional competence) but also has two other aspects to it: *intelligence* and *experience*. It is believed that these three elements together will allow a leader to respond effectively to any situation.

Functional approach

The concept of ability to influence underlines the functional approach to leadership. It is believed that the effectiveness of a leader depends on his/her ability to influence a group of people to achieve a specific goal or to complete a task. Thus, three elements are necessary:

- Leader
- Group
- Task

Leadership is, therefore, a function of their inter-relationship. In later research, the word "team" came into popular use and has since replaced "group."

The *functional* approach provides the intellectual basis for John Adair's Three-Circle Model (see Figure A.1) which he successfully used as "Action-Centered Leadership" (ACL) in his training programs.

Figure A.1: *Three-Circle Model*

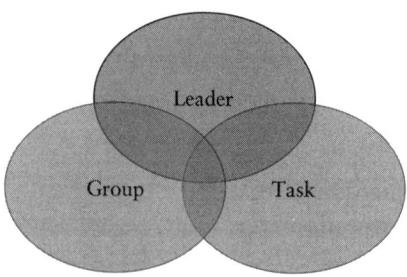

Source: Adair (2010).

The three interlocking circles illustrate that each area of need—Leader, Group and Task—exerts an influence on the other two. For example, if a task is missing, the leader and the group have nothing to act on or work together for. Similarly, if a leader is missing, a group with a task will most likely not be able to complete the task in any coherent or timely manner.

This model underscores the importance of various functions that need leadership in order for the objectives of the group and task to be fulfilled. This creates "areas of leadership responsibilities." Examples of these functions are

    * *Planning*   * *Initiating*   * *Controlling*   * *Supporting*
    * *Informing*   * *Evaluating*

This model gives leaders—with the necessary qualities and knowledge/intelligence/experience (*qualities* and *situational* approaches) —the opportunity to perform the necessary or appropriate functions so that the group can achieve its tasks as a working unit. In this way, by sharing information and knowledge as well as getting contributions from the group, this model strengthens the role of leaders.

Leadership styles in a nutshell

Much is demanded of leaders these days. They are seen to be playing or performing different roles. Are they visionary or strategists, politicians or campaigners, coaches or change agents? Clearly, they come in many different guises, depending on their own personalities and the skills and competences expected of them in their field or area of influence.

Leaders use different styles of leadership in response to different situations. A time of crisis would see a leader behaving very differently than in a less turbulent environment. The following is a list of six leadership styles suggested by Goleman et al. and what they aim to do:[10]

- VISIONARY

    o How it builds resonance: Moves people toward shared dreams
    o Impact on climate: Most strong positive
    o When appropriate: When changes require a new vision, or when a clear direction is needed

[10] Goleman, D., Boyatzis, R., & McKee, A. (2002). *The new leaders. Transforming the art of leadership into the science of results*. London: Little Brown.

- COACHING

  - o How it builds resonance: Connects what a person wants with the organization's goals
  - o Impact on climate: Highly positive
  - o When appropriate: To help an employee improve performance by building long-term capabilities

- AFFILIATIVE

  - o How it builds resonance: Creates harmony by connecting people to each other
  - o Impact on climate: Positive
  - o When appropriate: To heal rifts in a team, motivate during stressful times, or strengthen connections

- DEMOCRATIC

  - o How it builds resonance: Values people's input and gets commitment through participation
  - o Impact on climate: Positive
  - o When appropriate: To build buy-in or consensus, or to get valuable input from employees

- PACESETTING

  - o How it builds resonance: Meets challenging and exciting goals
  - o Impact on climate: Because too frequently poorly executed, often highly negative
  - o When appropriate: Get high-quality results from a motivated and competent team

- COMMANDING

  - o How it builds resonance: Soothes fears by giving clear direction in an emergency
  - o Impact on climate: Because so often misused, highly negative
  - o When appropriate: In a crisis, to kick-start a turnaround, or with problem employees

> **Pause for Reflection**
> Think of three leaders and identify their styles. Leaders have different styles but they all succeed. Why? Match styles to the context and tasks these leaders faced.

Exercise

Make a list of leaders you know or have heard of, and write down their accomplishments or major things they have done.

What is it about these leaders that we remember? Apart from their personalities or charisma, it is usually what they have changed or fought against that we remember. It could be as grand or dramatic as what Jody Williams and her landmine activists do, or it could be something as small-scale, quiet but needy as some community leaders do.

Being capable and possessing attributes of leadership is terrific, but capability must be put to appropriate and purposeful use. Effective leadership equals attributes × results. Leaders need to focus on what to accomplish (results) and how to accomplish it (attributes). Leaders who pay attention to only attributes will be ineffective. On the other hand, exclusive focus on results may be shortsighted and may result in a lack of ability to achieve results in the future.

Results-based leadership development would process with the need for analysis of health challenges and what is needed to address these challenges. These, in turn, would determine leadership competencies needed, as shown in the Figure A.2.

Figure A.2: *Results-based Leadership*

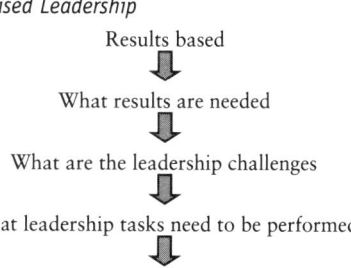

Results based
⬇
What results are needed
⬇
What are the leadership challenges
⬇
What leadership tasks need to be performed
⬇
What competencies will be needed

Source: Dave Ulrich, Jack Zenger and Norm Smallwood (1999). Results-based Leadership. Harvard Business School Press. Boston MA USA.

> **Pause for Reflection**
> Identify one health challenge and a leadership competency to address this challenge.

Leadership as performing different roles

The leaders need to perform several different roles to achieve results: visionary and strategist, politicians and campaigners, coach and change agents, as shown in Table A.5.

Table A.5: *Leadership Roles*

Organization	Inside	Outside
Future possibilities	Change agent	Visionary and strategist
Present operations	Coach	Politician and campaigner

Source: Burt Nanus and Stephen M. Dobbs (1999). Leaders who made a difference: Essential strategies for meeting non-profit challenge. Jossey Bass Publishers.

What leaders need to do?

A chain of events will happen when a leader decides to set a goal (or goals) in motion. Leaders will start with a vision that will set the tone and direction for the organization to follow. Then they have to show their own personal commitment through beliefs, integrity, trust, empathy, habits, and other character traits before they are able to persuade other people and get their individual commitments.

Thus, it is important for leaders trying to make a difference to have the much-vaulted "people skills." When people are excited by a leader's vision, capability within an organization or community can be easily mobilized (see Figure A.3).

Challenge the status quo

According to Kouzes and Posner,[11] the root meaning of the word "lead" is "to go, travel, guide" while for "manage," the root

---

[11] Kouzes, J. M., & Barry, Z. P. (1995). *The leadership challenge. How to keep getting extraordinary things done in organizations.* San Francisco: Jossey-Bass Publishers.

Figure A.3: *What Do Leaders Need to Do?*

Sets directions

Demonstrates personal character
(habits, integrity, trust, analytical thinking)

Mobilizes individual commitment
(engages others, shares power)

Engenders organizational or community
capability
(builds teams, manages change)

Source: Dave Ulrich, Jack Zenger and Norm Smallwood (1999). *Results-based Leadership*. Boston, MA, USA: Harvard Business School Press.

meaning is "hand" (handling things, maintaining order, etc.). In this sense leaders, by virtue of the meaning of the word, are pioneers, the "first," which complements very well the idea of leaders challenging the status quo to change, improve, or to bring in something new. The challenge of change is perhaps what drives leaders at a personal level, that there is something that matters so much to them that they have to act.

Leaders can challenge the status quo by searching opportunities to change, grow, innovate, or improve,[12] and they do this by

- Treating every job as an adventure
- Treating each new assignment as a start-over, even if it isn't
- Questioning the status quo
- Sending people shopping for ideas
- Putting idea gathering on one's own agenda
- Going out and finding something that needs fixing
- Assigning people to the opportunities
- Renewing teams
- Adding adventure and fun to everyone's work
- Always learning new skills

Leaders look for ways to radically alter the status quo, for ways to create something totally new, for revolutionary new processes, for ways to beat the system. (Kouzes and Posner)

[12] Ibid., p. 61.

Index

About the Authors

Jay Satia is Advisor to the President, Public Health Foundation of India (PHFI) and Professor Emeritus at Indian Institute of Public Health - Gandhinagar (IIPH-G). Professor Satia was previously a Professor at the Indian Institute of Management, Ahmedabad, India for more than 20 years and served as its dean from 1987–89. Professor Satia also served International Council on Management of Population programmes (ICOMP), Malaysia as its Executive Director (1993–2008). He received his doctoral degree from Stanford University and has published extensively and has been a consultant to many governments and international agencies including the World Bank and the United Nations Population Fund (UNFPA).

Anant Kumar is an Assistant Professor of Public Health at Xavier Institute of Social Service (XISS), Ranchi, Jharkhand, India. Before joining XISS, Dr Kumar worked as Program Officer with Institute of International Education's (IIE) Population Leadership Program in India. Dr Kumar obtained his Bachelor and Master degree in Psychology from University of Allahabad. He obtained his doctoral degree in Social Medicine and Community Health from Centre of Social Medicine and Community Heath at Jawaharlal Nehru University, New Delhi. Dr Kumar is also a Visiting Fellow at the Institute for Human Development—Eastern Regional Centre (IHD-ERC), Ranchi. He is a South Asia Representative for Canadian Coalition for Global Health Research Task Group on Global Health Research Partnerships.

Moi Lee Liow is a Malaysian national and Executive Director of Asia Pacific Council of AIDS Service Organizations (APCASO). Before joining APCASO, she worked with International Council on Management of Population Programmes (ICOMP), Malaysia as Senior Programme Officer (2002–2008). She has more than 16 years of professional experience in the NGO development sector, focusing mostly on leadership, population and development. She has a Bachelor of Economics degree from Monash University, Australia, and a Master of Arts degree in International Development from Clark University, USA.